GOOD MORNING

But The Nightmares Never End

By Charlie Dukes

Tales
Urbana, Illinois

First Edition, 1997
Second Printing, 2003

Library of Congress Cataloging-in-Publication Data
Dukes, Charlie, 1923-
Good morning—: but the nightmares never end / by Charlie Dukes.
p. cm.
ISBN 0-9641423-2-5
1. Dukes, Charlie, 1923- . 2. World War, 1939-1945--Personal narratives, American. 3. United States. Army--Biography. 4. Soldiers--United States--Biography. I. Title.
D811.D836 1997
940.54'8173--dc21 97-44486
CIP

Printed in the United States of America

To Gracie,
my loving and faithful wife of 48 years.
It was through her urging—no, her badgering—that I finally found the strength to write this book.

And to Deb, Laurie, Kent and Rob,
our four children, who now, perhaps, will understand why their dad is like he is.

Good Morning! To: Ed & Dottie
Booth

Thanks! Dottie, you gave me my whole future. - Have worshipped this Excellence for over 55 yrs.
Hope you can enjoy my story!
Gracie is really responsible for my writing of this story

Respectfully.
Charlie [illegible]
30 - Oct - 2001

Introduction

The first time I ever heard of Charlie Dukes, I had just come in from an afternoon run and checked the messages on my answering machine. A noncommital voice asked if I would call Charlie Dukes at a number whose prefix I didn't recognize. Initially, I thought he must be selling something and started to erase the message. But he didn't really sound like a salesman, and I dialed the number.

"Good morning," a cheerful male voice said in my ear.

"Good morning?" I asked, thinking he must be a shift worker who had his mornings and afternoons mixed up, or he just must be mixed up, period. "It's evening, isn't it?"

"It's always good morning to me," the voice said politely. "What can I do for you?"

I told him who I was and that I was returning his call.

"Oh, yeah," he said. "I saw a column you wrote about veterans. I was a POW in Germany during World War II."

He said his name was Charlie Dukes, that he was from Georgetown, Illinois. And he explained that he often talked with students about his experiences and wondered if my classes at Urbana (Illinois) High School, where I was teaching, would be interested in hearing what he had to say.

At first I thought he might be the man one of my students had told me about when we were working on the essay for the Veterans of Foreign Wars' annual "Voice of Democracy" contest. Although the contest deadline was past and we had moved to other assignments, I had told the student to give me the man's name and telephone number so I could have him speak anyway. So I asked Charlie if he was this man and if he had landed at Normandy.

"No, sir," he said, undoubtedly wondering what I was talking about after he'd told me he'd seen a column I'd written earlier and why I had asked about D-Day but addressing both questions with his reply. "We went in about D+80, with the 104th Timberwolf Division. I first saw combat in Belgium."

Speaking with him for a few more minutes, I could tell he had much to say that would be of benefit for my students to hear. So we arranged for a classroom visit the following week.

And although he didn't mention it until he spoke to my classes, it was in Belgium that Charlie had begun greeting everyone with a cheery "good morning" regardless of the time of day. Not long after his unit made contact with the Germans, he got pinned down one night by a machine gun crew that literally shot the pack off his back while he hugged the ground.

"I'm not really a religious man," Charlie told the students, "but I promised the man upstairs that if I ever saw the sun come up again, I'd say good morning for the rest of my life. When the sun came up, I said, 'Good morning.' I've been saying it ever since."

His company was overrun and he was captured on Thanksgiving Day 1944. Of the 78 casualties in the company, 12 others were taken prisoner along with Charlie. Most were wounded and were taken to nearby hospitals and prison camps by their captors. Later, many POWs were loaded in boxcars for shipment to eastern Germany. Twelve men on Charlie's car died en route and were stacked at one end until the destination was reached.

Charlie's feet were frozen so badly when he jumped off the boxcar that he immediately tumbled to the ground. He still had to help remove the dead from his boxcar, though, because he was one of the most able-bodied of the POWs. Standing around a bonfire later, he realized only after he heard the German guards singing *Stille Nacht* (*Silent Night*) that it was Christmas.

For the next six months, Charlie was confined to a small prison camp near the Polish border. The prisoners were beaten to enforce camp discipline, given little to eat and worked seven days a week. Charlie arrived in Europe weighing 178 pounds and was down to 110 at the end of the war.

After the war he said he always saved a piece of bread from his evening meal for the next morning. Years later at a reunion of the surviving men from the prison camp, their wives observed that all of the men did the same, a habit carried over from the POW time when a scrap of bread they would save was the only thing besides a cup of weak coffee for breakfast.

Throughout the 50-minute class, the students sat spellbound as Charlie shared his experiences. He passed around a tag that identified him as a POW while he told about watching the sky light up at night near the end of the war as Allied planes pounded Dresden, killing civilians by the tens of thousands. He spoke of the agreement the American POWs made with their German guards for safe passage through German lines when everybody knew the end of the war was coming.

Later, in Russian custody, rumors of Siberian gulags for the Allied prisoners influenced Charlie to escape and make his way to Allied lines 20 days after the war ended. More than 136,000 men were taken prisoner in World War II, Charlie says. About 110,000 of them were repatriated. That leaves more than 26,000 who weren't for one reason or another. He maintains that some 22,000 of his comrades in the Russian camps disappeared to those gulags.

"I'm not bitter," Charlie said, "because that eats you up. But I'm mad as hell at my government for leaving those men there. And that's where I'd have been if I hadn't decided to escape."

After his visit, one female student said, "You hear about people like Charlie. You read about them in books, see then in movies or on television, but you forget that real people lived the horrible things Charlie told us about so we can have the freedom we take for granted."

One senior boy said, "I'll remember the things Charlie had to say for the rest of my life."

I'll remember what he had to say, too. That's why he comes, of course. And with this book, many more people will have the opportunity to remember what he and thousands of others endured at a time when it was important to take a stand against the dictators who would deprive people of their freedom. Charlie's family and friends had been urging him to write the book for a long time. He feels an obligation to leave his story for young people after he is gone in much the same way he now feels obligated to tell his story to them in his classroom visits.

"I want to tell them the story they don't read in the history books," he said. "And I want them to know what the price of Freedom is so they can appreciate it."

For what he freely gives to these young people and for all that he's been through to guarantee our way of life, he deserves our respect and our gratitude. We all owe him and others like him a great deal. What you read in his book, I think, shows that.

And what you read has been softened by the years. Charlie still sees what he experienced very clearly, but it took awhile for him to let it out so we could see it clearly, too.

"I did a few things back in those days that I'm not particularly proud of," he said about the days after he left the POW camp and roamed around the country, trying to reach the Allied lines and home.

Undoubtedly. The war was still going on for him and thousands of others. People were trying to survive any way they could. And Charlie had just lived through what most of us can't even imagine.

Writing the book has been cathartic for him, I'm sure. But it's also been painful. When I agreed to help him and Gracie with the writing, I knew the story was there. It took a bit longer for the book to get to where it is now. It also took a lot of emotional soul-searching from a man who has paid so much.

"Your book is probably different at 74 (years of age) than it would have been at 24," I said to him one day.

"You're darn right it's different," he said. "I was really angry then."

More than 50 years later, he's still angry, but he's mellowed a lot.

"I'm no hero," Charlie says matter-of-factly, as he does about much of his experiences. "I'm a survivor."

You will see that in this story.

— *Ray Elliott*

1

My eyes were slowly opening, almost against my will. They focused on my surroundings in the dusky darkness of this unfamiliar place. Then came the realization that I was in the basement storeroom of the coal processing plant that had been our objective when we jumped off at dawn.

My "bed" was a coal pile. The chunks of coal were just as they had come from the mine, mostly large pieces–and hard with sharp, pointed and jagged edges that jabbed me every time I moved. My head was spinning. I felt as if I were floating on air. Then I tried to move my legs, and the pain shot through me. Both legs were throbbing, a burning sensation running up and down the backs of them where they were full of shrapnel. The pain subsided briefly, then another wave of pain hit with a vengeance. The burning and stinging was constant.

I shook my head in an attempt to clear the cobwebs from my brain, glanced to my left and saw 1st Sgt. Charles Williams lying nearby. How did we get in this place? I wondered. My last recollection was of being in a muddy trench with Pvt. Lou Vinduska, surrounded by German infantry after the artillery round had landed close by and sprayed shrapnel in my hands and the backs of my legs. I looked at Sarge again; he was awake, grinning at me. My legs needed attention–they hurt badly.

"Sergeant, I need a medic," I said through clenched teeth.

"There's your medic," he said, pointing.

I followed the direction of his finger. A German soldier was standing there, about 30 feet away, with his *Schmeisser*, an automatic rifle similar to the American Thompson sub-machine gun but with much more rapid firepower, pointed at us.

It suddenly became quite clear that I was now a prisoner of war and wouldn't likely receive the medical attention I needed. I knew that a wounded prisoner was a definite liability to our captors. So fearful of being shot, I said no more and gritted my teeth when the pain from the shrapnel in my legs made my whole body hurt.

As I drowsily lay on that lumpy pile of coal, I became aware of others from L Company being brought into the basement. My eyes slowly grew accustomed to the near-darkness of the windowless coal storage area. Only when the door was opened and a shaft of light was let in could I grasp the gravity of my situation.

And lying there trying to reconcile it, I suddenly remembered that picture of Hitler I'd stuffed in my shirt earlier to take as a souvenir. I quietly but quickly sneaked it from under my clothing and hurriedly buried it as deep in the coal pile as possible without attracting too much attention; I certainly didn't want that guard with the *Schmeisser* pointing my way to notice.

I also had taken a German Luger from a prisoner in Aachen. My next job was to get it buried and out of sight. It wasn't crystal clear what would happen if the enemy found these two items in my possession at the time of interrogation. But I knew we would all be interrogated shortly, once the Germans had corralled all our men together, and I didn't want to find out.

I placed the pistol under a large chunk of coal close to 1st Sgt. Williams, using his body to shield my digging. The German soldier standing guard in the corner was an older man who gave the impression he'd rather be any place else than standing in that corner. He didn't look menacing; rather, he looked bored. But then I didn't want to attract any undue attention. He seldom glanced my way, so I felt certain he hadn't noticed what I was doing. ...

After graduating from Georgetown (Illinois) High School with the class of '41, I took a job at Chanute Air Base a few miles away in Rantoul. The base was in a rapid expansion phase. It was the oldest air training base in the United States and was furiously being transformed into an advanced training base for airmen as the war in Europe raged.

I worked on a construction crew, building double-decker barracks for Air Corps personnel. It was hard work for 82.5 cents an hour, nine hours a day, seven days a week. But it supplied me with money to enter Indiana University in Bloomington in September of 1941.

Like most freshmen, I found the college experience different in numerous ways. All facets of college life were new to me: living in a fraternity house and being a member of the freshman pledge class, setting up my own study habits to ensure good grades, being away from parental influence for the first time and trying to make the right choices based on my own assessments.

The fall of '41 was uneventful, even though everyone was aware that the war in Europe was reaching disastrous proportions for most of the European nations Germany was rolling through. The United States had been drafting men and women into the armed forces for more than a year.

It was a typical, normal Sunday afternoon on December 7, 1941, when I took a date to the local theater in downtown Bloomington. Sometime around 4 p.m. the movie abruptly stopped and lights flooded the theater. It was safe to say that most people in the theater figured that once again the film had broken, would be spliced and the movie would resume when it was fixed. But not this time. The shocking, bone-chilling announcement that came over the sound system had nothing to do with the film:

"The Japanese have bombed Pearl Harbor, wiping out nearly our entire Pacific fleet anchored in the harbor. American forces have suffered catastrophic casualties, with the entire harbor area in flames. ..."

An eerie silence settled over the audience as everyone sat in stunned horror. Many of those in the audience quietly got up and walked out into the late afternoon sunlight. The voice filling the theater ended the announcement by saying that President Franklin Roosevelt would be on all national radio stations at 10 a.m. Monday to brief the American people on the fact that "a state of war now exists between the United States of America and the Imperial Government of Japan."

Conversations after that were subdued. The majority of moviegoers seemed to be in a state of shock at the news. I know I was. The impact of that day's bulletin will forever be with me, for it changed the course of my life, as it did millions of other Americans, abruptly.

The lines of all military recruiting stations seemed endless on Monday, December 8. Men and boys hurried to enlist in the service of their choice to defend their country and to bring peace and freedom around the globe. Patriotism was running high.

I finished my freshman year at Indiana University and started my sophomore year in late August 1942. Going back to college was a welcome relief from a long, hard summer of hard manual labor working for a mortar- and concrete-block construction company. Upon returning to school, however, I became restless and actually felt somewhat guilty about going to school. It seemed that all my buddies were rapidly quitting school to enlist.

With news daily of defeat after defeat of the Allied Forces in battles all over the world, I decided at age 19 to enlist in the Regular Army. That was October 26, 1942. But since I was still at the university and the pipeline was full, I was placed in the Army Reserve until I was needed and would be called to active duty.

During second semester, I took a reduced academic load because the Reserved Officers Training Corps (ROTC) was receiving extra training. When school was finally out and I could no longer tolerate my guilt feelings, I went to the Marine Corps recruiting office with six of my fraternity brothers. The Marines always wanted good men, and I wanted to be one of them.

My nearly 6-foot, 130-pound frame didn't quite fit in with Marine Corps expectations, though. So I was rejected as were four of the others who had decided with me to do our bit for the war effort. Only one of the six was accepted by the Marine Corps. The rest of us, with our pride completely shot, traipsed on down the block and entered the Army recruiting office.

"What do you boys want?" a voice thundered from behind a

mammoth desk and from an equally mammoth and tough-looking sergeant.

Since we had been humbled by our experience at the hands of the Marines, we respectfully chorused that we wanted to fight for our country. Our patriotism was still at a high pitch.

The sergeant eyed us rather suspiciously, I thought, for what seemed to be several long minutes. Without a word, he finally reached into a desk drawer and pulled out five sheets of paper. Thrusting them our way, he gruffly commanded, "Sign here."

We did. Although later, as the five of us discussed the scene, we were all just about ready to chicken out. Our pride kept us in place as each one took his turn to sign the papers. That was it. The United States Army had just inducted five more very green recruits.

On this momentous day, June 4, 1943, I was still 19 years old–a very scared 19-year-old. The decision I had made to fight for my country was to forever change the course of my life. Little did I realize just how much. Like everybody else in the military during the war, my life and allegiance belonged to Uncle Sam for the duration. Once I put on the uniform and was in the Army, I couldn't wear civilian clothes, except when the situation was beyond my control. To be out of uniform during wartime was considered cause for a court-martial.

Since my ROTC training at Indiana University consisted of infantry training, I was automatically placed in infantry basic training when I reported for active duty at Camp Fannin near Tyler, Texas. The camp was new and not yet completed, so we spent many days completing minor projects around the camp. Along with that, we did some conditioning training and calisthenics and took increasingly longer hikes with full field equipment.

This period was a real toughening-up process. We were subjected to Marine Corps-type training. Who needs to be a Marine when you can get the same training in the Army? I wondered. As part of an experimental training group, this part of basic training lasted 17 weeks instead of the normal 13 weeks. We were going to be the best when we finished.

The last week of training consisted of a bivouac in tents, located along a small lake way back in the boonies. On the second day out, I was called to the command post (CP) for an urgent message. My mother had just entered the hospital back home and was diagnosed with throat cancer. Dad had contacted the Red Cross to get word to me. I was given a 72-hour emergency pass to go home and see her.

After a rough jeep ride through the piney woods and hills of Texas, I boarded a train for Danville, Illinois. Dad picked me up at the station, and we rushed to the hospital where I was able to spend about two hours visiting with Mom and Dad. She was weak from the radiation therapy, a new tool in medicine, and seemed very tired, but my sudden appearance at her bedside brought a glow to her eyes. I was glad I could make the trip.

I hadn't seen my parents for several months. We sat around her bedside, and I responded to a steady stream of question about Army life while they told the latest goings on on the home front. Gas and food rationing were in effect. Coupons and/or tokens meant almost more than money, but everyone wanted to do his part for the war effort, so people all tightened their belts with little complaining. Dad and I carried most of the conversation. Mom was too weak to say more than a few words in a sentence, but she was alert to our chatter.

The time flew by. My short leave was soon up, and I bent down and gently kissed Mom goodbye. With tears bubbling from my eyes, I abruptly turned and hurried out the door. I knew she was crying as I bolted away, but I was too overcome to look back. My mind was awhirl with the terrible thoughts of possibly kissing her for the last time in my life. Her illness was life-threatening. I figured that I would face a similar situation in future combat.

Then it was back to the train for the return trip. Dad and I drove the short distance to the train terminal in complete silence. Once there, I jumped out of the car quickly. Due to the emotional state we were both experiencing, Dad had a difficult time letting me go as we shook hands. I jerked away and headed for the platform to await the arrival of the next train for St. Louis with the other travelers. I never looked back.

This was my first visit home since enlisting, and the uncertainty of Mom's condition, plus such a hurried trip with practically no sleep, left me a little dazed. It all worked out okay, though. Mom recovered with the new therapy, and things eventually worked their way back to normal.

Back in camp, I returned to my tent late at night in time for an early-morning forced march through the swampy woods. I hardly missed a beat. That's Army life. We had a few days of rest, "laying around" between calisthenics, short hikes, classes on Army discipline, policing the area and whatever else soldiers do. A soldier must not be allowed to have too much free time. He must be kept busy, even if it's just picking up cigarette butts and other bits of debris–anything to look busy.

Our training battalion was soon broken up and shipped out in small groups to other military installations throughout the United States. I had been tapped to attend infantry Officers Candidate School (OCS). But I argued that I didn't think I was capable of leading troops into combat, which is what you learn there. Incredibly, the officer in command bought my plea, and I was shipped, instead, to the Army Specialized Training Program (ASTP) unit at Fordham University in the heart of the Bronx in New York City.

At Fordham, I was housed on campus in a nice, warm, comfortable dormitory, Dealy Hall. I studied physics, chemistry, calculus, history and other courses related to engineering. And I was transferred into the U.S. Army Engineers, trading my infantry blue braid for the red of the engineers. Our daily schedule included seven to eight hours of classroom instruction.

In addition to attending classes, we also had an hour of calisthenics that included strenuous exercise with our M-1 Garand rifles. The common Army slang term for this drill was "Butts Manual." After another hour or so in the gym, we were free to work out on the parallel bars and other gym equipment. As an added attraction, we organized several basketball teams. Some of the men had played ball in high school and on intramural squads in college, so we had some lively contests.

I decided to try my luck at boxing, which was another physical activity encouraged in the gym. One of the trainers had been a bantam-weight boxing champ. Even though he seemed a bit old and skinny–a little past his prime, I thought–he was still lightning fast and could really sting with his blows.

On a few occasions, former world heavyweight boxing champion Jack Dempsey would drop in and give some of us a few pointers. As he and I squared-off against each other during one exercise, I made a near-fatal mistake by somehow landing a lucky punch to his jaw. His defense penetrated, his instincts came into play immediately. With one blow, he sent me flying across the floor on my back.

He hurried to me, bent over my prostrate body and helped me to my feet. He apologized, thinking he had really hurt me. Whether I was actually getting into great physical shape from our rigorous training or whether I was merely hit by a glancing blow from the champ, I don't know. But I bounced right back and was never the worse for wear.

Whatever it was, though, there was a side benefit to the incident for me. Jack Dempsey's Bar was located on 51st and Broadway in New York City. When I happened by on a Saturday night, there was always free beer for me.

The ASTP schools all closed their doors in March of 1944, and we were all shipped out by train to infantry divisions. Most of my buddies and I were sent to Fort Carson, Colorado. Upon arriving there, I was assigned to 3rd Platoon, Company L, 413th Infantry, 104th Timberwolf Division.

We were immediately sent into intensive training. The snow cover was several feet deep, but that was merely a minor, inconsequential inconvenience. In other words, tough shit. All the new arrivals for the next month were put into special training companies, and then assigned permanent spots as replacements in the rifle platoons.

Training consisted mainly of long marches with full field equipment and company-sized maneuvers. The initial problem facing the new arrivals was getting acclimated to the shortage of oxygen in the air more than 5,000 feet up in the mountains, making breathing labored at best. After a few days in camp, however, everyone became used to the thin air.

True to form in the infantry, the second day of training included a nine-mile forced march in two hours. Many of the men never made it to the end. We averaged 4 1/2 mph with full field equipment weighing about 80 pounds. Of the men who smoked, not a single one made it. Many days later, we hiked 25 miles in full field gear in eight hours, averaging a bit more than 3 mph.

It didn't take me long to discover that this was a really tough outfit. During our first month, we were restricted to camp. No leave of any kind. A new commander had just been assigned to the Timberwolf Division. His name was Terry DeLamesa Allen. He came to us via campaigns in North Africa, Sicily and Italy. He was a major general who had commanded the 1st Division in Italy. The second in command was Brigadier General Bryant E. Moore who was fresh from the Guadalcanal combat zone.

General Allen's objective was to turn the Timberwolves into a new concept of highly trained night fighters who would use only bayonets, hand grenades, K-Bar knives and bare hands. Accordingly, we spent many hours in bayonet training and judo for hand-to-hand combat. The major part of the training took place at night in simulated combats situations.

Our commander evidently had little use for the Air Corps. We were ordered to always wear our winter wool olive-drab uniforms (ODs) whenever we left Camp Carson. The order was given, in effect, because General Allen wanted to distinguish the Timberwolves from all other military personnel. Since the Air Corps always wore their suntans, the Timberwolves in ODs really stood out. In Colorado Springs or Denver during the summer months of our training, a Timberwolf could always be spotted in winter wool ODs.

The Timberwolf Division was activated in September 1942 at Camp Adair, Oregon, and had had extensive training in Oregon and California in addition to maneuvers in the Arizona-California desert area. When the division started desert maneuvers, Company L consisted of 327 men, including attached elements (anti-tank companies, tank destroyers, combat engineers, artillery, signal company, ack-ack, trucking company and field kitchen).

At the completion of the nine-month training exercise, Company L moved into Fort Carson with only 98 men. Only one man was killed during maneuvers, but many were injured. The rest just wore out or became ill and were transferred out to other outfits or were given Conditional Disability Discharges (CDDs). Those who were left were the really tough soldiers. Our role was to fill in as replacements. With the Timberwolf reputation for toughness, those were mighty big shoes to fill.

I actually didn't realize what a reputation the Timberwolves had until I finally got a leave to go into Colorado Springs. Walking along a street, an airman or a sailor would just step aside and let us pass as we approached. Whenever we walked into a bar, the other military personnel would leave.

The girls in town also had heard of our prowess. You could hear a gasp when one of us asked one of them to dance. They even appeared to be reluctant to talk with us. Obviously, our reputation preceded us. Even the Denver newspaper remarked that if the Timberwolves fought as well in Europe as they did in Colorado Springs, the war would be shortened by quite a bit.

I felt proud to belong to this tough outfit. They would be good men to have on my side when we got into combat. And the way we were training, it was obvious that we would soon have our chance. Training became furious as we forged through our Preparation for Overseas Movement (POM) requirements. During this period, I qualified for and was awarded the Expert Infantryman's Badge. It wasn't the badge I cared so much about, but the $5. extra per month came in handy. Part of the test included a nine-mile forced march in two hours and a 25-mile hike in eight hours, all within a week of training.

The Normandy Invasion on D-Day, 6 June 1944, put the Timberwolves on high alert as a reserve stateside division. All men who were due for a furlough were immediately granted leave time. Training became even more intense than before as we made our final preparations to ship out. Our equipment was checked and loaded onto trains headed east.

Orders for overseas movement came to the division on 16 July 1944 while the 413th Infantry Regiment was in the middle of preparing to seize Hill A on the Camp Carson reservation. We were ready. Before leaving Camp Carson, I donated all my civilian clothing and articles to the pile in the center of our barracks to be given to the Salvation Army in Colorado Springs. Orders from General Allen had been specific: No civilian attire whatsoever was to be worn or taken overseas.

We moved out of Camp Carson by rail on 15 August 1944 in 24 separate trainloads, heading for Camp Kilmer, New Jersey. For security reasons, the trainloads of Timberwolves followed several different routes across the Unites States to arrive at the Port of Embarkation. Some trains even went a northerly route into Canada, then down through New York to New Jersey.

One incident on the trip stood out in my memory. We stopped at McCook, Nebraska, detrained and did our calisthenics on the platform and the area surrounding the station. Gradually we became aware that a crowd of townspeople was assembling, quietly, and were observing us as we went through our paces. The activity was a welcome respite from the monotony of the trip.

Although we weren't allowed to speak with anyone in the crowd, we did appreciate their clapping and cheering for us as we boarded the train to resume the journey. Patriotism was so high, and this was one way they could relate their thanks to us. They didn't even know that we were on our way to ship out to Europe to go into combat.

Five days after leaving Camp Carson, my train arrived in Camp Kilmer. One of the first things we had to do was line up for all those horrible shots a soldier had to endure before leaving the States. I had a 72-hour pass into New York City and enjoyed a final look at my old haunts from my days at Fordham University.

Then we boarded our ship, anchored out in New York Harbor, at night. The ship was named the "USS LeJeune." She carried the 413th Regiment, Headquarters and Headquarters Battery of the 104th Division Artillery and the 385th Field Artillery. Daylight found most of my squad gathered along the ship's railing, taking in a final view of the New York City skyline. Most impressive of all was the sight of "The Grand Old Lady" herself, the Statue of Liberty. We were exhilarated by it, but also emotionally affected. Would we ever see her again? And when?

We heaved anchor and were on our way to only God knew where.

A strange silence befell each man, as if, suddenly, we all realized the true implication of what was really happening. We exchanged fleeting glances and quietly, one by one, slipped away from the railing. Tears welled up in my eyes, and I had to turn away. I didn't want other soldiers seeing me crying like a whimpering child, even though I heard some muffled sobs from them, too. It was a sad time, saying goodbye. But it was a proud time, too, as we embarked to serve our country in the cause of Freedom. Along with the others, I was thinking, how many of this 12-man squad who had trained together for all these past months would return to say "hello" to this Grand Old Lady?

The culmination of those long, hard days of preparation had brought us to this point. We felt we were well prepared for whatever lay ahead. Only time would tell.

Fifty-six ships made up our exceptionally large convoy. Included were troop transports, freighters, aircraft carriers, destroyer escorts, battered tankers, destroyers and merchant ships. The tankers carried millions of gallons of gasoline and aviation fuel. They were so loaded that they sat very low in the water. You could barely see their superstructure rising out of the ocean.

I later learned that we were one of three combat divisions in the makeup of the convoy. We were the first convoy to proceed directly from the United States to France. The 13-day voyage was uneventful except for a few submarine alerts from the German subs that patrolled these waters all the time. These alerts marked the first time we had to face real danger.

The troop transports were patrolled by destroyers and destroyer escorts, a smaller version of the Navy destroyer. But the troop transports were always safely tucked into the middle of the entire convoy, leaving us relatively safe from the action. We must have lost a few tankers and merchant ships out of the convoy. I'm not sure how many. Still, the subs made a few kills on nearly every convoy that crossed the North Atlantic.

Life aboard ship was monotonous for the 3,000 of us in the 413th Infantry Regiment that were aboard the old French ocean liner. We would rise early, stand in long lines for chow. Shortly thereafter, we'd be back in line for our second of only two meals per day. This was no luxury line. And as always, in the Army, it was "hurry up and wait."

2

We arrived in the English Channel off the coast of the Cotentin Peninsula, France, in early September 1944. Nothing could have prepared us for the devastation we saw in the harbor and in the city of Cherbourg itself. The constant pounding from the air raid attacks prior to the D-Day landing up the coast at Utah and Omaha beaches had reduced the entire area to complete shambles.

The only way we could reach land was to go over the side of our ship, down cargo nets in full field gear and into Landing Craft Infantry (LCIs) for the short hop to the harbor area. This turned out to be more than a little difficult. The seas were extremely choppy, and the LCI rode up and down the ship's hull rather high and fast. We would descend the cargo nets, four at a time, until such time the order was given to kick free and drop into the small craft.

Sometimes, if you were lucky, you caught the LCI on the way up. Then your fall into it was not so bad. If, however, you kicked free at the wrong time, just as the craft started down in the swells, you would drop an extra 10-12 feet into the steel bottom. Some men received leg and ankle injuries in the process. Regardless, with 80 pounds of field equipment on your back, you became a crumpled mass on the floor of the craft one way or the other.

Once ashore, we immediately headed inland through the bombed-out ruins of Cherbourg to the interior of the peninsula, which was to be our holding area. We covered many miles that day. Since we were short of transport trucks, 6x6s would load up at the rear of our column, haul the troops up ahead several miles, deadhead back to the rear and repeat the process—sort of leapfrogging our way into France. In doing this, we didn't have to march the entire way. We were spelled by the short truck rides, and it helped us regain our land legs after those 13 long days at sea.

Preparing for more intensive training before being assigned to combat, we set up tents in a bivouac area that consisted of an old French apple orchard. We were just getting settled in when orders came to prepare to move out on our first mission. On 26 September we embarked on one of the longest marches in our history: a distance of 30 miles, in full field gear, to reach our beach positions. Our mission was to protect the French shoreline from a strong German garrison located just offshore in the Jersey Islands. We conducted day and night patrols, established outposts and prepared defenses to drive off any raids initiated by the Germans. While there was very little action, we had to stay alert at all times.

War was at hand for the Timberwolves.

Rumor had it that we would be going to head for the front lines in just a few days. The probability of impending movement was verified by a Sunday morning free of training. Many of us were free to leave the camp area until noon chow.

I'd heard some of my squad talk about a wine shop in a small village several kilometers up a narrow road, inland from out bivouac area. About eight of us decided to scout around and try to find the village. The thought of securing a bottle or two of wine spurred us quickly on our way up the road.

After nearly an hour of walking, we came up over the rise of a fairly steep hill. Looking down the far slope brought us face to face with a small church building. It was made of wood and was topped with an imposing tall steeple. We approached the quaint little church, amazed that it had survived the war that had been so recently waged in the area. Two tiny stained-glass windows rather high up on each side of the two large entrance doors were amazingly intact.

While we stood in awe, gawking at the two beautiful windows, someone walked up beside us and opened one of the heavy wooden doors. Our curiosity got the best of us at this point, and we walked into the church. The building was nearly full of people sitting on rather primitive benches, all in several rows facing away from the door.

The minister stood on a wooden platform at the far end of the room. Seeing us through the opened door, he quickly motioned us to enter. Sheepishly, we walked inside. By now we were just a bit embarrassed by our rather brash intrusion. An elderly man seated on the end of the back row of benches immediately arose, gently took the arm of the lead soldier and led us down the center aisle to the front of the church.

There he indicated that we sit on the bench on the front row. I felt awkward and totally out of place sitting in front of all the worshipers. Because we were in full battle dress, the other men undoubtedly felt much the same. All we lacked was our combat packs. Upon entering, we had removed out steel helmets but still had our M-1s slung over our shoulders.

Sitting ramrod straight with our rifles between our knees, we listened as the minister continued his sermon. Since it was in French, we couldn't understand a word. About twenty men in French navy uniforms sat directly in front of us on a raised platform.

Five minutes after we sat down, the minister offered a closing prayer. All heads, including ours, were bowed. As words of prayer faded away, the French sailors stood. One of them stepped forward and led them in song without musical accompaniment.

I sat absolutely stunned by the beautiful harmony of the men's voices. The service in this out-of-the-way place was affording us a tranquillity we didn't know existed. Although the words were in French, I easily recognized the song as "Ava Maria." When the last strains died away, the congregation rose and silently filed out the front door. The people moved as if a spell had been cast over them. I was caught in the spell, too.

Slowly standing, my eyes blurred with tears, I hugged the first sailor I could reach. Although no words were exchanged between the sailors and us, they understood our feelings of gratitude for their efforts. We were foreigners in their land, but we shared a common bond with them. And hearing them sing a beautiful song surely had beaten the heck out of finding a couple of bottles of wine, which had been our initial goal. I left that little church on that Sunday morning filled with a renewed spirit.

That renewed spirit helped carry me through the tough battles for survival I would face in the next 10 months. Many, many times during the long frightful days and nights ahead, I would hearken back to those few minutes of being embraced by the strains of "Ava Maria." When we left the church, I couldn't envision the number of instances this lonely, homesick soldier boy, far from home and in strange surroundings would need all the inner strength he could find to continue the struggle. "Ava Maria" was later the song I requested for my wedding to Gracie. No song was ever more appropriate for such an important milestone in my life.

It wasn't long afterwards that we were to move-out again; this time for real. After another forced march to the village of La Haye-du-Puits, we boarded dilapidated French boxcars and headed for Belgium. I got to see Gay Paree through the cracks in the boxcar as we hurriedly slipped through the city during early evening.

Reaching the city of Mechelen, Belgium, we disembarked and immediately prepared to relieve the British 49th Polar Bear Division in the line. As we took over the 49th's positions, some of the men were actually looking forward to making our first contact with the enemy and going into battle. The men were stir-crazy and ready after nearly two long years of intensive infantry combat training.

Every man in the 104th Division had known that combat was inevitable someday. When we first committed to battle, the thought that was uppermost in my mind was that this is the final test of all our training, the final test of ourselves. Questions raced through my mind, as I'm sure it did those of other men. Will I be able to stand it? Will I be wounded? Will I be killed? Can I physically and mentally survive the hell that is soon to come?

Never entering my mind was the thought or possibility of being taken prisoner. It was the last possibility for me—I never even thought of it at all. "Wounded" or "killed," they were part of my vocabulary and were very real to me. "Prisoner" was not.

I soon realized that a soldier learns more in the first few hours of battle than he learns in all of the long months of maneuvers stateside. The realization sets in when he witnesses his first combat casualty. This is especially true when it happens to be a buddy that he had known and trained with for the previous several months. The first sight of real blood seeping through a uniform really puts the situation in immediate perspective. It's truly a life-and-death scenario, and he's in the thick of it.

My most lasting impression of that night of combat was what it was like to have fear. It is difficult to put into words just exactly what fear is and what it does to you. The constant roar of the big guns is deafening. The sky is lit up like a giant fourth of July fireworks display. But this display is spewing forth death and destruction over the landscape.

Your senses play tricks on you in combat, especially at night. Stationary objects seem to move. Little sounds are somehow exaggerated into a roar. Your stomach is queasy. I couldn't eat the first five or six days in the line. Others felt the same. After that, there was seldom enough food to alleviate our hunger. We lived mostly on K rations, which were barely enough to keep us going.

I went to sleep in my foxhole that first night, not knowing whether it would be forever or if I would wake to the dawning of another day. The period of waiting preceding a battle is the most nerve-racking and frustrating time for an infantryman. Each of us had to be sure our rifle was spotless, our gear squared away and we had all the ammo and grenades that could safely be carried. Then the seemingly eternal waiting began, along with the continuous griping among the troops, until the order came to move out.

It was during this waiting period that my mind played tricks with my senses. I always imagined all possible scenarios when I was waiting for the battle to begin. But after the firing started, all attention turned to survival, and I had a clear head. Of course, we continued a steady barrage of bitching and griping, even during battle situations. Perhaps it was only out loud and addressed to no one in particular, but expressing ourselves in this manner sort of helped ease the tension of the moment.

We made never-ending complaints about our living conditions, the muddy foxholes and the lack of food. None of our complaints received any attention, but it relieved the nagging fear that tore at a man's guts. We vented our anger at the rear-echelon troops who received food and shelter and, most of all, mail, everyday. I was lucky to get a mail call once a week during my days on the front lines.

We pushed hard up through Belgium and crossed the border into Holland at night, not even knowing when we crossed into another country. The 413th Regiment, plus support troops, were covering an area more than 8,000 yards wide, leading north through Holland.

Because Holland had been reclaimed from the sea by the building of large dikes, the water table was about 1 foot below ground level. In addition, the terrain of boggy fields was crossed by canals that were about 8 feet wide and waist deep or more with a double strand of barbed wire running down the middle just below the water line. The banks were steep and more than a little slippery.

As soon as you got tangled in the wire, a machine gun would open up at one of the canals, sending bullets ricocheting and tumbling off the surface of the water. So we were forced to do most of our fighting along and on top of the dikes. All dwellings were situated along the built-up dikes. This afforded plenty of cover for the enemy, who was very well dug in by now. Also, the dikes were heavily mined.

Battle casualties were extremely high. And a lot of men were sick from the continued exposure to the cold, wet conditions. We were soaking wet for the entire Holland campaign unless we could find refuge somewhere out of the rain. During one of the instances I was in reserve during the campaign, I did just that. I was wandering around in the small village of Breda, just looking at the quaint Dutch houses. The day before, we had pushed the Germans out of the area, and the local inhabitants were just beginning to emerge from their basements and other hiding places. Most of the townspeople spoke English, so conversation was easy and friendly. They were thankful to us, their liberators.

I was admiring an especially large house, ornately decorated with hand-carved faces of humans and animals. As I stood entranced by its beauty, untouched by its beauty in such utter destruction, the lady of the house appeared in the doorway and beckoned me inside. Darkness was approaching as she asked me to stay for supper. I eagerly accepted. Although the amount of food was rather meager, its taste was exceptional to me.

After supper, I sat around with the entire family, consisting of the mother, the father and their 13-year-old daughter. They spoke of life in the village before the Germans came; I talked about my home and family. It was enjoyable, and the evening passed quickly. The village was small and sat in a dense forest. The hour was late, and it was dark outside. I was invited to spend the night, "if it was not against Army regulations."

"To hell with Army regulations," I said. "No one but my foxhole buddy will miss me. I stay."

Shortly afterwards, I was led to a large upstairs room which held a large, hand-carved, four-poster bed, complete with a thick, soft mattress. The electricity had not yet been restored to the house, a result of the fighting that had taken place. There wasn't anything to stay up for, so I stripped down to my shorts, climbed into that bed and pulled up the big, fluffy comforter and was in happy dreamland in a matter of minutes.

Although occasional artillery fire rattled the windows, I think I slept soundly for the first night since landing in Europe several days before. I awoke at daybreak and was treated to a hearty home-cooked breakfast in bed, served by a pretty Dutch maiden. This will surely be the high point in my European travels through picturesque Holland, I thought, as I enjoyed the meal.

From there, it was back to the life in the field and the horrible living conditions that went with it. The mighty Air Corps was the recipient of its share of our disdain. On another day we were on reserve duty just behind the front lines and not actually in the thick of battle, Pvt. Bob Polanko and I stretched out on the ground behind the shell of a bombed-out building. It was a rare sunny day in Holland, and we were soaking up the sun. It rained most every day during our campaign in Holland, so this was really a treat. We were trading gripes about everything that was wrong with the war.

The sky was clear as far as we could see. Bob caught sight of the vapor trails first. They were approaching from the direction of Germany. He immediately launched into a tirade about the Air Corps.

"Look at those lucky bastards, sailing for home base in England."

"Yeah," I piped up. "As soon as they land, they'll all rush to the pub for a shot of whiskey to calm their nerves after that long, stressful flight over enemy territory. Then to a nice, warm, dry bed instead of a muddy foxhole. Hell, they're only in actual combat over their assigned target area a few hours. Then clear flying home."

"Cripes, Dukes, we're under stress 24 hours a day."

Bob was getting more fired up by the minute. He kept on.

"I was told they only have to fly 25 missions and they can rotate back to stateside. Damn! Wish we had that option, Dukes."

"Yeah," I said. "What do we have to look forward to? Killed in action; wounded or severe illness; survive through to the end of the war; possibly be captured by the enemy. Some future, huh, Polanko?"

Bob, a Mescalero Apache from an Arizona Indian reservation, was usually very quiet. But today he was wound up. Raising his voice, he leaned over close to me and said, "Do you realize that every one of those flyboys up there is a sergeant or an officer? I'll bet most of them haven't been in the Army any longer than you and me. How long you been in, Dukes?"

I quickly added up the months in my head and replied, "I've racked up 24 months and six days."

Bob shot back, "You got any stripes yet?" But he answered his own question before I could even utter a word. "Damn it, I've been in longer than you have, and we're both lowly privates!"

I could only laugh.

"Maybe your bravery in battle will win you a combat promotion," I said, jokingly.

At first he didn't take the joke too kindly, but he finally grinned and said, "Why did you enlist in the goddamn infantry instead of the mighty Air Corps?"

Before I could come up with a smart reply, our gripe session ended abruptly as we both dove headlong into the nearest foxholes. Debris from the nearest building was flying all around us.

"Damn it, Polanko! I thought we were in reserve! Why in hell are they picking on us?"

As we burrowed deep into our holes, I could still hear Polanko bitching about the "goddamn Air Corps" before the noise of exploding artillery drowned him out. I crouched, shivering, in that muddy hole. I thought of the guy from home who had shipped out to England, having flown his 25 missions, and was back in Georgetown, medals and all, before I finished training. For him, the war was over.

The shelling became more intense around me. I heard Bob yelling and cursing. I hollered above the roar of exploding shells, "Polanko! You OK?"

"Yeah, I guess so," was the reply. "The friggin' brick bats from that building are about to cover me up!"

"Hey, ol' buddy, I'll dig you out," I said. "After the artillery lets up, of course."

"Gee, thanks a lot," came a low, muffled voice.

We both came out of that barrage with only minor bruises from flying bricks. The building in front of us was reduced to a pile of rubble.

Sure looked like we were in a war zone.

The few roads in the region ran on bare dikes high above the surrounding fields. Dutch towns were strung out for a mile or more along each side of the highway. These towns, being situated on the raised dikes, gave the enemy full observation of all the surrounding meadows and canals. Many times we were caught in the open fields where we were subjected to murderous small-arms and machine-gun fire as well as mortar and artillery fire, too.

Vehicular traffic was impossible except on the high-dike roads. And every house along these roads had become a fortified strongpoint that had to be systematically cleaned out. We did the cleaning out with our bayonets and hand grenades. Casualties suffered along the way usually had to wait until dark to be evacuated. Then it was comparatively safe to drag the wounded to a waiting jeep at the roadside.

Throughout the day in Holland, the 413th Regiment was in reserve. Nevertheless, we were still subjected to intense mortar and artillery fire. So when the orders came to move out at 2100 hours for another night attack, we almost felt relieved for getting out from under the heavy barrage that had been landing in our area. Little did I know then just how tough the next three days and nights would be in my first big battle in Holland.

I was lead scout on a platoon-strength patrol. We were sent out to safeguard us from any ambush. The rest of L Company was to follow at a 1,000 yards behind, but our advance guard was stopped by intense automatic fire 50 yards from enemy lines. The Germans either didn't detect me or were waiting for me to walk right into their position to capture me for interrogation.

When they opened fire, though, Pvt. Fred Keeler, the second scout who was just a few yards behind me, was killed instantly. The night was dark, foggy and murky. He and I had been walking fairly close together to maintain contact with each other and the rest of the lead platoon. Upon hearing the machine-gun fire, I immediately hit the dirt and crawled into a shallow ditch at the side of the road.

The company then closed up to within 100 yards behind us and deployed to attack the strongpoint or the Main Line of Resistance (MLR), which was now definitely located, at dawn. The firing was sporadic all night long. Occasionally, there would be a round of mortar fire, or 88s and a new sound I had never heard before. It sounded like some sort of big gun but without the terrible muzzle blast of the German 88 cannon. (After we had taken the strongpoint later, I saw the source of the new sound. It was 20mm Ack-Ack guns that had been firing anti-personnel rounds point blank into our positions.)

This other big gun was to my direct front and was firing straight down the center of the road that I had just walked up. One of the first shells landed about 80 yards behind me in the ditch. My squad leader, Sgt. Russ Phillips, was killed instantly when he took a direct hit in the head from the exploding shell.

Most of the mortar fire was coming from my right flank. The Jerry mortar crew continued to lay down a salvo across the road and the ditch, which was now filled with the rest of my platoon.

Just to my right front about 50 yards, a machine-gun nest was laying down grazing fire across the road, too. I was lying flat in that shallow ditch, so flat that my backpack was sticking above the bank of the ditch. That machine gunner kept firing away at me until my pack was completely shredded and ripped off my body.

At first, I thought the force of the shell fire might roll me completely out of the ditch and onto the open roadway. If this happened, I knew Jerry could cut me into small pieces. I was finally able to shed what was left of the backpack. The firing stopped then because he could no longer see the bulge sticking up out of the ditch.

But then the mortars started dropping all along the road and into the ditch. All I could do was hug the ground and try to dig in with my hands to get my body below ground level in the ditch as protection against the mortars. The Jerries kept up the firing all night long, so I was unable to get any sleep.

As I lay on my stomach in that shallow ditch all night, I said many a prayer to the good Lord above. I made a promise that if He would allow me to survive the night and witness the light of another day, I would say, "Good Morning," for the rest of my life regardless of how long it was or what time of day. And I did see that beautiful sunrise the next morning.

For more than 50 years, I have continued to use that phrase in greeting 24 hours of every day without explaining my reason—except to those who seem truly interested—and without being concerned about the criticism. Try answering the telephone in the evening with a "Good Morning" in a cheerful, happy voice and see how many people hang up on you.

At dawn, we made a frontal attack but were thrown back with heavy losses. I continued to fire from my forward position, barely 50 yards from the German emplacements. The company made several more daylight assaults, all ending in failure and with heavy casualties. Eight men were killed in the attempts made to penetrate the entrenched German force.

The enemy defenses were well camouflaged, which made it difficult for our men to locate targets. Meanwhile, enemy snipers were having a veritable field day. In addition to those killed, the company suffered more than 20 men wounded. Later that morning, a company of five British Churchill tanks blasted a hole through the German lines, providing us with the support we needed.

About that time, my company commander, Captain Marshall Garth, crouched, with an M-1 in his hand, came running along the ditch where I had lain through the night and said, "Let's go, soldier. Get up and go get 'em."

I jumped up, glad to be out of the shallow ditch, and followed the captain toward the hole the tanks had made in the strongpoint. Our company took it at about 1000 hours and was able to put the enemy in flight, pushing the Germans into a big woods. At nightfall, we halted and dug in for the night. From there on, we were in intense and continuous combat, night and day, until we reached our original stated objective: the south banks of the Maas River. During one stretch, I continued four days without ever stopping to sleep and found myself sleeping as I walked. Unquestionably, life on the front was drab, dreary and scary. It seemed as though there was no beginning or end; everything just ran together. Light moments were few and far between. When one did come, you savored it and remembered it.

On one such incident, I was sitting alone in a dugout. My foxhole buddy, Pvt. Don Tase, had been hit two days before and, as usual, replacements were slow in arriving. The dugout was located at the edge of one of the numerous canals that crisscrossed the broad landscape in this section of Holland. Mother Nature was providing a steady downpour while the Jerries were providing the thunder by lobbing in a steady barrage of mortar rounds. One round landed so close that I was partially buried when part of the dugout caved in on my legs. I couldn't move my legs from the thighs down and got right to work with my entrenching tool to get that weight off my legs.

After several minutes of frantic shoveling, I was gradually able to move first one leg, then the other until I finally was nearly uncovered. About that time I spied the abbreviated overseas edition of *Reader's Digest* that I'd tossed aside when the dugout caved in. I had been reading all about how rough conditions were in the jungles of the Pacific Islands. Maybe so, I thought, but it's rough here, too. When the last mortar had hit, I was beginning to panic. I had had the urge to jump out of the hole and run, not walk, to the rear. It was called "deserting your post." But, fortunately, as I was digging myself out, the company runner approached my position and hollered, "Dukes, mail just arrived. You have a package from home."

"Okay," I said, shouting while thinking perfect timing. "Thanks."

I grabbed my M-1 and fairly flew to the rear, heading straight for the CP and out from under the mortar fire. If it's food, it'll take me at least an hour to eat, I thought. I was going to delay my return to my post as long as possible.

Pvt. Pete Lobue, the mail clerk, saw me coming and retrieved my package from his jeep. I eagerly tore off the wrappings and opened the box from my mother. There, in all its glory, was a pineapple upside-down cake. Mom knew it was my favorite. But what a broken, crumbly mess it was. I couldn't figure out what was upside-down or down-side up. What the heck, though, I thought. It didn't matter, and I grabbed a handful and ate it as though it were my last meal. It was delicious!

I was immediately transported back to my mother's table, gorging myself on this same cake, smothered with real whipped cream. Poor Mom. She obviously didn't realize the cake would arrive in such poor condition. But I knew she knew I would savor and appreciate it. At that point in my musings I was rudely jolted out of my daydreams by Lt. John Meader Jr.

"Get back to your post immediately, Dukes," the lieutenant said. "Prepare for an advance across the canal. Enemy forces are headed our way."

I gave a hasty "Yes, sir," slung my M-1 over my shoulder, picked up my box of cake and headed out, slipping and sliding across the muddy wasteland. As I went, I balanced the box as best I could, but the condition the cake was in, nothing short of a direct hit could have made it look worse than it did.

Back at the foxhole, I ate as much of the cake as I could in 15 minutes. Then orders came to move out, and I left more than half of the cake in that muddy foxhole. There was nobody close to share it with. Mom must have been with me that afternoon, because I ran, dodged and hit the ground many times. But I survived about 300 yards of open terrain that was being saturated with artillery and mortar fire. I lost several of my buddies that afternoon before we secured our objective and dug in for the night. Later, I shared the cake episode with the some of the surviving men in my company. By then I exaggerated the whole thing to make it all the more bizarre and humorous.

In our approach to the Mark River crossing on our way to the Maas, we were moving through one of the small villages along a main dike road and came under heavy fire from the German 88 mm cannons. At about 3,500 feet per second, the 88 round traveled so much faster than anything in the American arsenal that our movement slowed to a crawl. To avoid high casualties, we had to stay off the road and cross it only when necessary.

When it was necessary, we tried to time our crossing of the open road between salvos of cannon fire. One man would cross to the safety of a building and then signal for the next man to make a mad dash to the other side. Just after I made it safely across, Pvt. George Will, the machine gunner, started and tripped with the heavy gun. As he got up and started on across, an 88 caught him within a few feet of where I was waiting for him. Blood covered the roadway where he had gone down.

The explosion was so close that it almost completely demolished the small building I was crouched behind. I was nearly buried by the rubble the blast created and suffered a few bruises and small cuts but no shrapnel wounds. So I was able to crawl out and drag him to the safety of the small building by the side of the road, leaving a wide trail of blood behind us. After hollering for a medic, I tried to calm the man's fears. His face quickly grew pale as his life blood poured out through his shattered body and soaked his uniform. I knew he was hit badly but initially had hoped he had a "million-dollar wound" and would be sent stateside for recuperation. He knew otherwise.

"Would you take my watch and get it to my mother?" he asked in a soft voice, his eyes almost closed. "She lives in Queens. New York City."

"Sure, I know," I said and gently removed the watch and put it on my right wrist. "You can get it from her when you get home."

I didn't know what else to tell him under the circumstances, wanting to believe that he was going to make it home but knowing the 88 had made almost a direct hit and that he had caught the full weight of the exploding steel. He died right there in my arms before the medic ever got to us. Had the man not stumbled and fallen, he surely would have made it to safety and maybe back to Queens instead of becoming another casualty.

Crossing the Mark took a heavy toll of casualties for the 413th Regiment, too. Using rubber boats to cross, we had to go in the river and cling to the side of the boat with our heads barely above water because of the intense fire from the well-fortified German positions. Several rafts were sunk, forcing the men, who were heavily weighted with equipment and ammo, to attempt to swim or wade to avoid drowning in the swift, muddy stream. Being more than 50 yards wide, the river became quite an obstacle for us.

At another time, we made a forced crossing at night with a full battalion. Using rubber boats again, that crossing of the Mark River was successful after one of the most awesome displays of high explosives I ever witnessed during my time in Holland. High explosives were ripping apart the town of Standaarbuiten to our immediate front. The town seemed to rise and fall with each successive barrage, as though it were undergoing a series of earthquakes.

The use of timed fire from artillery battalions was the most devastating cause of the casualty rate among the enemy forces. Both sides employed this type of fire in combat. The timer on the shells would be set to explode several feet above ground level. It was especially ravaging if a man was caught out in an open area or even down in a foxhole where the shrapnel would rain in on him.

Some of the shells were armed with steel shrapnel, while others contained the nightmarish white phosphorus. The stuff would eat into your uniform down to the bare skin and continue burning its way deep into the flesh. This white powdery stuff caused us, on occasion, to dive into one of the many canals to escape its devastation. With water, we were able to wash away any remnants that clung to our uniform. White phosphorus was one of the most fearful and painful weapons of World War II.

The Timberwolves were under the command and control of the 1st Canadian Army. I don't know why, but it seemed that we were always out in front of the forces on our right and left flanks. We had already gained a glowing reputation as a fighting force in our early engagements with the enemy.

Field Marshall Bernard L. Montgomery, commander of the 21st Army Group, gave our regiments the toughest assignments. Being night fighters and jumping-off after dark, the next morning would find us 2,000-2,500 yards in front of the British 49th Polar Bear Division on our left flank and the 1st Polish Tank Division on our right flank.

Although we were fighting alongside seasoned veterans from the British and Canadian armies, the Germans employed all kinds of ruses. They knew we actually were green troops, fresh from the United States. One of their machine gunners would place overhead fire down a highway. When an infantryman attempted to cross the road, he would be cut down by another machine gun firing grazing fire.

A German soldier would stand up and shout, "*Kamerade*," wave a white flag wildly in the air. Surrender? Just as an infantryman stuck his head out of the foxhole to take command of the "surrender," the comrades of the flag waver opened fire on our man. One of my close buddies, Sgt. Albert Knorr, was literally cut in two by a German *Schmeisser*, a sub-machine gun, in one of these scenarios.

The German soldiers attempted to make us believe that our own artillery was firing on our positions by shelling us as soon as our artillery opened up on them. They timed their barrages so that we might blame our own guns for "short rounds."

As an advancing army, we had the advantage in one area. If you were wounded on the battlefield, you had a good chance of being treated by your own medics. But a retreating army was not always able to evacuate its own wounded.

The Germans, however, as they retreated back north toward the Maas River were very adept at laying mines and booby traps all along the restricted avenues of our advance. This caused much havoc among our forward units. Any item a soldier would want to pick up as a souvenir was nearly always booby trapped. Many a casualty resulted from these well-placed booby traps; many an inviting path through a forest, more often than not, was covered by trip wires that would set off a Bouncing Betty, our name for these treacherous mines.

These beauties consisted of a small canister filled with pieces of nuts, bolts, nails and assorted other scrapes of lethal iron. They were placed at ground level, well camouflaged, with four or five trip wires emanating in all directions from the canister. By tripping one of the wires, the device would detonate, sending a small charge under the mine. This boosted the mine about waist high. The canister would then explode, spewing its deadly charge in all directions and taking a man down before he had a chance to take cover.

Occasionally, we encountered another type of German contraption called a "SCHU" mine. This was an especially scary device because it was constructed of wood; therefore, it could not be detected by any of the mine detectors in our arsenal. When you stepped on one, the pressure would activate the detonator and the mine would explode when you lifted your foot off and relieved the pressure. Sometimes you would hear the click of the activator, but as soon as you moved and released the pressure, the thing would explode.

This mine, too, was placed at ground level and was well camouflaged. It contained just enough explosives to shatter a soldier's ankle, knee or hip joints. In some cases, the explosive would mangle a soldier's foot to such a degree that amputation would be performed right on the battle field in order to save a man's life from the loss of blood.

Across the bleak and forbidding, marsh-filled plain, intersected everywhere by such obstacles as canals and dikes, and with penetratingly cold winds blowing in from the North Sea, our pursuit of the enemy continued for the next three days and nights without any letup in sight. Although the enemy suffered high casualties, the Germans continued to contest every foot of territory. They had to be flushed out, foxhole by foxhole and house to house until they were finally pushed back across the Maas River, our assigned objective since entering combat.

At this point, the mission was accomplished.

We dug in along the south banks of this mighty river and prepared to take advantage of a chance to rest and regroup. I had just barely finished digging what I considered to be the finest foxhole in all of Holland when orders were issued to mount up and move out for a much-deserved seven days of rest.

Loading onto our division 6x6s, we were all full of vim and vigor and eagerly looking forward to our first night free from combat in a long time. Our destination was Liege, Belgium. Upon arriving there, we piled out of our trucks, jabbering like idiots at the prospect of maybe a few nights with a roof over our heads.

Sitting around a small garden area which surrounded a water fountain, it didn't take us long to relax and get comfortable. The fountain was such an elaborate piece of architecture that some of us just sat and stared at the cascade of water pouring over the mostly red-colored mosaic tile that formed the base of the whole structure.

But then we looked out at the winding road on which we had just arrived and saw another convoy of trucks rapidly approaching our area. The trucks roared to a screeching halt and an order again rang out: "Mount up."

I had left that prize-winning foxhole at 1000 hours on 6 November, thankfully looking forward to relief. By 1800 hours, I was crawling my way to a foxhole which had just recently been vacated by the 1st Division. The 444th Quartermaster Truck Company that had transported us back to the front lines wasn't the most popular outfit around after taking us away from our little time off.

We were dropped off on the outskirts of Aachen, Germany. No sooner had I settled into my new home when orders came to prepare for a night assault on the German positions. I guess we had to prove to the enemy that we were just as good as the soldiers of the Big Red One. With only token resistance from the Jerries, we did push out more than 2,000 yards.

As I finally settled down in a new dugout that first night in Germany, I thought about my first big battle in Holland. It seemed like so many, many days ago. At the time, I had had a wool blanket and shelter half hung over in back of my ammo belt. Then the machine gunner had literally shot the pack off my back, and I lost them and all my personal possessions. What will I lose here? I wondered.

3

The 104th Timberwolves had been in Aachen for slightly more than a week, mopping up following the downfall of the city at the hands of the 1st Division, now on a well-deserved rest. As our patrols went back to the command post (CP) for food and supplies, they'd run into pockets of Jerries and had to flush them out. Mines were everywhere, and the rubble from fierce fighting and bombings that had taken place made the whole scene eerie.

We were waiting for replacements and supplies to arrive for the start of the winter offensive. Each soldier was caked in mud because of the unrelenting rains. Weapons were not in the best shape, either.

After several days of mopping up some pockets of diehard Krauts, we pushed to the outskirts of town along the main *Autobahn* going east out of the city. Our outposts were strung along the top of the ridge a few feet from the extreme edge. From this vantage point, we were able to overlook the large valley and observe the enemy, yet the Germans could not actually see our dugouts. And we had full observation of their positions across the valley.

They had been there awhile and were well dug in; so well, in fact, that they had our area "grid coordinated," meaning that when they spotted any activity from our men, they would immediately pinpoint it and zero in their 88s. The muzzle velocity of the German 88mm cannon was so powerful that by the time you heard the report from across the valley, the shell had landed. It was almost faster than the speed of sound. If they were coming in close, a man couldn't hit the dirt fast enough to beat the blast.

During our occupation of Aachen, we had time to build elaborate dugouts, big enough for three men to live in on outpost (OP) every night. The dugouts were deep and long, with a hollowed-out space on one side so that the number-three man in the rear could squeeze by the middle man to replace the number-one man at the front of the dugout. Thus, you had one hour of duty and could sleep two hours. Of course, you were squeezed in the back with your knees pulled up to your chest. If you had a hint of claustrophobia, this was no place to spend the night.

We continued to send out five-man reconnaissance patrols every night, always probing for a weak spot in the German defenses. Actually, this proved to be a rather futile effort since we were smack up against the pillboxes and other fortifications of the well-fortified Siegfried Line.

We also sent out a patrol to the rear every night to pick up supplies. The total destruction of Aachen prevented supply trucks, or even jeeps, from reaching our forward positions. Casualties had to be carried out by litter bearers.

Top priority on the trips to the rear was to bring back as much ammo as supply would allow. The next priority was Jerry cans (five-gallon, all-purpose cans) full of water. The last item on the priority list was K rations and an occasional box of C rations. The latter were in cans and could be heated for a hot meal; the former were dry rations.

These forays to the rear were quite an undertaking. For fear of mines and booby traps that seemed to be everywhere, we had to avoid the roads and walk or crawl over the rubble of the bombed-out buildings. A cold, tired infantryman loaded down with ammo and rations, carrying a five-gallon can of water and stumbling around in the darkness of the shell of a city made quite a picture.

When a man fell, which I did on several occasions, the water can made an unbelievable racket as it bounced around in the rubble. Actually, it was the noise that did the bouncing against the piles of rubble and the walls still standing on some of the buildings. The eerie echoes from the deserted area were unlike any sound I had ever heard. You lay where you fell for several seconds, waiting for the sound of German small-arms fire that was almost certain to come in your direction. I was sure the echo from the fall could be heard all the way back to France.

We were at least a mile forward of any reserve troops, which made the round trip to the rear last most of the night. No one else was in our area except us and the Jerry patrols. Our ranks were so depleted that every man was on constant duty day and night. But L Company had been shorthanded since we had suffered those 29 casualties during our first big battle in Holland. The Army never seemed to have enough infantry replacements to keep our company at full strength; the Army seemed to have plenty of men for the Air Corps but were woefully short on foot sloggers.

I was still wearing my original uniform, including my regular GI shoes, when winter descended upon us. None of us was issued any extra winter clothing: no high-buckled combat boots, no overshoes or rubber boots to ward off the mud and water. I had no raincoat; I did have my heavy wool overcoat, which was completely soaked. But I never had a chance to dry it out.

Since day one, the Germans had continued to shell our forward positions until all structures were reduced to rubble. We were forced to hole up in deep basements or the dugouts. During the nighttime hours, Jerry would fire a salvo into our positions about every 20 minutes just to keep us awake and on edge. Although a direct hit was a rare occurrence, just the chance of one kept us in a state of high-nervous alert.

Now, the weather was cold and rainy with occasional snow showers. And the sun hadn't shined since we entered Holland. Having lived in the mud and water all through the Belgium-Holland campaign, I felt right at home in the same conditions on the outskirts of Aachen.

I slogged for many days and nights without ever taking off my shoes. Eventually I was unable to take them off for fear my feet would swell up and I wouldn't be able to put them back on. All of us were suffering from trenchfoot, one of the scourges of the infantry.

In my last letter home to my folks, on or about 15 November 1944, I wrote that the letter might be a bit smudgy because I had only the stub of a pencil and had not washed my hands in more than six days.

Everyone drank water out of shell craters, using Halazone tablets for purification. Hot coffee? I quickly learned to heat one-half canteen cup of water just by tearing up the K-ration carton into small bits and feeding the blaze. Those cartons were about the size of a Cracker Jack box and helped provide the ingenuity to get by with what was available.

You never got a full stomach on K rations, but they sustained life. I used everything but the cigarettes. Since I never smoked, I traded them to my buddies or an occasional civilian for extra food.

Coupled with those adverse conditions of existence was the Germans' relentless infiltration of our positions during the night. Consequently, we were sometimes forced to slip back into the edge of Aachen to clean them out of the buildings. On one such foray, most of my platoon was sent into the city to flush out some bombed-out buildings, suspected of concealing a few of the enemy.

I was going from room to room inside a large old apartment building or what was left of it, looking for any stray Germans. Approaching the last room on the top floor, I thought I detected a slight noise. Immediately tossing a grenade, I then leaped through the door, rifle at my hip. I had only a split second to scan the entire room and caught a movement on my right flank. Instinctively, I whirled to the right and fired my M-1.

To my amusement, a large, framed picture came crashing to the floor. It slid right down the wall, glass shattering in all directions. Evidently the force of the exploding grenade had shaken the picture enough that it was still wiggling when I entered the room. That was the sound I'd heard. Walking over to the mess, I took one look and fell to my knees and began laughing hysterically at what I'd done.

On the floor, still leaning against the wall, was a large picture of *Der Führer*, Adolf Hitler, himself. Nothing unusual about a picture of Hitler in the house. They seemed to be on every wall in Aachen.

The thing that had caught my eye in this picture of him was the small hole right between those beady eyes that were staring up at me. My one shot had caught him squarely—and I just lost it. I poured out my pent-up frustration about this whole mess of a war like a babbling, laughing idiot. My laughing subsided after a few seconds, and I bent down and took the picture of Hitler, folded it up and stuffed it inside my tunic. This is a real souvenir of war, I thought as I turned and walked out of the room.

I heard a creaking sound coming from another room I had bypassed earlier and went on about the business of cleaning out the buildings. As I quietly walked back down the long hall to return to the street below, I stopped before the closed door and listened intently at the sound for a few seconds before bursting through the door firing my M-1 in the direction of the sound. A frail, gray-haired woman rocked backwards onto the floor out of an equally frail, squeaky rocking chair. An awful, sickening feeling came over me as I saw what I had done. I knew the sight of that helpless old woman now laying slumped on the floor would be with me for a very long time, haunting me every step of the way, before the reverberating echo of the M-1 rounds I had pumped into her faded away.

I turned and bolted out the door. Had I not been so hungry, I'm sure I would have spilled my guts right there. I had seen so much death and destruction in these last few months that I thought nothing could bother me any more. But I'd never seen or done anything like killing an old woman up close. Nothing I could do about it, though. For one fleeting, horrific moment, I seemed more like a civilian again. Then the soldier in me kicked back into gear, and I was able to get on with what I had to do.

Finally, after days of waiting, the morning we had been waiting for finally arrived. Weather conditions had been so bad with rain, snow and low cloud cover that the Air Corps had been unable to get off the ground for some time. We had had to wait until the weather cleared to get that air support needed to soften the line of fortified pillboxes. And the weather had finally cleared. It was 17 November 1944.

For several days before, we had been sparring around with the enemy in preparation for the big push into the Siegfried Line we knew was soon to start. We had sent out both combat and recon patrols, mostly at night, and hurriedly trained all the new replacements and formed 14-man assault teams to attack the pillboxes and other fortifications.

That morning we began to hear, vaguely at first, a low roar coming from the rear. As the roar became increasingly and incessantly louder, we soon saw a most beautiful sight approaching over the horizon: American planes. Hundreds of them. The sky was literally filled from horizon to horizon with aircraft. What an exhilarating sight!

The noise was deafening as they roared overhead, wave after wave of American B-17 and B-24 bombers, British Halifax bombers and literally hundreds of fighters buzzing around as cover for the big planes. A few miles ahead, behind German lines, the earth seemed to erupt in explosions and fire as the armada unloaded its devastation on the enemy positions.

A combat infantry soldier's greatest fear is the waiting. As you prepare for the battle, your mind starts spinning with all sorts of thoughts of what might happen. Once the battle begins, however, you have to concentrate on the job at hand and struggle to survive the hell that is war. Now the waiting was over for us.

We jumped off immediately as soon as the bombs began to hit and moved out in the early light of dawn. My platoon objective was a strongpoint about 400 yards to our immediate front. Reconnaissance had alerted us as to what to expect in the way of Jerry's defenses. Our objective was a typical German house constructed of concrete and mortar. The Germans were well dug in around the house and had two machine-gun emplacements inside the building.

This was going to be a tough obstacle because there was little or no cover all the way to the house. We would have to use heavy mortar fire along with approaching fire from every man in order to overrun the position. All went relatively well, though, and we successfully captured our objective while losing only one man to a wound.

If everything else went as well, I thought, maybe we would "have Berlin for Christmas." That was the master plan. Only the Siegfried Line stood in our way.

The Siegfried Line was well fortified with machine guns and 88s that were so placed as to have covering crossfire in all directions. Each pillbox was interlaced with connecting trenches and completely surrounded by barbed wire. The area was also densely sowed with mines and bobby traps. Large steel and concrete barriers were spaced out well in front of the pillbox line to prevent the use of tanks and tank destroyers.

After several minutes of heavy concentrated fire from our artillery, our assault teams would move out under an umbrella of small-arms and mortar fire. We attacked the pillbox by blowing a hole in the barbed wire surrounding the perimeter, using a bangalore torpedo. This device consisted of three or four sections of steel pipe crammed full of TNT. The sections could then be screwed together and shoved underneath the wire.

The team would immediately assault through the gap with the objective of reaching the top of the fortification to throw satchel charges into any and all openings in the pillbox. The hail of our covering fire would keep the enemy pinned in the trenches, leaving the machine-gun fire from the pillboxes as the biggest obstacle to overcome.

With enough withering firepower, we could usually keep the machine gunners occupied for the time sufficient to gain the perimeter of the pillbox itself. Then it was a matter of getting grenades and satchel charges inside the structure. This was no easy task and resulted in many casualties for us.

Once that line was pierced, though, we would be able to fan out and advance into the Fatherland. And from that dreary dawn morning that this big push jumped off, my full regiment was to see continuous night assaults on strongpoints around the many small villages and farms. Every inch of German soil was contested. Nevertheless, the regiment continued to keep up the pressure with constant attacks and infiltrating patrol activity.

The Timberwolves were engaged in some of the heaviest fighting on the entire front. The relentless pounding of the German artillery and mortars on our position was taking a mighty toll on our troops. Ammo became a problem. Our supply trucks were unable to keep up with our forward advance, primarily because of the axle-deep mud and numerous potholes.

It was still necessary to send patrols to the rear every night just to keep a supply of ammo, water and what little food that could be scrounged at the CP. More often than not, the troops had to drink water right out of the shell holes. Many of the men got sick from this. Not sick enough to be evacuated to the rear, however, because we were always so shorthanded. It took a major epidemic or a severe wound to get to the rear.

Day and night sort of blended in the continuous battle. We had little or no chance to rest, shave or even wash our hands. In fact, my last bath occurred somewhere back in Holland. As for shaving—forget it. I didn't even have a razor or any soap to use. Personal items were nonexistent.

I often marveled at the combat movies I saw when I returned home after the war. The soldier was always shown loaded down with a huge backpack. His load was so unwieldy that it would be impossible to do the type of fighting I was engaged in, especially with all the mud and continuous movement in battle.

The equipment I carried consisted of my web-cartridge belt holding 10 clips of ammo, K-Bar knife, first-aid kit, canteen, trenching shovel, a wool blanket or shelter half tucked into my belt in back and usually two bandoliers (each holding 10 more clips) of ammo crisscrossing my chest. Throw in a few more hand grenades hanging from my body at any spot I could hang the handle.

I was never burdened down with equipment. I always ate my rations as soon as I received them. First, I was always hungry; and second, I didn't want to die leaving any rations on my body.

After six days of non-stop night-and-day battle, L Company was again assigned yet another tough job of taking two large, nameless hills. The map designated them as Hill 303 and Hill 272. The same old story came down from the CP: "These two hill masses are very strategic and of the highest priority and must be taken at all costs." I had heard that same priority stuff a few time before.

Grazing fire was possible for hundreds of yards in all directions because the area was a continuous hill mass. Because of that, taking the two hills would be an extremely rough operation. The enemy position consisted of four strongpoints: Lohn, Putzlohn and Hills 272 and 303. These were all connected with continuous trenches and communication lines running the entire length of the defensive setup. Later developments proved this was an extremely important strategic defensive line in the enemy's defense for the Inde River.

On the night of 22 November 1944, we moved into position on the rear slope of Hill 303 near Durwiz in preparation for a pre-dawn bayonet attack. In moving up, we encountered a steady barrage of mortar and artillery fire. I think I must have dug eight or 10 slit trenches that night before I reached the jump-off line where I dug my foxhole for the night.

I had just finished scraping out a shallow foxhole in the mushy, muddy ground just below the crest of the hill when I heard something or someone crawling up the hill to my position. God! I was so exhausted from the continuous fighting of the past six days. Then the long march in complete darkness through the muddy fields. Now my foxhole was barely deep enough to hide my whole body. The night was ink black. A steady rain muffled all sounds. But whatever or whoever, friend or foe, was coming directly toward me. I could tell that and buried myself as deeply as I could, rifle in hand, safety off, finger curled around the trigger and prepared for the worst.

"Fertilizer," I said, whispering the first part of the password as the crawling sound got closer. My finger tightened on the trigger.

"Compost," a voice I recognized as my platoon lieutenant said, whispering the correct password in response just a few feet from the end of my rifle.

"Sir, that was a close call," I whispered hoarsely and reset the safety. "I was barely able to hear you coming in, let alone see you."

"Sorry, Dukes," Lt. Meader said, apologizing. "I should've walked up to your position."

But we both knew the Jerries had a nasty habit of dropping a salvo of 88s on our lines about every 20 minutes all night long, and nobody wanted to be spotted. It was harassing fire, but accurate. The 88 crews had our positions grid-coordinated and could place concentrated fire about anywhere they wanted.

"There'll be a turkey dinner tomorrow at 1700, Dukes," the lieutenant said. "We'll celebrate Thanksgiving with all the trimmings."

After we capture our objective, of course, I thought. But a hot meal! I can't remember the last time I ate a hot meal. It sounded wonderful, and I was looking forward to sleeping in that muddy hellhole with happy thoughts of hot food the next day, Thanksgiving Day. I knew, though, that the lieutenant didn't crawl to my foxhole this time of the night just to bring me the good news that we would get a hot turkey dinner the next evening.

"Right now, I want you to go down to the CP and bring some new replacements up for my 3rd platoon," Lt. Meader said and disappeared into the murky night without giving me any idea of the location of the company's CP.

I crawled on my belly part way down the hill. Finally I said, "To hell with this" and stood up and walked to the base of the hill. The Germans had observation of the whole valley below, but it was so damned foggy and rainy that I could barely see five feet ahead.

As I was stumbling around in the darkness, completely lost as to the direction or location of the CP, a shadowy figure suddenly loomed out of the night. Not knowing for sure whether I was still behind our lines or behind German lines, I dropped to my knees, low to the ground. If I could catch the silhouette of a helmet against the sky and it looked like a coal scuttle, I'd know it was a German. But there was no sky, only an inky black curtain. I held my breath and froze as the figure walked toward me. With rifle in my hand, safety off, I took the risk of softly uttering the password again.

"Fertilizer."

For what seemed like an eternity, there was only silence.

Then the soldier said, "Compost."

I heaved a big sigh of relief, clicked on the safety and approached him. He was on CP guard duty. I had miraculously walked right up to the headquarters.

"Lt. Meader sent me for replacements," I said.

"Follow me, soldier, but watch your step," he said, cautioning me as he led me through the rubble. "This area hasn't yet been cleared of German mines and booby traps."

I followed him through a bombed-out building and down a long stairway into a basement. At the foot of the stairs he parted a GI blanket. All of a sudden I was in a well-lighted, warm room. My company commander, Capt. Garth, was seated behind a makeshift table. Several company non-coms were standing around with a group of clean, well-groomed American soldiers.

"Private Dukes needs three replacements," Capt. Garth told them.

The replacements eyed me (suspiciously, I thought). I could readily understand their reluctance to go anywhere with the likes of me. My 10-day heavy beard growth was dirty and soaked, and I was wet and mud-soaked from head to toe. I hadn't realized how bad I did look until I saw these bright, clean uniforms. Two of the men wore combat ribbons, and all wore corporal or sergeant stripes. All of them had been in the service for half the time I had served, and they were already sporting stripes.

They'll just be common foot sloggers in this outfit, I thought. What're these guys trying to prove at a place like this? All those ribbons are so out of place. The Army always seemed to have plenty of Air Corps personnel and rear-echelon garrison troopers, but the lowly infantryman was forced to fight with a constant shortage of manpower. L Company had been reduced from the normal 187 men to dangerously low numbers several times, and we still had to cover the whole company front.

About that time I noticed the shoulder insignia worn by the whole group: Eighth Air Corps. My heart sank. It was tough enough to survive out there with combat training. Without it would be almost impossible. I immediately felt that the Army was doing a terrible injustice to us all by sending three of these men into the battle situation they would soon be facing. But I was just a private.

"Have any of you men had any firing practice with a Garand?" I asked, confronting them with my concerns anyway.

Everybody shook his head.

"We trained with the carbine," one of the men said.

"You have any tactical training under combat conditions?" I asked.

Their only response was to shuffle their clean-booted feet and look away from me.

"Sir, we've been short of replacements since our first battle in Holland," I said, turning to confront Capt. Garth. "We've been getting good infantry-trained replacements up 'til now. And now I have to take *this* into battle. These guys will be dead by the end of tomorrow night. They don't stand the chance of a snowball in hell."

Capt. Garth just shrugged his shoulders and volunteered three men to step forward. "You three men are now assigned to 3rd platoon, L company, 413th Infantry, 104th Timberwolf Division," the captain said, standing to give the orders. "Dukes, they're now in your hands."

One of the men immediately walked over to me and stuck out his hand. I slapped my filthy, mud-soaked glove onto his nice clean hand and squeezed as much mud out of my glove as I could. He winced for a second and then said, "Hi, my name is Joe—"

"I don't want to know your last names," I snapped and jerked his hand as I abruptly stopped him. "Only your first because I've already cried too many times over the bodies of my dead buddies. I don't think I can stand to cry any more."

I was beginning to get cozy and warm in the CP out of the elements, but I knew it was time to get back out there. Looking at the three men, I gruffly gave the order to move out and said, "Grab your

M-1s, load up all the extra bandoliers you can carry and put on that overcoat. That'll hide those flashy Air Corps ribbons. Anyway, it's damn cold and rainy outside. I'm in a hurry to get back to my foxhole for a few winks of sleep. Two or three hours of shuteye a night this past week or so just isn't enough."

"Oh, a big, tough sergeant, huh?" a redhead named Harry with a chest full of ribbons said, popping off as we lined up to leave.

His remark caught me off guard, and I whirled around, angered by his tone. I realized he was a tech sergeant, outranking me about five grades. But he was at my mercy in this situation.

"No, I'm not a sergeant," I said quietly and politely. "Even if I were you wouldn't see any stripes on my arm. The Germans concentrate on soldiers wearing stripes. They figure that if they kill our leaders, the rest of us will just collapse and surrender. They just don't understand that most of our non-coms rise up from the ranks."

That off my chest, I turned, saluted my company commander and the four of us headed up the steps and into the dark night. Just outside, I halted, and we stood in silence for a few minutes in order to adjust our eyes to the darkness. Huddled together, I explained our predicament. We had to cover about 300 yards of slippery ankle-deep mud, all uphill.

"Stay very close to me," I said. "No talking, not even a whisper. Sounds carry at night. I got totally lost coming down from that hill earlier."

Since L Company had earlier moved into position in the black of night, there had been no way to establish landmarks. So absolutely no reference points existed to guide me back to our lines. When we had buttoned up for the night earlier, the Jerries were just 50 years over this big hill mass. They had well-fortified positions that were going to be tough to break through. Our positions were so close that I had heard their muffled conversations drifting our way now and then.

An error to the right or left would put us smack into German positions. I was getting groggy from fatigue and knew we had a long way to go. I had to be careful to steer a straight line because of the tendency to walk in a circle when walking in complete darkness or a blind situation such as we were in. At times, I'd take a step forward and slide back two, but I had to keep trying.

With Divine Guidance from above—and that's the only way I could explain it—I managed to come within a few feet of my foxhole. I turned the men over to the sergeant. Then without one word, I eased into my foxhole and was fast asleep within seconds, my rifle across my chest, bayonet fixed, ready for the morning attack.

With I Company on our left flank, L Company spearheaded the attack at dawn with bayonets and hand grenades. The surprised Germans were caught still in their foxholes. Initially, we took about 77 prisoners and had the situation well in hand.

We had engaged the 385th Field Artillery Battalion to give us covering fire by using a rolling-barrage technique. This kept the enemy pinned down as we followed behind each salvo of artillery. At one point in the attack, we had the Jerries on the run down the hill towards a large building, which turned out to be a coal-processing plant. A giant, gaping, open pit on our right flank apparently supplied the coal.

During the headlong flight, the forward observer (FO) was wounded by small-arms fire and his SCR 300 radio was silenced. This type of radio was carried on a man's back and gave better communication than a walkie-talkie. Accordingly, he was unable to raise the next round of artillery.

Not knowing of this problem, we continued pell-mell in pursuit of the Germans and ended up running right through our own artillery barrage. I was running as fast as I could, considering the mud was deep and a hard rain was coming down.

Although I heard the shell coming at me, I didn't hit the dirt quite quick enough. The shell exploded behind me and sent me flying into the mud face first. Probably the soft muddy field saved me from more serious wounds: The shell dug deeper into the soft earth before spewing its lethal shrapnel around the area.

As it was, several pieces of steel shavings tore into my legs and hands. Since I had the heavy wool overcoat on and a blanket hanging from my belt, the steel did not penetrate my back. It just tore holes in the coat. I also had about an inch of caked mud all over the wool overcoat. The mud acted like armor and kept most of the shrapnel out of my back and upper legs. But several pieces did penetrate my legs below the overcoat, and I could feel the hand wounds through my mud-soaked gloves.

I knew I had been hit but was too scared to think about it or to examine the extent of my wounds. Anyway, shock set in and dulled the pain for the first several minutes. But I hurriedly extracted myself from the mud and continued on down the hill when, abruptly, I found myself again hugging the muddy ground.

A tremendous amount of small-arms and machine-gun fire was pouring out of concealed positions around and inside a big factory building at the base of the hill. Most of our men were within about 50 yards of our objective before we were completely stopped cold.

I started crawling around to find cover and fell into a newly vacated enemy foxhole. This hole was well constructed, I could tell, as though the previous occupant had spent quite some time preparing it. It was quite obvious that the enemy had intended to hold this line of defense for some length of time.

Trying to make contact with the rest of my squad, I crawled through the mud to where I thought I could find them. I found only one man, Lou Vinduska. We attempted to regroup to decide our next course of action. But the enemy quickly made that decision for us.

Just then, I heard the roar of tank motors. Oh, God, I thought. My morale sank to a new low. The lowly infantry soldier has absolutely no defense against armor. And the monstrous Tiger tank suddenly came veering around the corner of the factory building immediately to my right front, followed by a second tank. A third, then a fourth, then a fifth Tiger appeared from around the building to my left front.

They methodically formed a line, five abreast, and proceeded to advance up toward our thin line of defenders. All the while, the tanks were pouring machine-gun fire into our positions, forcing us to keep deep in our foxholes. Some of the men trying to regroup now were caught out in the open and were immediately cut down while attempting to seek some sort of cover.

Then the big 88mm cannons opened up firing the anti-personnel shells point-blank at anything that moved. The firing reached such a deafening crescendo that I felt as though I was starting to float away on air. The ground shook, and the lead showered down around me as though I were in a hailstorm.

Looking for some way out, I witnessed a gruesome scene that curdled my blood. With one tread, a tank rolled over a foxhole occupied by one of the replacements whose name I never learned. Then with the tread still on the foxhole, the tank spun around and around, literally grinding a Timberwolf into the ground. Nothing I could do about it. But as I went back to looking for a way to avoid a similar fate for myself, I knew his screams would be with me forever.

I yelled to Vinduska, in the foxhole nearest me, and we both decided to make an attempt to withdraw a few yards back up the hill to a series of zig-zag trenches. By sheer guts and a bit of luck thrown in, we both dived headfirst into the long trench. We figured and hoped that we would be safe from the tank trying to grind us up, since the trenches were fairly wide, and it would be forced to go straight across. The firing continued, and finally the lead tank passed over us.

Lou suddenly realized that he had an anti-tank grenade in his belt. We started fumbling around, attempting to screw down the wing nut on the grenade adapter at the end of his M-1. This was usually a simple chore, but in our anxiety, it became a monumental task. But finally we were able to mount the grenade.

With a Tiger bearing down on our left flank, we prepared to take a crack at hitting the tread—the only vulnerable spot that we had any chance of doing any damage to the monster. We became so engrossed in trying to latch that damn adapter that we failed to notice the advancing German troops until they were within only a few yards of our position.

Instinctively, Vinduska took his attention from the tank, whirled around and fired the grenade at the first enemy soldier who by now was bearing down on us, bayonet in hand, shouting something in German that neither of us understood.

In our haste and excitement, we hadn't had the sense or shown the presence of mind to pull the pin that would arm the grenade. That stupid blunder undoubtedly saved our lives. The projectile hit the German and peeled a layer of hide from the side of his head just under his helmet. Had we pulled that pin, the grenade would probably have exploded and killed us all. If not normally, surely the impact on that hard-headed German would have detonated the grenade.

Vinduska had had to remove his bayonet in order to clamp on the grenade launcher. Quickly reattaching the bayonet, we both jumped out of the trench to engage the infantry following the tanks. I was so groggy and unstable from concussion that I really don't know what happened for the next several minutes. I only recall being somehow knocked to the ground on my face. Apparently I was dragged down the hill and into the basement of the coal-processing plant.

I never saw those three replacements I brought to the hill again, although I think one of them was killed by tank fire to my rear in the morning's attack. Nor did I ever see Lt. Meader alive again. He was one of the L Company men killed that morning. That hot turkey dinner he had been promising the company would have to wait for many of us. And more than a few of us would never get a hot turkey dinner again.

It was only after I came home after the war and had discussions with my father that I learned the 13 original men I knew had been taken that day. He obtained their names from a "Buddy Book" that I'd kept all through training and sent home prior to overseas shipment. Dad personally contacted the next of kin of all 38 members of my platoon. Through these contacts he learned that 13 men of the 3rd Platoon were listed as MIA on 23 November 1944.

Throughout the winter of 1944-45, Dad learned the fate of all of the men in the platoon. Some were killed; some were wounded; some were still fighting. Those of us who were captured were scattered among several different prison camps. I was the last one of the group that was reported alive. After the war, I learned by reading the history of the 104th Division that L Company all but disappeared that Thanksgiving Day. The company suffered a total of 78 casualties, including 22 killed and the rest missing or wounded. The Thanksgiving Dinner was "celebrated" by the 43 survivors of L Company

Many strange, almost unbelievable, stories pop up from time to time concerning little incidents that happened during the war years. The strangest and most interesting of all was related to me in July 1997, just as I was putting the final touches to this book. A local woman (a young girl in 1944) spent a lot of time at my house back then. She and my sister were best friends. When she learned of my book, she related this story:

"Putsy," my dad, was cashier of the First National Bank in Georgetown at the time. Occasionally, after closing time, he stopped at the local pool room, which was adjacent to the bank, and played in a friendly poker game with several of his cronies. He relished this time with his friends and had always enjoyed a good card game.

As a hand was dealt along in the evening, Dad suddenly became silent, almost detached. Looking down at his untouched cards, he quietly pushed his chair away from the table and slowly stood up. Without a word or a look back, he left the pool room, checked the bank door and drove home.

Everyone was astounded. Hugh Sanders, the owner of the poolroom, said he had never known Putsy to leave a card game, whether his luck was good or bad. And Hugh and the rest of the card players all felt that Dad had had some intuition about me. According to the woman, this happened on 22 November 1944 at about the time I was going into my last battle. My exact situation was unknown to him then, but that was when I was captured,

It wasn't until 10 December 1944, late on a cold and icy winter night that a knock at my folks' door got Dad out of bed with that news. When he opened the door, three Army officers stood before him. Dad ushered them in out of the cold, and they introduced themselves. The senior officer handed Dad "The Telegram," the dread of every family in World War II who had a loved one overseas.

Dad tore open the envelope, fearing the worst, I'm sure. He was somewhat relieved to read "Missing in Action" rather than the finality of "Killed in Action." The officers had done their duty and prepared to leave. When they opened the door, four of Dad's card-playing cronies from Danville were standing on the porch. They had learned of the telegram—somebody always had a friend at Western Union—and wanted Dad to know their foremost thoughts and prayers were with him and the family. They knew there hadn't been any letters from me in nearly a month and realized Mom and Dad had been under a strain.

Although the news was a shock to all, there was still hope that I was alive. All were thankful for that mercy. The men stayed until the wee morning hours and were a great source of support then and throughout the remaining months of the war.

4

Not long after I had stuffed the picture of Hitler and the Luger under some lumps of coal, and without much rest, we were ordered out of the basement of the coal-processing plant, lined up behind the building and immediately marched off. I was somewhat disoriented and was having trouble keeping my balance.

The Germans had requisitioned a long ladder and had put it to good use. By laying the ladder on short poles and placing a man at each end, the ladder became a makeshift stretcher. I was ordered to handle one end of the pole. The added weight caused me to fall several times into muddy water holes along the road.

Besides the sergeant I first saw when I regained consciousness on the coal pile in the basement, I had no recollection of who survived that bloody mess. After endless days of combat, my platoon had lost many of the original men with whom I had trained. So I really didn't know about half the guys that were brought in as replacements. Under combat conditions, we never got in a group together to socialize and knew few of the men that came into the platoon.

Several of the men marching along in this ragged formation were wounded, but we were walking wounded and were forced to march at a rather rapid pace. By this time, the shock had worn off, and I was in severe pain as we trudged through ankle-deep mud on what passed for a road. Many of us fell time and again but got up each time, fearing what would happen if we didn't. I was already soaking wet and caked with more mud, so the slop made little difference. In fact, I was so encrusted with mud that the blood never did seep through my uniform.

We moved rapidly to the rear of the enemy lines in a ragtag group, dropping off a couple of men at a small field hospital tent. These men were too badly wounded to continue.

As we moved farther to the rear, we occasionally added one or two newly captured soldiers to our ranks. I quickly noticed that the farther behind the line of combat we got, the tougher and meaner the treatment became. Our initial captors were decent soldiers and treated us as one fighting man to another. It was the rear-echelon soldiers who became abusive and tended to exert authority.

During one of several encounters with these rear-echelon troops, I was searched and relieved of my two watches and ID bracelet. But even these Germans always returned my wallet with the American silver dollar bearing my father's 1892 birth date. The idea that it was my good-luck charm always seemed to touch a soft spot in everybody, and the coin was returned.

By nightfall of that first day and after several stops for these searches, our column had grown to about 30 men, all Americans. Some were from the Big Red One and some were from the 30th Old Hickory Division. These two divisions had been on our right and left flanks during all of our battles since leaving the city of Aachen.

With only an occasional break to rest, we continued marching through the Rhoer Valley for the next 10 days, heading toward the Rhine River. We wound around through numerous small villages that were completely destroyed by the continuous raids of the Allied bombers. The roads and fields were pockmarked for miles around, attesting to the many months of warfare. By the proliferation of bomb craters, we could always tell when we were approaching a village or town.

About this time, some of us lowly foot soldiers began wondering about the mighty Air Corps and its supposedly great part in winning this war. The fly boys must have called it saturation bombing because this area of the Rhoer Valley was saturated with bomb holes.

Since most of the buildings, including houses, had been destroyed from the air, the surviving inhabitants would come pouring out of the rubble, armed with broom sticks, mop handles, ax handles and anything else that would work. These surviving German civilians would beat on us as we slowly trudged through the town—we weren't exactly marching anymore in the strictest sense of the word. They would hurl epithets in German and sometimes in guttural English. And they spat on us to vent their anger and frustration. I then began to realize that I was the enemy. Since the villagers couldn't reach the Air Corps that had brought on this devastation from 30,000 feet overhead, the civilians could take their hostility out on us.

At this time, we all still had our full uniform and steel helmet and could cover our faces with our hands and stumble along, absorbing the blows on our arms, shoulders and backs. Fortunately for us, most of the villagers left around these parts were old men and women, so the force of the blows was not as hard as it could have been.

The most degrading part of it all was having the people spit on us. The blows I could take, but being spat upon was difficult to accept. As we approached a new village, we would take turns walking on the outside lines of the column to take our turns at being exposed to the townspeople. A couple of the more badly wounded men were always kept in the center of the column to give them more protection.

Throughout the 10-day period, we continued to trudge along from dawn until dark in what seemed to be an indirect route through the countryside. We bedded down wherever we happened to be after nightfall. Some nights we slept out in an open, snow-covered field. If we were lucky enough to be near a village or a farm, we would spend the night in a farmer's barn along with the cows, chickens and hogs. What a treat to be able to burrow into a big stack of hay!

On a couple of occasions, we gorged ourselves on raw potatoes or any other vegetables we could scrounge. Our only other food consisted of an occasional bowl of watery grass soup and a few small slices of black bread. And we only ate when we stopped for the night.

Not only did we have to contend with the wrath of the villagers, but we were subjected to several strafings from our own Air Corps. The fighters would be returning to England from missions over German-occupied territory and seemed to enjoy strafing anything and everything that moved on the ground. Since we were an exposed column of men marching in formation, we became an easy target.

Realizing that the pilots didn't know that they were strafing their own men, we would stagger our lines, shift into columns of four instead of the normal three. Then we would wave our arms in hopes the pilots would understand.

The guards would always head for cover when the planes approached, forcing us to stay in the roadway. On some occasions, we would break for cover in defiance of orders. But since we were usually in open areas, no man was ever able to escape during one of these strafing runs. Several of the men in my group were hit by the 50-caliber bullets, though. The guards would then simply roll them into a ditch and force the rest of us to continue. A couple of times the guard just yanked off both dog tags and shoved them in his pocket.

That soldier then became one of the 78,000 Americans that is carried as "Missing in Action" in World War II. These men had not lived long enough to arrive at a regular POW camp to be registered as having been captured alive. In my own case, I did not become a registered POW until sometime after Christmas 1944 when I reached a permanent camp, Stalag *IV A in Hohenstein, Germany. This was some 30 days after I was captured.*

After walking for some 10 days, we finally reached and crossed the Rhine River at Bonn. From there, we headed in a southeasterly direction to Limburg where I was ushered into my first POW camp, *Stalag* XII A and had my first night's sleeping with a good roof over my head. I also had some of the first food I had had for a while. It consisted of grass soup, two small boiled potatoes and a slice of German black bread. This, I later found, was to be my diet for the remainder of my captivity and the war.

At this point, I had told no one except the sergeant back in the basement of the coal-processing plant about being wounded in both legs. I was afraid the enemy might shoot me in case I became a burden on our march. Fortunately, the bleeding had stopped rather quickly, and my wounds healed almost as quickly. Undoubtedly, the extremely cold weather helped coagulate the blood.

But as soon as I got situated in one of the barracks in XII A, I inquired around, hoping to find an American medic who could check out my wounds. Luckily there were several in the camp, so I moved to a so-called hospital barracks where they could work on me.

Two medics determined that my case was not too serious, at least not serious enough to waste any of the extremely scarce morphine. They had me lay on my stomach while they tried to extricate the shrapnel from the backs of both of my legs. The substitution for morphine was one man sitting on my back while the second one held my feet.

Despite the primitive methods, these medics were awfully kind. They extricated only the pieces of shrapnel that were close to the skin and didn't probe too deeply, leaving several small shards that were more deeply embedded in my legs.

These small pieces of shrapnel left in my legs would eventually surface. Through the years, I would be popping them out one at a time as they worked their way to the surface of my skin and festered. One of the last ones came out in 1994, 50 years after it entered that Thanksgiving Day. The last one came out in January 1997 as I began this account of my POW days.

Because there was an acute shortage of bandages, my legs were tightly wrapped with some scraps of cloth. And I got a glass of milk after the "operation." Then I was discharged "to go home" to the regular barracks.

As I was recovering from my bout with the medics and trying to keep warm, a runner came through my barracks hollering for all men who had arrived that morning to form up in front of a large raised platform on the west side of the camp for an indoctrination "talk." During my three-week stay at *Stalag* XII A, we were subjected to these daily tirades about rules and regulations that we must obey or be severely punished, maybe even shot. That threat of execution was always in every utterance.

Crowding around the platform, we pressed close together for warmth and protection from the brisk, cold wind blowing across the area. Typical of Army routine—German, American or any other, I suspect—that morning and all the rest, it was hurry up and wait. Twenty, 30 minutes, we milled around, stomping our feet and moving to keep warm. The crowd of POWs began to grow ugly, shouting all sorts of rude, insulting things about Germany. But we were abruptly quieted by the approach of four armed guards, marching arrogantly, in their usual manner, toward the platform.

In the center, an American paratrooper, a staff sergeant with stripes, ribbons and all, strode only slightly less arrogantly to mount the platform. He did not display any identifying shoulder insignia that I recall; he did look as though he had just stepped out of a stateside military administrative assignment with his spotless uniform, clean-shaven face, polished boots that reflected like mirrors and air of arrogance that made us sick to our stomachs.

I'd been asked several times by some of the men who had been in camp for a few days if I'd heard my welcome speech from the trooper yet. And when the call came to report to the platform, one of the men said he would accompany me.

"I always go," he said. "It's interesting and gives me a chance to vent my frustration with this place."

Once the trooper got started with his indoctrination speech, I understood the point the man with me and the others had been making. He appeared to be an American and spoke without the guttural accent of a German. But he didn't sound like any Americans I knew.

"Men," the trooper said, launching into the speech he seemed to relish giving, "you are now prisoners of the German Republic."

The grumbling began immediately, but the trooper ignored it and continued with a list of the rules and regulations by which we must abide. He droned on with a long list of dos and don'ts, always ending with "or you will be shot." The Germans seemed to be obsessed with that one statement, ending nearly every sentence with the threat of shooting someone.

As the trooper droned on and on, the grumbling grew to a shouting torrent of epithets emphasizing our opinions of the great Third

Reich. Our catcalls and shouts soon drowned out what he was saying. When that happened, he made a hasty retreat, surrounded by the same four guards who had ushered him to the platform.

Rumors were rampant as to his identity. Was he a German mole planted within the camp? Had he turned on his fellow soldiers to keep from being shot or just capitulated under the same pressure we all felt? Had he been born in America of German parentage but returned to fight for the Fatherland? Nobody seemed to know anything for sure about his background. Whatever, he was living the good life with shelter and sufficient food.

Had he been caught roaming the camp, I'm sure the men would have made mincemeat of him. Compared to the grubby, grim, unshaven faces surrounding me, this American dandy stuck out like a beacon in the night. Many times I wondered what would happen to him. Would the Germans eliminate him near the end of the war when they were through using him? Or would he survive? I knew that if any of us met him back in the States, he would physically feel the anger of his fellow POWs. It gave me something to think about during the depressing days.

And life at Limburg was very depressing, extremely depressing. Nothing of any consequence ever happened to break the monotony. The days were long and cold; the nights longer and colder. I slept on the hard floor, on straw, with one ragged, thin, blue blanket.

Little or no heat was provided in any of the barracks. During the day, I huddled under my blanket or walked around the perimeter of my compound to keep warm. It seemed to be raining every day, so I wasn't able to walk as much as I wanted. Besides being depressing, life was just simply miserable.

During the middle of the afternoon of my first day in Limburg, I was called out and escorted by two German soldiers to what I determined was the headquarters building. Upon entering the building, I was led to a small room and told to wait. The room was bare of furniture, so I sat down on the floor and leaned against one wall. I had no inkling of why I was brought to this room

Shortly afterwards, the door swung open and a stern-looking corporal ordered me down the long hallway to a door at the end. He virtually shoved me through the door into a large room with a desk at the far end. The floor was carpeted and the walls were covered with portraits of all sorts of German officers with a few scantily clad women interspersed among the gallery. A stern, scowling SS captain behind the desk reading from a pile of papers glanced up when I entered the room. His glance caught me red-handed, staring at an extremely beautiful blonde.

"How would you like to spend an evening with that lovely lass?" he asked, a tight smile tugging at the corners of his mouth. His casual manner and smile brought the color to my cheeks.

"I-I would," I said, stammering and stuttering, then managing a meek, "Yes."

I think I was embarrassed by his question.

"I might arrange for such a meeting," he said, motioning for me to sit in the chair at the end of his desk, "if you cooperate fully with me."

That helped me see through the facade. The woman in the picture probably didn't even exist, just a ruse by the officer to get me to believe he was a nice guy.

Then the questioning began. I was thoroughly interrogated by this German officer who tried everything to get me to say something of interest or significance about the American forces. The session went rather smoothly, I thought. I followed the rules of the Army Code of Conduct, repeating only my name, my rank, my serial number. Nothing else!

But he continued shooting questions at me: "Where were you born? What state? When did you join the Army? Why did you chose to fight Germany when the Russians are the real enemy?"

After what seemed like an eternity of one question after another, the questioning stopped—not without some scary moments, however. The officer was big and gruff and had kept up a steady stream of questions, always trying a different angle to catch me off-guard. He was real nice and friendly one minute and a tiger the next. I kept repeating the same sentence after every question he threw at me: "Charlie Dukes, Private, 15304102."

Never once did I say anything except my name, rank and serial number. This held true during this interrogation and the other numerous times I was questioned while I was on my way to a permanent camp. I never wavered.

After he stopped asking questions, he began to tell me more about myself than I knew myself. He had taken my complete history from my wallet and dogtags. I continued the same name-rank-and-serial-number routine until the officer finally gave up and called his orderly to get me out of the room and back to my barracks.

To this day, I think my demeanor kept the Germans from pestering me any more than they really did. They were always looking for the slightest break in a prisoner's composure that I never gave them.

Just a day or two before I was to be transferred out of XII A, I had a more harrowing session with the same officer. Evidently one of the new replacements from back in Aachen had been taken in the same battle that I had. He somehow referred to me as being a sergeant. This information had to come from a replacement, because all of my original buddies knew differently. At any rate, this time the interrogating officer's mask was off.

"You lied to me, *Schweinhund*," he said, snarling at me and calling me a pig dog. "You're masquerading as a private to keep from giving any pertinent information."

He kept repeating that I was lying because non-commissioned officers knew more than privates. I was really frightened this time. But I kept up my same line.

"Charlie Dukes," I said, trying desperately not to show my growing fear. "Private, 15304102."

The officer had an entirely different personality than he had shown during my first encounter. The longer he questioned me, the louder he shouted. Finally, he flew into a rage and grabbed a pair of heavy, cuffed leather gloves that were laying on his desk. With a tremendous back swing, he caught me full in the face with the gloves and knocked me backward off of the chair and sprawling across the room.

Without even a glance my way, he called an orderly and ordered him to send in another prisoner. The officer then began questioning the next man in a calm, quiet manner. I was a bit stunned by the blow and could feel the blood running down my cheek and taste it in my mouth. I had a bloody nose, a couple of small cuts inside my mouth and another gash in my lip. But afraid to move, I lay quiet and still.

In a few minutes, he called his orderly back into the room and told him to get me out of his sight. For once, I heartily agreed with his order. I heaved a big sigh of relief once the orderly grabbed me, and I got through that door. He was none too kind as he hustled me back toward my barracks.

Once there, he opened the door with one hand and gave me a such a hard shove with the other that I went sprawling on my face. The idea obviously was to use me as an example of what happens when you don't cooperate fully during interrogation. Several men came to my rescue and helped me up, full of questions as to what happened to cause my beating.

I tried to explain the best I could. Many of them had yet to be interrogated, and they were curious. I didn't want to put too much fear in them and didn't want them to think that all prisoners got this treatment. But I did want to let them know what had happened and why.

Early the next morning, I was called out and taken to a remote section of the compound where I was forced to stand at attention facing a high barbed-wire fence. A guard stood behind me with his bayonet just inches from my back. I got the idea: I would stand until I passed out and then fall forward into the barbed wire or backward to be impaled on the bayonet.

Standing in the cold wind, I first tried to think of the good times I had had while I was stationed in New York. Then because I wasn't sure I would survive the punishment but felt I had to control my showing of fear, I just let my mind wander to all sorts of thoughts. The fear of being shot hung heavily over my head.

I didn't have any idea how long I stood at attention. After awhile, time and the barbed-wire fence blurred together on the same continuum. But I felt myself begin to crumble. I woke up lying on the floor of the barracks with only a couple of cuts on my face from the wire. Because of the Geneva Convention—Rules of War, you know—I was now fairly certain the guard wouldn't have stuck me in the back. Apparently, the period at attention was just additional punishment for my insubordination during the last interrogation.

Regardless of what the punishment was for or what lay ahead, I was ready to move on. I had had enough of *Stalag* XII A to last for a long time.

5

Early on the morning of what I thought had to be about 19 December, we were rousted out, lined up and counted, then counted again. I was beginning to think that the Jerry soldier's could not count more than 20 of us at one time. But after the second count, we were quickly separated into groups of 65-70 men each and herded into a large brick building where we were told to undress and put our uniforms in a neat pile along the wall. It looked as thought we were going to be treated to a hot shower.

The building was bitterly cold, so we were slow shedding our uniforms. This seemed to push the guards into a frenzy of shouting, shoving and striking us with a few well-placed rifle butts.

Since I had a severe case of trench foot, extending back to my days of living in the muck and water of Holland, I shed everything but my shoes, socks and skivvies. With a great deal of shouting and pointing, I was finally able to convince one of the guards of my condition. Losing his temper but acknowledging, he pushed me through the door and into the shower room.

We all huddled under the four shower heads along one wall, trying to find a handle to turn on the water. When it finally started dribbling out, everyone tried to get wet at once. Man! The hot water turned out to be ice cold and dribbled down for only a brief time. Some of the men never did get wet. All of us were screaming for some soap, but there was no one around to hear us.

As soon as the water was turned off, a door on the opposite side opened. Wet and shivering, we were herded into another large, bare room. Along one wall, we saw a large pile of nondescript clothing. We were ordered to get dressed.

At this point, we were really freezing. Everyone started fighting and clawing after the clothing. I was finally able to grab a shirt which was a couple of sizes too large. Finding a pair of trousers was a bit more difficult. These "clothes" weren't heavy winter trousers, shirts and coats. They were lightweight cotton rags, and they were all we were to have to keep us warm until only God knew when.

I tried many pairs of trousers in pawing through the mess, but all of them must have belonged to short, fat men. The waistband would go around me twice, but the pantlegs would only come down between my knees and ankles. The guards were getting testy again, so I finally settled on the best pair I could find and grabbed a wool-stocking cap and a short, wool-like scarf. Then I hastily dressed.

Somebody handed me a lightweight, light blue coat that hung halfway to my knees. It was so thin that you could actually read a newspaper through it. The back of the coat had an orange triangle painted on the left side of center. It was conveniently where a bullet would go through the heart. The triangle was approximately 10 inches high, affording a perfect target for anyone running from a guard.

Some time later, I discovered three or four bullet holes in the back of the coat. Buttons were non-existent, so I just had to let it hang open. Several days later, I was able to find a small piece of rope which I used as a belt to tie around my waist.

My new shirt did have two buttons, but the trousers had none. I was forced to hold them up by trying a piece of string through the belt loops. Later on a work detail, I scrounged another piece of rope that I used as a belt.

It was a stroke of luck that I had insisted on keeping my shoes. Those who took them off to shower were issued wooden shoes to wear. Besides being cold, the wooden shoes played havoc with the soldiers' feet. Blisters were a constant problem.

After every man was dressed, we marched out to the railroad that ran through one edge of the camp. There we stood for several hours in the cold, waiting. Waiting for what, we didn't know. Rumors ran rampant through the ranks that we were going to be moved to a permanent camp deep inside Germany.

Still, we waited and wondered about our fate.

Then we saw a small steam engine approaching, pulling about 20 small boxcars. The train came to a halt and we were immediately herded into one of the boxcars. All 65-70 of us were crowded into this small space, not knowing what lay ahead.

During our long hours of waiting, we had been counted and searched a dozen or more times, each time by a different group of guards. We had nothing but the clothes on our backs. The searches were nothing more than a harassing tactic.

The guards kept pushing, shoving and shouting at the slow-moving Yanks until the whole group of us was crammed inside the boxcar. These boxcars were about one-third the size of their American counterparts. Then the doors were closed and we could hear the chains and locks clicking. We were locked in. And we were crammed in so tightly that it was impossible for few, if any, to be able to sit down. I was pinned in the left front corner of the car—a spot that I would not vacate for the next six days and nights.

A flat car with an Ack-Ack gun mounted in the center and a small crew manning the gun as a defense against an air attack was positioned near the middle of the train. The gun crew and guards had a closed boxcar similar to what we had, but I'm sure they had much better living conditions than we did to spend their time.

Again we waited for what seemed like hours before moving. Well after dark, a sudden, loud crashing jolt nearly threw me to the floor. But there was no floor on which to fall. Not an inch of floor was visible because of the mass of humanity crowded into this inadequate space. We moved in slow, jerky motions as that small engine tried to get up steam to pull our car and several more boxcars full of POWs and German troops.

Throughout the night, we continued moving in a swaying, jolting motion. I slept as best I could on my feet, leaning on the side of the car. It was extremely difficult because the drunken motion of the train kept jostling the men around like ping-pong balls in a large box. This kept everyone in a foul, angry mood, swearing and cursing at the slightest provocation. Fights broke out, although no real blows were struck because of the severe crowding. A man had no room to swing his arms.

The small outbreaks would be quickly broken up, and the combatants hustled away from each other to the far ends of the car. These outbreaks became more frequent as the days and nights stretched endlessly on into one big blur. Nerves wore thinner and frustrations continued to build.

I had been standing for so long that my feet no longer had any feeling in them. Desperately trying to keep my mind off of the possibility of frostbite, frozen feet or their amputation, I simply concentrated on keeping alive and as warm as possible. To survive, I knew I had to put any negative thoughts out of my mind.

Along the way to none of us knew where, the train made frequent stops. Sometimes the stops were in the middle of nowhere. But each protracted stop brought out the guards who were housed in one car in the middle of the train. I'm sure it was heated and had all the amenities of barracks life. We could hear them parading through the snow, up and down along the side of the tracks on each side of the train. They would stomp loudly as they walked on top of the cars, just to annoy us and let us know they were ever present.

Always during those delays en route, the POWs entombed in the boxcars would set up a continuous chorus of profanity and catcalls. We'd beat on the inside of the cars. But this was all to no avail. The guards ignored us and methodically clopped back and forth on their rounds. I wondered how anyone could have thought we'd get out and where we'd go if we did.

The boxcars had two small 8-inch-by-10-inch windows at each end, high up near the top, that provided some ventilation. Besides that, the boxcars were well ventilated by the numerous cracks in the walls. The only advantage of this was that it enabled us to catch glimpses of the countryside occasionally. Of course, that was limited since we traveled mostly at night and spent most of the daylight hours along some siding way out in the country. It hadn't taken more than a couple of days before I learned why we were traveling mostly at night. Traveling this way helped cut down on the strafing attacks by American planes.

One entire day was spent holed up in a long railroad tunnel somewhere up in the mountains. At night, the wind whistled through the tunnel. I was getting a bit claustrophobic by then, thinking about those big American bombers that we heard overhead every now and then. I kept hoping they didn't know this tunnel existed.

Another day, we had heard planes going both ways overhead, seemingly no cause for alarm until the roar of a fighter sounded much too close. Then we heard the staccato sound of 50-caliber machine-gun fire. The guards were screaming, jumping off of the train and diving for cover. We instinctively crouched down as low as possible while the rounds came flying through the length of the car. I could hear the screams of the wounded as the plane groaned overhead. Supposedly, there was a large "POW" painted in white on one or two of the boxcar tops to point out to the fly boys that the train carried some of their own men. In most cases, those air jockeys were low enough to read the big white letters and would buzz off.

On four or five occasions, however, the character would squeeze off a few rounds before he realized that he was shooting up a trainload of American POWs. Sometimes, though, I think some of the fly boys strafed the train anyway, maybe trying to hit some of the guards that were scurrying for cover.

I quietly listened to a few fly boys later at some of the pubs in England and learned that they were beginning to run out of targets at the end of the war. The Luftwaffe was rapidly becoming a memory. So with ammo leftover, the pilots would hedgehop over the German landscape, shooting at anything that moved, military or not. Some of them bragged about shooting at cows and other animals roaming the fields and even an occasional civilian running for cover.

The days and nights dragged on slowly, one after another. I was having a difficult time keeping my feet from freezing. I tried stomping them while standing in my meager space. After a couple of days, I'd already completely lost all feeling in both feet. But still I continued to pound away, hoping to keep some circulation going.

At each stopping point, we would holler for food and water. None was forthcoming. And as the train continued on eastward, ever deeper into the Fatherland, the misery grew even worse. One or two men in our car died each day. We made a little room against one wall and stacked them on top of each other.

Hunger and thirst were driving some men to desperate measures. One GI in particular tried to quench his thirst by licking the hoarfrost from one of the iron hinges on the boxcar door. Apparently he didn't understand the consequences, that a warm tongue would immediately stick to the iron surface.

The swaying motion of the train soon tore him away from the hinge, and he fell back with most of the surface of his tongue still stuck to the hinge. Infection set in and he died a horrible death from strangulation in 18-24 hours. His suffering was unbearable, but we were powerless to help him. And the Germans paid no heed to our cries for help.

Some of the prisoners had suffered wounds during their capture and were growing weaker by the day. At least 15, maybe more had been wounded or killed during the strafing runs. So by the time this excursion ended six days and nights from the time we left Limburg, we carried 12 corpses from my boxcar and lay them to rest alongside the railroad tracks. They were picked up the next morning by a prison burial detail. I was never able to find out how many POWs died just in this one trainload.

The boxcar ordeal ended at 2200 hours in the dark of night and, seemingly, in the middle of nowhere. When the chains were removed from the doors, we tumbled out, mostly headfirst, into a snow bank along the tracks. According to what we had already heard, the winter was the coldest, snowiest in Europe in recorded history. The snow banks were all of 4 to 5 feet deep.

Barely half the men could navigate under their own power. Although I later learned that my feet were frozen, I was determined to walk away from that pitiful mess of humanity created by the long train ride. But I fell to the ground, too, when I jumped off the train.

Being one of the last POWs off the car, I was "volunteered" with three other men by the guards to help carry out our dead. That meant 10 to 12 trips back into the smelly car. With no blankets or stretchers at our disposal to use in supporting the corpses, we had to use our bare hands to pick up and carry the bodies off the boxcar. Fortunately, the severe, cold weather had helped slow the deterioration of flesh. The bodies were stiff and, except for our own feebleness, they weren't too difficult to handle. It was all we could do to empty the boxcar. The activity drained us. But it was the last humane act we could do for our fellow prisoners.

After completing this sickening detail, I was then forced to help carry those too weak to walk. I did happen to be one of the most able-bodied men at this point. Helping each other, we had to cover a distance of about 200 yards to a glowing, hot bonfire in the middle of a grove of large trees. The bright, glowing fire was like a beacon on that dark, cold night. I was drawn to the heat like a firefly to a light bulb.

"God," I said, murmuring to nobody in particular. "The thought of the warmth from the fire will give us a new lease on life." I heard a couple of "Amens" from the mass of stumbling humanity around me, then complete silence as we pressed on toward the source of the radiating heat. We moved as fast as possible through the knee-high drifts of snow to the warmth ahead.

Although the weather was bitterly cold, the winds were calm. The moon shone above the scene; the stars glittered like thousands of diamonds in the black sky. I was trying to help another soldier, who was very weak and unstable on his feet, toward the glowing source of heat. Reaching the perimeter of the glowing coals, I just dropped the man to the ground in the snow. By then I was too weak to even help him stand. Six days and nights on that boxcar without food or water had taken its toll on all of us.

Gradually the warmth from the fire soaked through me. I began to slowly revive to where I almost felt human again. It was then that I first noticed the large black iron kettle hanging on a tripod over the coals. Steam was billowing up from the kettle, and I caught a faint aroma of tea.

Several British Tommies and Canucks were stirring the contents of the kettle. Then they reached into the kettle with long-handled dippers and started passing around big tin cups full of hot, but very weak, tea. Because it was the first liquid we had had since starting the train ride, it was the best-tasting tea a man ever had.

As I was sipping the tea, trying to make it last forever, the Canucks passed out to each man a small square sandwich of black bread with some kind of what looked and tasted like cottage cheese. Except for a small tin of molasses and three slices of black bread I'd smuggled onto the train in the beginning, this was my first food in six days. The bread and molasses were gone at the end of the first day on the train. I didn't know then that it would be such a long time until the next meal.

With that small sandwich and cup of hot tea in my belly, I was revived enough to look at my surroundings. The trees were big and tall. And as I looked up at that beautiful sky full of wonders, I swear I felt a hand lightly touch my right shoulder for just an instant. I glanced to my right; no one was standing near me. Was it the hand of God, reassuring me that He was right there beside me all the way? Was my imagination playing tricks on me? Was I losing my senses of the real world?

Imagination or not, I suddenly felt a surge of adrenaline and looked to the heavens to say a silent prayer. I felt a renewed hope that I would survive this ordeal. Little did I know what lay ahead in the next five months—the suffering, the cold, the hunger. But I had gained a different perspective of my situation, and I felt a renewed strength for whatever I would be faced with from here on out. I felt that whatever was in store for me now could not possibly be worse than the last six days of inhumane treatment I had just endured.

The fire was burning down; the sandwich had been consumed; the tea cup was empty. "Sorry, boys, only enough for one round each," we were told. Quite suddenly a rather old, rotund Jerry guard threw back his head and started bellowing. The character had a good bass voice, and I soon recognized the song to be "Silent Night." In German, he was singing, "*Stille Nacht, Heilege Nacht. ...*"

It dawned on me just then that this had to be Christmas night. Sure. Six days and nights locked in that lousy boxcar. No food or water. Forced to relieve ourselves through the cracks or right where we stood. Such inhumane, stinking treatment. At Christmas time, no less. Certainly there had been no adherence to the Geneva Convention on the conduct of the treatment of Prisoners of War.

But we all joined in song. Any music director would have stopped us because we were all off key. Had our lives depended on it, we couldn't have done any better: We hadn't used our voices in nearly a week, except to shout out obscenities at the guards on the train. We droned on for several minutes, singing the first verse over and over. It was the only one most of us knew or could remember. What had started out as a lusty songfest faded to a whisper as the men's voices gradually grew hoarse. Yet the whole scene was quite an uplifting experience. Many of the men who had been lying in the snow had roused up as the heat from the fire had penetrated their bones, and the singing had roused their spirits.

For a while, I felt relaxed and totally detached from the gruesome scene surrounding me. I let my thoughts wander back to the tranquillity of small-town life in Illinois, to familiar Christmas times. For a few moments, I was completely transformed into another, quite peaceful, world. The shouting of the guards abruptly brought me back to the reality of my predicament. And I felt sadness at seeing the brief moment of peace disappear.

Then the remaining embers of the fire were stomped out, and we got orders to move out. The guards were screaming and shouting again. I came to believe that the Jerries had only one tone of voice—angry. They never addressed us in a normal tone. It was always an angry tone and usually included, "*Swinehundt.*" I became too familiar with this lousy word before the war was over.

At any rate, our Christmas party was over.

We had arrived at the outskirts of Hohenstein, Germany, at about 2200 hours. The party under the tall trees where we were given the much-welcomed food and drink had taken another hour, so our guards were becoming tired and jumpy. We seemed to be about 400 yards outside the barbed-wire fence of a prison camp, *Stalag* IV A, and were surrounded by armed guards.

They were having a difficult time with us, trying to get us to move toward the big open gate to the prison compound. As usual, we were slow to follow their commands, always forcing them to shout the orders several times.

"Nix verstehen," we kept repeating the German words, indicating we didn't understand what the guards were saying until they would lose their tempers.

At that point, we tried to move quickly enough to avoid the butt end of the rifles they were sure to use on us. I was too slow on many occasions during my time as a POW and wound up either on my butt or flat on my face.

These tactics of being slow to move and "not understanding" an order were only a couple of ways that we could harass the enemy. The Army Code of Conduct states, "If you become a prisoner of the enemy, you must resist at all times, in any manner possible." The code also states that a prisoner must make an attempt to escape should the opportunity present itself.

By now I was probably 1,000 miles behind enemy lines in eastern Germany, smack up against the Czech border. I had no idea where this POW camp was located; I couldn't speak the language. So I had to bide my time as far as planning any foolish move to make an escape attempt.

Finally, we were all herded through the gate. It was slammed shut and locked. This *Stalag* covered a large area and had several rows of one-story wooden buildings with few windows. The buildings were sitting up on concrete piers. This enabled the guards to survey under the buildings to see any tunnels or other hidden material.

The building toward which we were walking, however, was not set on piers. Instead, it was a dilapidated structure, flat on the ground, with some of the roofing flapping in the wind. Most of the windows were boarded up, and the building had only one small door at each end.

And there we stood. The guards who had been in such a hurry to get us through the gate and this far now forced us to stand outside, near the front of the building in about two feet of snow, until daylight. One of the guards indicated they were getting the place ready for us, since we weren't on their schedule for new arrivals.

What's another six hours at this point? I wondered.

Once the door was opened, we were lined up and counted—then counted again. Finally, after some discussion, some shouting and some more discussion, we were allowed to slowly file, one at a time, inside the building. Inside the door, we were stopped, searched and checked as to identity. Then we were each issued a POW metal dog tag which was to be worn around our necks at all times.

I also was issued a *Personalkarte*, a half sheet of blue paper containing all my pertinent personal information. As I studied it in the dim light of the barracks, I wondered where they had gotten ahold of all this personal data. All I had repeated in any of the interrogations was name, rank and serial number. Then I remembered. During my first appearance before the *Kapitän* back in Limburg, I was ordered to empty my pockets of all belongings. My wallet, which had been returned, contained such information.

At the top of the paper was my new prison number, 311162 IV A. After that came my Social Security number, religion, name and date of birth, weight, stature and hair color. Even the fact that I had been a student and my father's name and home address was included.

Also, I was listed as an *Amerikaner Infantrio Soldat,* captured on 23-11-44, *Deutschland.*

It had been more than 30 days since I was captured, and I was just now being registered as a POW. I wondered about those who died along the way. Were they officially counted as Prisoners of War or would they be added to the some final listing of Missing in Action?

As my eyes grew accustomed to the dim, grim interior of the building, I also wondered what took them so long to "prepare" this place for us. It had holes in the roof; half of the windows were boarded up; and a dirt floor was covered with a thin layer of straw. Big deal. Water could be obtained from a hand pump located outside the back door.

The toilet facilities consisted of several five-gallon buckets and two or three "relief tubes." These were pipes sticking through the wall that drained into a hole outside one end of the building. Drinking and washing were done at pump side.

With the one blue blanket in hand that we had been issued as we filed into the barracks, I surveyed the interior and quickly decided on a spot along one wall to spread the blanket. Because I hadn't made friends with any of my fellow prisoners, I was forced to entrust my blanket to a guy who had flopped down on the straw next to me while I went to the pump. When I got back, I would watch his blanket while he took his turn at the pump. Although none of the POWs had anything of value, we had to be eternally vigilant to protect what little we did possess.

Stripping bare to the waist, I vigorously washed and scrubbed as best I could without any soap. It became a comedy of sorts after a time with men jostling for a position at the pump. We'd slosh bitterly cold water over ourselves, trying our best to remove some of the stinking grime from our bodies and our wretched clothing.

Soon the area around the pump became a muddy quagmire with men slipping, slopping and occasionally falling into the mess. By this time, I was beginning to accept the fact that I would be cold for the duration of the winter. The bath, however, was a morale booster. My hands that had been nearly black with dirt and grime were now less dirty and less grimy. Luckily, I had been one of the first at the pump. I missed most of the squabbles that happened later.

6

Nothing was available to occupy a man's mind. It was so cold inside and outside that we mostly just lay around, curled up in our blankets. I kept working on massaging my feet and walking when I could to get some feeling back in them. I had no trouble walking, but the feeling never returned to any degree.

More than 50 years later, I still have very little feeling in my feet. They were, and are, continually cold with an occasional hot flash going through them. But I feel extremely fortunate that I am still able to walk.

At night we would huddle, three together, to make the best use of our blankets and to conserve body heat. We would take turns being the lucky guy in the middle. That was the only time I could stay warm.

In moving about the compound during the following days, I noticed that the men in our barracks were the only ones without uniforms. We were still wearing the thin, nondescript clothing issued to us after the shower back in Limburg. Why had our uniforms been confiscated and not those of anyone else in this camp? I wondered.

I later learned the answer but it was some time after the war was over. What I learned came from soldiers who had fought in the Ardennes in what became known as the Battle of the Bulge.

The war was now going badly for Hitler as the Allies were fast penetrating into the Fatherland. The German leadership was grasping for straws and had promised to take back Aachen before Christmas and to be in Antwerp, Belgium, by the end of 1944. But it was the end of 1944. And Antwerp had finally been cleared of all enemy forces by the Canadians. The city was rapidly being rebuilt and put into use as the main supply port.

The big Allied offensive into Germany was grinding to a halt for lack of matériel—especially gasoline for Gen. George Patton's tanks. Ammunition was in short supply, even during my last several days of fighting. In fact, several times during late November of '44 we had to be most judicious in our use of bullets and hand grenades. When I was taken prisoner, I was completely out of ammo and hand grenades. I had only my bayonet and knife for protection.

As the tempo picked up in December, so did the action on the front lines. A brilliant, but stupid, plan had been hatched by the German High Command: The Germans would confiscate the uniforms of newly captured American prisoners and use them for English-speaking Jerries who were to infiltrate American battle lines.

In retrospect, maybe I was allowed to live rather than be shot by the troopers following those Tiger tanks because of that strategy because of my outfit. The Germans would need only the uniforms from those divisions that were in the immediate area of operations. That meant the 104th Timberwolf Division. Mine! The Timberwolves were the main troops on the Aachen front. That must have been the reason we were separated in Limburg.

The stupid part of the plan centered on the masquerading German soldiers. Many German people could understand and speak English. It was taught in most schools throughout the entire country. By using English and sign language, we could communicate with most everybody. The idea for this bold plan, dubbed "Operation Werewolf," was for the German soldiers who were fluent in English to infiltrate American lines in American uniforms. These uniforms obviously had been taken from American POWs who had previously fought in the area.

Two pertinent facts that spelled doom for this operation from the very start, however, had been overlooked by the German High Command. For one thing, no German I ever talked with during the war who spoke English spoke it like a true American. His English was good, sometimes even better than mine. But there always seemed to be a guttural sound to his speech. Either that or else it was frightfully British.

Any front-line soldier who had to be alert at all times could easily spot the accent. We always had German patrols sneaking through our lines at night. When they were challenged, one of them would always respond in English. So the troops were used to this ploy and constantly on the watch for it.

Secondly, the biggest handicap to the infiltration by the German was the use of American slang. My last recollection of passwords were fertilizer and compost and Yankee and clipper. If we threw out a slang term that didn't trip them up, we could always throw out the latest baseball or football trivia from back home. This did the trick nearly every time. What little information we did receive from home through letters helped us on sports happening in the States. Also, the command post (CP) would send down the latest stories about football or baseball that weren't published or the latest news stories. The front-line German troops could not get the latest stuff that we could.

Regardless of these obstacles, however, Operation Werewolf was successful to some extent and disrupted some of our units in the area of the Battle of the Bulge. Road signs would be switched and mines were replanted in roads that had been previously cleared by our engineers; truck tires were slashed; and an occasional burp gun splattered some of our men from behind, causing momentary panic.

But most of the intended results did not pan out, especially after a few Germans were taken alive. The word spread quickly among the forward and rear echelons, and all U.S. troops were on high alert for the penetrations.

However unreasonable the feeling, I have always felt a little pang of guilt because some GI may have gotten killed by a Kraut wearing my Timberwolf uniform. At the time, I had no idea why it had been taken from me, couldn't have predicted its intended use and could have done nothing about it if I had known. Still, I felt some guilt and some remorse. My suffering from the extremely cold winter was made much worse without the warm uniform, too. Especially, I missed that wonderful long, wool overcoat and the wool blanket.

The use of American uniforms was all part of the big operation that Hitler planned as his last chance to win the war. The Americans named it the Battle of the Bulge because it created quite a dent or bulge in our lines in the Ardennes Forest region.

The battle raged from 16 December 1944 to 17 January 1945. Although the enemy was eventually stopped and driven back, the cost in American lives was tremendous. During this one bloody month, our casualty rate totaled 78,000 men: 8,000 killed, 48,000 wounded and 22,000 missing in action. Two complete regiments from the 106th Division were annihilated.

The flood of prisoners into Limburg had been the cause of our hasty shipment out, without provisions, for the long train ride.

The rations at Hohenstein were no different from those at Limburg. We would fall out to be counted, then march to the kitchen area. There, we were handed a metal bowl and a spoon and slowly got in the chow line. The big, fat cook—all German cooks seemed to be so fat, but they surely didn't get that way eating the stuff they gave us—would dip a long-handled ladle into the black kettle of soup, one ladle per man. On down the line someone passed out two or three small boiled potatoes or *Kartoffel.* Next came a slice of that horrible black bread.

It became quite a chore, trying to balance the potatoes and bread without spilling that life-saving, hot, watery, tasteless soup. Some men would squat in the snow and hastily gobble down the soup, while others would make it back to the barracks before eating. Since there were no tables, we sat on the floor to eat.

This camp was typical of most of the camps in Germany. It was situated on an open, treeless, windswept plain, guaranteeing visibility for hundreds of yards in all directions. This enabled the guards in their high towers to view any and all activity in the camp at all times. The towers were spaced periodically around the perimeter. They were a depressing sight.

After about the third day in *Stalag* IV A, several of us were moved out of the area into another compound about two barbed-wire enclosures away. These new quarters were a luxury compared to what I had just left. Instead of one big open building, the barracks was divided into small rooms, each housing eight men in double-decked bunks, four bunks on each side of the room. A small, narrow wooden table stood in the center aisle. The table had narrow benches which allowed a place for the men to eat, read or whatever.

I instantly recognized the uniform of the men already living in the barracks as Canadian. I had fought beside the 4th Canadian Division in Belgium and Holland. When I first walked into their quarters, I noticed some apprehension from them. They were eyeing me with a hostile look in their eyes, I thought. But with my greeting, "Good morning," the hostility quickly receded as they realized I was speaking English.

The man on my right immediately stuck out his hand in welcome. "Are you an American?" he asked in a rather dubious and subdued voice.

My answer in the affirmative brought a big sigh of relief from the rest of the men. "Good God, man," one of them said. "I thought they were putting the bloody Russians in with us."

The Canadians noticed that I was weak and unsteady on my feet. One of them grabbed a rag hanging on the edge of a top bunk, put his arm around my shoulder and gently tugged and half carried me out the door. "We'll go down to the wash-up area and get some of that German grime off your face and hands," he said.

Gosh, I thought, am I that dirty? I thought I got pretty clean when I splashed under the pump a couple days back. Guess not.

The Canadian led me into the washroom where six spigots stuck out of the wall over a derelict-looking tub for a wash basin. We walked over to the spigot in the far corner. After scanning the few men in the room, he sidled up to me and slipped me a very small sliver of soap.

"Use just a mite, quickly," he said in a low whisper, "and give it back to me without letting it be seen. Soap is more precious than lites (cigarettes)."

I nodded and took a couple of swipes at the thin sliver and slipped it back to my new-found friend.

"Can't let any of these blokes know I've got soap," he said, muttering as he took the soap and backed away to let me scrub away at my hands and face.

That bit of soap did manage to cut away some of the dirt from my hands. As for the face, the soap was useless. I now looked like a hairy ape covered with whiskers and long hair. But it was another minute before I knew what I really looked like.

As I raised up from the tub to splash cold water on my face, I was suddenly gazing into a metal mirror that hung above the spigot. Although the mirror was cloudy and scratched and the piece of metal was uneven, I was not prepared for what I saw. And what I saw was an apparition that terrified me so that I had to look away.

"What's the matter, Bloke?" the Canadian asked, his tone not nasty but merely attempting a little joke to break my stunned silence. "Don't like what is peerin' back at you?"

I managed a feeble grin and reluctantly looked in the mirror again, hoping not to see the same grotesque animal as before. But there it was, a gaunt face with hollow eyes—eyes absolutely without any spark and face covered with dirt and black coal dust, highlighted with filthy matted hair and beard. It was the first time I had seen what I looked like since I was captured. I had no idea I looked so terrible. The past six weeks had taken their toll.

My clothes were filthy from the boxcar ride, and I reeked with smelly body odor. I shouldn't have been so surprised at my appearance, though: Every man around me looked just as bad.

I spent little time trying to untangle the matted hair and beard. Instead, I used that precious bit of soap on my gritty hands. I managed to turn the black to a dull brown. When I was finished, at least I felt a lot cleaner. And I had made a friend. He was the first person that I had actually talked with since Limburg.

After this refreshing respite, my new buddy and I returned to the room because it was about chow time in the barracks where I was given a lower bunk—the last man in the building always got the lower bunk because, being closer to the ceiling, the top bunk always received more of the heat that filtered through the building. I was exhausted, so I lay down in my assigned bunk and immediately passed into a deep sleep. What little heat there was in the building had made me warm and groggy. It was the first time I had been even remotely warm since winter began.

Sometime later, I was awakened by my Canadian friend. Although he touched me gently, I still bolted upright in my bunk. In doing so, I cracked my head on the bottom of the top bunk. I saw a few stars dancing around for a bit, but they quickly cleared at the call for chow.

Since I had only a thin blanket and the clothes on my back, one of the Canadians scurried about and somewhere came up with a *Shüssel,* or a bowl, and a spoon. Then we lined up inside the cubicle. Knowing that I had had only about three meals in the previous 10 or 11 days, the Limeys and Canucks placed me first in line.

As the chow line formed in the hallway, a knock would come on the door, and the men in each cubicle would file out and join the group. From there we continued down the center hall of the barracks and out into the yard. There sat the chow wagon, a two-wheeled cart with a large, black pot of steaming soup precariously balanced in the middle.

This was the same procedure every day. A ladle of watery mixture of chopped kohlrabi and beet tops cooked in a bland gruel of some type of grain—the same old stuff everyday. It wasn't seasoned, but it was nourishment. That and a couple of small potatoes, a slice of that blessed black bread and we were on our way back to our cubby hole.

The table was so small that it barely accommodated eight men plus the eight bowls of soup. I took a seat at one end of the table, stuffed one potato in my mouth and swallowed it in one gulp. It was then that I noticed the two men on either side of me. They had not started eating and seemed to be eyeing me suspiciously. Unsure of why they were looking at me, I quickly took two or three spoonfuls of soup, slurping like a starved animal.

A man slowly reached over and gently, but firmly, took a hold of one of my wrists. "Take it easy, Yank," he said. "We know how hungry you are; but you must take the food slowly, or it will all just come back up. Now you wouldn't want to waste this lovely bowl of broth, would you?"

"No," I said, beginning to understand why they had been eyeing me so closely. With their gentleness and calm voices, my fear abated and left me weak. I babbled an incoherent thanks.

From then on, we ate and all talked and joked of happier times. That seemed to help all of us relax and eat more slowly. After all, there was no hurry. We weren't going anywhere. I thought I could become accustomed to this place without any problem. It was warm; I had made good friends.

Other than meeting these good friends, my short stay at Hohenstein was uneventful—except for the one day I was called out on detail. The English had told me that there were only about three jobs to be done around the compound. You could get the lucky detail of pulling the potato wagon and distributing potatoes through five or six separate enclosed areas. At the time, I had no idea of the scope of this camp, how many prisoners it contained or what nationality they were.

But on my first trip outside my enclosure, which contained mostly British and Canadians with a few Americans, Australians and New Zealanders, I discovered separate areas that held Russians, Polish and French. One compound was even full of Italians. Each group was separated from the others by a 20-feet high barbed-wire fence.

I was supposed to go on the potato-wagon detail to take the place of a man who had been run over by the wagon. I was led through the gate into the Russian compound to take my place at the rear of the wagon as a pusher. The Germans used six men on the tongue and another four men as pushers at the rear. Just as I leaned against the wagon and had begun to push, pandemonium broke out on the other side of the wagon. The wagon was piled high with boxes of potatoes, so I couldn't see what all the commotion was about.

Suddenly, several shots rang out. I automatically hit the dirt and crawled under the wagon. Peeking out from my hiding place I could see the results of all the shouting and rifle fire. Four Russians lay sprawled in the mud, dead, beside the wagon. To the Germans, Russian life was cheap. The bodies of these four were hustled off and buried in the prison cemetery before they were even cold and without as much as a grave marker.

As we went about our business of dropping off boxes of potatoes at the several compound kitchens, I tried to figure if there was any way I could quickly rescue even one or two small potatoes. But after witnessing the callous way the guards mowed down the four Ruskies, those thoughts vanished. From then on, I was very careful to keep my hands in full view of the guard at all times while delivering potatoes.

Later that day, I was told that this killing was not uncommon in the Russian compound. The Russians were subjected to much harsher treatment than the rest of the Allied prisoners. The death rate from disease for Russian POWs was also several times higher.

To die for the sake of stealing a few small extra potatoes gave me some insight to the terrible conditions fostered on the Russians. In the following months, however, I found myself taking a few chances to steal extra food at the risk of being shot on sight. Starvation causes a man to take desperate measures just to survive. But this time I came away with no potatoes.

The next day I was again called out on detail. It was early morning. My Canadian bunkmate told me it would probably be a burial detail coming this early. Most of the deaths occurred during the night, he said, so the Germans wanted to get the bodies underground early and quickly.

"When an American is called for burial detail," the Canadian said, "it means a fellow Yank has died."

I nodded apprehensively and was ushered into the American area to load the body, fearful that it might be someone I knew, although I hadn't seen a familiar face since shortly after I was captured. Fat chance anyway, I thought, as I looked at the body already wrapped in a dirty, tattered GI blanket that was already bound with a rope.

Only four men had been called for the detail. By the time I'd sloshed through the snow and mud to the prison burial plot, I was staggering. It wasn't from the weight of our dead comrade—he weighed less than 100 pounds. It was the lack of strength in my own body, at this point.

The cemetery was located on a slight rise in the ground at the far east end of the camp. Thank God they already have a crew digging the grave, I thought as we staggered up the hill. Upon our arrival, however, we were handed picks and shovels and ordered to help finish the digging.

By this time, the digging crew had already picked its way through the heavily frozen surface. So when I started with the shovel, the digging was fairly easy. To my relief, the earth was pretty sandy. The chore was still difficult, however. I had expended most of my strength just getting to the site.

After we had finished and had lowered the man's body in the hole, one of the men in the group muttered a few words as a prayer. We stood silently with our hats in our hands, each of us deep in our own thoughts as we said goodbye to another good soldier. Then, grabbing the shovels, we worked quickly to cover the body.

To get our circulation going so we could warm up, we probably worked more furiously than was really necessary. Also, it wasn't a pleasant task, and we wanted to get it over with as soon as possible. I'm sure each man was deep in his own mind, wondering if or when he would end up in a barren hole after such an untimely and inglorious death.

With a great deal of gesturing on his part, the guard finally got the message across to me to go get a small pile of sticks from the corner of the cemetery. I hurried over, picked up a couple of sticks and with a short piece of wire, furnished by the guard, fashioned a crude cross and placed it at the head of the grave. We had been given the dead man's dog tags when we picked him up and now draped them over the crude cross. These would be his only means of identification.

This whole process had taken its toll, both physically and mentally. It had only been two hours since we first picked up the body. But I was exhausted and emotionally drained. Back in the barracks, I hit the sack and immediately dropped into a deep sleep.

The American compound became full quickly as the Germans brought in a flood of men from the Bulge area. They had been arriving at the rate of one or two trainloads a day. Judging by some of the wild tales being passed around by the new arrivals, we thought the Germans had destroyed half of the American Army. I was fortunate to be spending my days in the British compound. These men had been POWs for four or five years and helped me prepare for what might lie ahead.

Some of them were captured in the English fiasco at Dunkirk in 1940, some in the North African Campaign in 1941 and 1942. They all had ingenious ways of fighting the boredom of prison life. Of course, they had no tools and precious little material to work with. Yet they managed to confiscate a few items—the bare essentials—on the occasional trips out on work details.

The most astonishing pieces of equipment were the small stoves. These stoves were fashioned from tin cans received in some Red Cross boxes. Above what served as the small firebox was a set of fan blades, turned by a hand crank. By cranking the fan, it would force the warm air from the firebox through a small tunnel-like opening at the other end of the firebox.

Actually, the device was a small forge, an idea used in the Dark Ages. By adjusting the speed of the fan, the operator could heat water or a small can of soup in short order with a minimum of fuel. The fuel was small wood shavings, scraps of paper, wood from bunks, wood scraps from a work detail or anything else that would burn or was available.

All the men took daily walks around the inside perimeter of their own compound, continuously avoiding the electrified wire that stretched just five feet inside the high wire. Usually there were two or sometimes three barbed-wire fences about 20 feet high with several electrically charged hot wires running through the fence. One touch and—Zap—you're done. Step over that first wire and you would be gunned down immediately from one of the high guard towers that were spaced all around the outside of the camp.

What more preparation for the days and months ahead these British and Canadians could have helped me with was cut short by the Germans. I was going on the move again.

7

After about three days of relatively easy living, I was suddenly ordered to pack my bags and get ready to move again. Since all my worldly possessions were on my back, packing up to move was easy. I was ready before the significance of the order moving me hardly had time to register.

But I bid a sad farewell to the English and the Canadians and was led out of the compound through three gates to an area just inside the main gate to join 15-20 other Yanks who appeared to be waiting for me. I stood around with the group of men, waiting for what I thought was just another work detail. After about an hour of milling around there, two guards approached from the outside, and we were released into their custody.

The other men and I stood around in the cold morning air, discussing the possibilities we now faced. Rumors are the lifeblood of a POW camp, and they were flying fast and furious among this small group. The betting was heaviest that we were heading to an outlying *Arbeitskommando* (work camp) farther into Germany or maybe Czechoslovakia—maybe even Poland. None of us knew a thing, but that didn't stop the speculation.

Finally, after what seemed like at least two more hours standing in the cold, we were herded down towards the railroad tracks. Oh, no, I thought. Not another boxcar ride.

As we approached the long string of boxcars, we were abruptly ordered to crawl between the cars to the other side. On the adjoining track sat a passenger train. We boarded one of the cars and were actually put in a heated compartment with plush seats.

Wow! I thought. Is the war over? Are we being shipped back to Allied lines by first-class coach? But those fantasies were soon squelched. By looking out the window at the position of the sun,

I learned that we were headed east—farther into Germany.

This train ride was actually very peaceful, rewarding even, as we sped through some beautiful countryside in a heated car. We made three brief stops and were shunted onto a siding to allow a fast freight or a troop train to speed by.

Two hours later, we pulled into a small station and were hurriedly ordered off. Passing through the station door, I glanced up to read the sign that said, "Runddorf." The two guards who had accompanied us from Hohenstein presented a sheaf of papers to a German officer. After much shuffling and yakking, we were lined up and counted. Something seemed to be causing a problem.

After more paper shuffling, yelling and counting again, the *Kapitän* gave the order to move out. Later that day we learned what the problem had been at the station. The orders were for 20 men; only 18 were on the train. The *Kapitän* wouldn't take the word of our guards, so the train was ordered to stay put while a squad of German soldiers searched the train from one end to the other. Finding no prisoners, the guards gave the order to march.

The train station was situated on one edge of Runddorf. We were marched to the other side of town and out into the countryside about three-fourths of a mile. There, out in a big open field, stood my new home. It consisted of four or five wooden buildings, surrounded by two high barbed-wire fences with cross fences dividing the interior. The larger, main building turned out to be our living quarters.

We were halted at the main gate and waited for someone to open the big gate so we could enter. But no one appeared, so we stood in formation and just waited—and waited. We waited for more than an hour out in the cold and snow, as usual. Since no one in our group could speak or understand German, our questions got us no answers. All we got was colder and the usual blank stares and the hunching of shoulders.

All the while, the guards made no attempt to find out the problem. They were too busy stomping their feet and flapping their arms to keep warm. We were forced to stand at attention in the blasted snow.

Because we were standing facing the camp, we didn't notice or hear a small group of men approaching us from the rear, from Runddorf, until they were right behind us. They were the reason for our delay. This group of POWs totaled 18 men, equal to our own. They had come into Runddorf by train from Mühlberg, *Stalag* IV B, which was located several kilometers to the north.

A few words, mostly complaining about their tardiness, were exchanged with the new arrivals, all Americans. Of course, they had no more control over their movement than we did, so we soon cooled it. Still we waited, though, until finally a short, pot-bellied German corporal appeared from a small building which we presumed to be a headquarters.

For the next 30 minutes, the scene was one of pure comedy, although in reality, there was nothing for us to laugh about. We were lined up at attention and counted, then counted again. And we had to remain standing at attention during the entire period of time.

The guards that brought us from Hohenstein handed over to the corporal a sheaf of papers; the guards from the new arrivals did the same. Papers were exchanged, read and reread, signed and shuffled around several more times, before somebody came up with a solution to whatever kind of problem that all the attention was directed.

After counting and recounting us three or four more times, we were finally allowed to proceed toward the barracks that was to be our quarters. Another gate had to be opened, however, before we reached the building. Once inside the gate, we were lined up and counted again. I was beginning to wonder if these Germans could count or if they were just stupid.

It seems that this camp had previously held 40 Russians, I later learned. Our count always came to 36 men, and none of the Germans could figure out why. And this discrepancy was the reason for all the shuffling of papers and incessant counting. The little corporal berated the guards for allowing four men to escape during the train ride. Communication had broken down somewhere—there were no escapes.

Eventually the corporal settled down, and we proceeded to receive our first indoctrination speech. He introduced himself as *Kommander Führer* Wilhelm Mueller. After strutting up and down our line for several minutes with us still standing at attention, he abruptly wheeled to face the line.

"Mann sprechen die Deutsche?" he asked, growling fiercely.

"*Jawohl,*" a voice from somewhere in the ranks answered.

"*Herkommen,*" the corporal snapped, happy that he could at least communicate with at least one of us.

Since we were all strangers to one another, we were pleased as well to have one of our own who could understand what was expected of us. I discovered in ensuing talks with the German-speaking American that he could speak the language fluently because he had been born in Germany. His parents immigrated to the United States when he was 12 years old. None of the family ever returned to their homeland.

In one of our later long talks, he inadvertently let slip a secret of his past. He was Jewish, a situation that really worried him. After his family arrived in the United States, they changed their last name to a common English or American family name. This proved to be a blessing for this 19-year-old soldier. If a POW even had a Jewish-sounding name, he was yanked and sent to a much tougher camp. Many American Jews died in those camps.

On at least two separate occasions during our time in Runddorf, the dreaded *Gestapo* paid the camp a visit. Each time they carefully, thoroughly and separately interrogated us at length regarding our family tree. True to our Army Code of Conduct, no man uttered a word beyond his name, rank and serial number. The *Gestapo* eventually got disgusted with our stubborn attitude and quit bothering us.

Years later I learned that I was the only man in the group who knew the man's background, and I never once gave any hint of his secret while in the hands of the Germans. I did discuss it at our first reunion some 40 years later in Arkansas.

Because of his knowledge of the language, the German-speaking

POW spent a lot of time at the *Kommander Führer* headquarters. He became our only source of information of the outside world. Even then, we actually received little information that presented the true picture of the progress of the war.

All radio broadcasts were rigidly controlled. Only the propaganda spewed by the Third Reich was available. Some of the prisoners in the larger Stalags *were reportedly able to build small radio transmitters and picked up some bits of information from BBC out of London. But I was completely lacking in any outside news of any consequence during my entire six months of captivity.*

Our interpreter may have gained a few extra favors by fraternizing with the *Kommander Führer*, maybe getting an extra bit of food and, at times, staying in camp rather than going on work details. Whatever he did to get these favors, I think was motivated by the fear of his Jewish lineage being discovered. And I don't think he ever did anything that would harm one of us.

We remained friends throughout our prison days, but I avoided his company as much as possible. I always had that gnawing suspicion that he might reveal too much someday in order to curry even more favors; I was especially concerned about the nightly discussions of escape plans among the men.

As the days dragged on, I think he was beginning to believe some of the propaganda espoused by Herman Göbbels in his endless tirades about the indestructibility of the Third Reich and its great leader, Adolf Hitler. I would politely listen to my fellow prisoner and then dismiss it from my mind without comment.

The first day's orientation was the typical German line. But introductions came first. The camp personnel consisted of 13 German soldiers, eight of whom would be our guards during daily work details and sentries during the night. The remaining five included the cook, the cook's helper, a valet for the fat little corporal and a couple of other flunkies or reserve sentries.

Each guard stepped forward as he was introduced. We paid little attention to their names but would scrutinize each man, trying to get an inkling of his bearing and attitude toward POWs. About half of the guards were young, previously wounded soldiers from the Russian front and had been rejected for front-line fighting.

In some, the bitterness shone like a chip on their shoulder. These guys were to be avoided as much as possible. The other rejects, plus the older Germans, were for the most part resigned to their task. Chasing after a few unarmed men was certainly much less life-threatening than front-line combat. We lost no time attaching our nicknames to each guard in accordance with his general attitude toward us and treatment of us.

Following the introductions came the rules to be followed. We were informed that this was a work camp, an *Arbeitskommando.* We would be working in a variety of jobs, all non-military, in different locations close to the camp. The food would be adequate. Our treatment would be determined by our attitude and our compliance with orders. We would work in small groups under the control of a guard, sometimes accompanied by a dog. These dogs were trained to run you down should you stray too far from control of your guard or try to make a run for it.

A German police dog scares me to this day.

All guards carried long blacksnake whips. For some reason, these whips were seldom used on Americans. I was whipped on two occasions for minor infractions and did not witness the use of the whip on any of my fellow prisoners. But I did witness many uses of the whips on the political prisoners that we occasionally encountered in the town of Hoyerswerda, our main work area.

The previous occupants of this camp had been the 40 Russian prisoners we had replaced. They had been good workers, the *Kommander Führer* said, and had caused no trouble. As a result, camp life had been very smooth. Supposedly they had all survived and had been moved to another camp. No explanation was ever forthcoming as to why they had been moved, leaving us to wonder about the real truth.

And why were we sent here when the place was already inhabited? I wondered. I knew I'd never know for sure but was told when I left Hohenstein that in all probability I would be staying here until the end of the war or starvation caught up with me, whichever came first. Grim prospect, that latter scene.

The *Kommander Führer* kept droning on and on, faster and faster, forcing our interpreter to scramble to keep the interpretation as plain as possible. I had heard all these rules and regulations, interspersed with threats, several times before, as had all the POWs standing there. So I focused my attention on my surroundings and the study of each guard. The idea of escape was always uppermost in my mind at this time. Later in my ordeal, survival took charge—just staying alive was the challenge.

We were standing inside the main gate but outside the inner gate to our barracks. The camp contained about 2 square acres surrounded by two 10-12-feet-high barbed-wire fences about 4 feet apart. Two strands of barbed wire about 3 feet in diameter protruded from the top of the fence. One strand pointed inward on the inside fence; the other stand stuck out from the outside of the fence, both making it impossible to ever climb up and over the fence. The space between the two fences was used by the guard and his dog for patrolling the perimeter at night.

The largest building in the compound where we had been placed upon our arrival was our living quarters. The rest of the camp's interior consisted of the *Kommandant's* personal quarters, a small cook shack and two other buildings. One housed the guards; the other was used for storage. The area was cross-fenced, with our barracks isolated at one end and with only one entrance.

After what seemed like hours of standing in the cold and snow, we were finally dismissed. Man! Did we all make a beeline for cover. The cold was in our bones by now, and we were all shivering pretty badly.

The entrance to the barracks was through one door into the middle room where we would eat. Long wooden tables occupied most of the space. A single-shuttered window was on the south wall next to the outer fences. Immediately to the right and left upon entering this outer door were the doors leading into the sleeping quarters.

Each room was small with 10 double-decker bunks on opposite walls and a little pot-bellied stove in the center. Each bunk had a mattress made of gunny-sack material stuffed with straw and wood shavings. Only one thin blue blanket and no pillow was issued per man.

The other two walls had windows, one looking out into the compound and the other onto the perimeter fence. The windows were without bars but were securely locked and had blackout shutters to be closed at night. While the building was solid enough, it certainly wasn't insulated for winter. Wind howled through cracks in the walls and ceiling.

Three briquettes were allowed us for each stove. The small briquettes were about 6 inches long, 2 inches wide and 2 inches thick and were made from coal dust mixed with clay, then compressed into these small briquettes at factories like the one where I was captured. We always had a difficult time securing a bit of kindling to get them to burn.

Once burning, however, they would produce a surprising amount of heat that lasted from two to three hours—after which the room would turn bitterly cold for the remainder of the night. The time we hit the sack coincided with the time the briquettes turned to ashes. Our only hope of any warmth at all was in our bunks.

Following the orientation, we gathered around the tables in the center room to decide who would sleep in each room. There were bunks for 40 men, and, as the count-happy Germans learned upon our arrival, there were only 36 men in our group. We decided to split it evenly with 18 men per room. Since we had all been thrown together after capture, there were no real buddies; there'd been no opportunity or reason to form a bond with anyone else.

Discussion then centered around our situation. We wondered about the kind of work we'd be doing, how we'd be accepted by the townspeople if we came in contact with them and how we were going to be treated by the guards. As more questions were voiced, none with answers, the door suddenly flew open and the little *Kommander Führer* burst into our midst.

He was accompanied by the one tall guard who stood about 6 feet 6 inches tall and had the scowl of a mean-looking tiger. His stare was enough to chill your blood as he glanced about, sizing up each man. Behind these two was a really huge man, so fat that he could barely squeeze through the door. I was afraid the buttons were going to pop off his tunic as they strained to hold it together over his huge expanse of stomach as he took big, gasping breaths. He was introduced as Corporal Rorsch, the cook.

"He needs two men to work in the kitchen," the *Kommander Führer* said, motioning at the cook. "Those chosen will move their gear into the room next to the kitchen and stay there permanently as kitchen helpers.

The burly guard asked if there were any experienced cooks among us.

A few men sheepishly held up their hands, hoping to get near the food source. The most cooking most of us infantrymen had ever done was heating up a can of beans in a foxhole.

Rorsch squinted over the men and chose two. As the *Kommander Führer* and his men left with the two new recruits, he turned and said to send two more men to the kitchen to bring back our evening—and what turned out to be our daily—meal.

Twenty minutes elapsed before they returned, carrying a big black iron pot full of soup, a bucket of boiled potatoes and two loaves of black bread. Enough to feed 36 men, I wondered. Or even the 34 that were still in our barracks? Apparently it would have to be enough.

We had been issued a *Schüssel*, or bowl, and a spoon upon entering the barracks. Since we had no knife to cut the bread, we broke it off in chunks, being careful that each man had an equal share. One man took charge of carefully dipping out the soup, being sure each ladle full was the same. He continued this process until the pot was emptied.

Nobody got seconds. There were none. The potatoes had been previously counted by the cook so each man would get three, sometimes four, small potatoes. This was the only menu during our entire stay at Runddorf. And it was served in this manner every time. Breakfast consisted of a tin cup full of hot ersatz, or imitation coffee, made from some sort of grain. That was it. Most of the time I would save a small chunk of bread from my supper to at least have a morsel in the morning to absorb some of that awful-tasting ersatz coffee.

As I said, I usually saved a bite of bread from my supper, hid it in my bunk and had it for breakfast. Forty years later, at the first reunion of Runddorf survivors that I attended, I realized that for several years after I was married, I continued to leave that small piece of bread or some morsel of food on my plate after my evening meal. My wife noticed this habit and asked why.

"Oh, I'll eat it later," was my stock reply.

I didn't realize until she told this story at the reunion and several other men's wives said their husbands had done the same thing that the habit I had acquired in prison camp was so ingrained in me, that I continued to save a morsel from the meal so I wouldn't be hungry later.

Likewise, when we planted potatoes in our garden and it came time to dig them, she would toss the tiny ones aside. I "rescued" every last one of the nubbins, each one represented a bite of food for me. None was too small to keep.

After all these years, I'm sure my wife understands why now.

Thanks to the Russian who had been the previous occupant of my bunk, I started itching and scratching after only one night in Runddorf. He had left scores of his nasty friends behind: lice.

I had never seen any of the loathsome little creatures before and didn't realize the cause of all the scratching until I saw one crawling on the neck of another man as we sat down to our daily meal one evening. On my first work assignment the next day, I had scratched my head and beard over and over again. Not knowing what else to attribute the scratching to, I thought perhaps the diet we were eating was having some kind of effect on the roots of my beard.

After discovering what the lice were, we tried everything possible to rid our bodies of the pesky things. Nothing seemed to work. We dusted our clothes with ashes; we put our straw bedding out in the freezing cold. But as soon as the straw and shavings warmed up, the pests would become hyperactive again.

Some nights, I would sit close to the pot-bellied stove in my underwear and chase those suckers up and down the seams of my clothes. Whenever I managed to catch one, I'd squash him between my thumbs. But finally, it just came to the point of mind over matter. It was the only answer. I was obliged to contend with the eternal itching and crawling as a fact of life at Runddorf.

By the time I occupied that bunk, the straw and wood shavings were a pulverized mess, allowing very little cushion between the hard wooden slats and me. On several occasions, we asked the Germans for new straw, but of course, none was ever forthcoming.

The lice lived on my body until I reached the hospital in Rheims, France. And I still squirm when I think of them and that filthy mattress, the gunny sack cover which undoubtedly had never been changed, let alone washed, since it was laid on the bunk.

I sometimes get amused at all the regulations on cleanliness in the United States today, all in the name of good hygiene and good health. By today's standards, my fellow POWs and I survived some of the most filthy living conditions imaginable. But in some of the nightmares I've had over the years, I awake with the sensation of those crawling devils in my hair.

8

Although I was extremely tired, cold and hungry, I spent a restless first night in Runddorf. And it wasn't because of the lice yet. I was awake long into the night, thinking what might lay ahead in our work details. I tried to visualize what kind of treatment I was going to get at the hands of the guards. Since I had just met them a few hours earlier, I really could only speculate what their attitude was going to be toward each prisoner. But I knew we wouldn't have a pleasant time of it.

My dreams were real that night, though. Maybe this was because I felt that I was in the first stable environment since my capture. I felt relaxed and snug with the thoughts of a roof over my head every night and some food. Poor as it was, I thought it would sustain life for the present. In this tranquil state of mind, I mentally wandered through happier times at Indiana University and all of those wonderful times roaming New York City. The fire in the pot-bellied stove had long since died out before I fell asleep. When I finally drifted off to sleep, I was deep into a wonderful dream of being back home, working in the hay fields.

This reverie was interrupted when I was rudely awakened by the bright light shining in the center of the room and by someone beating on the soles of my bare feet. Startled, I bolted upright in my top bunk that I had chosen because I knew what little heat was generated by the stove would rise toward the ceiling.

Then the other shocker: I was staring into the ugly face of that 6-foot 6-inch guard, shouting, "*Aufstehen! Raus mit dir!*"

Now he was beating on the end of the bunk with the butt end of his blacksnake whip. What a hell of a way to start the day, I thought. We couldn't even guess what time it was, since nobody had a watch. But I could see through the door, as I jumped from my bunk, that it was still dark outside.

We quickly dressed and filed out of the barracks and lined up in the snowy darkness to be counted prior to being led off for a work detail. While waiting to move out of the two gates to the road, our two kitchen men showed up with a black kettle of hot, steaming coffee. As we were issued a tin-cup full of the stuff, we were informed that this would be our breakfast each morning before marching off to work. All I can say for the coffee is that it was hot, strong and bitter. But it sure warmed my gut.

This tin cup was the only utensil we carried—the bowl and spoon stayed on our bunks in the barracks—and we carried it tied to our belt from that day on. I always felt like the proverbial beggar, sticking out my tin cup for an occasional bit of coffee whenever it was offered. It was nourishment of a sort.

The German army was no different from its American counterpart here, either. It was still hurry up and wait. Only this time it was hurry up and wait in the cold and dark morning with a strong wind blowing in our faces. About 10 men were marched off toward Runddorf with one guard in front and one behind the column. The rest of us headed off in the opposite direction.

We took a narrow dirt road heading directly toward a huge forest, thick with large pine trees. The snow was about 2 feet deep. Since we were the first ones on the road, we had to plow our own path. The snow was light and powdery, but we still had to take turns breaking a path. We had no idea where we were going or how far, so each man took short spells in breaking trail.

Actually, that's what it was, a narrow trail, not a traveled road, so we could only walk in two columns. We must have plodded at least two miles in this dense woods before the trees thinned out. At that point, we left the trail and took a path in a northerly direction.

Just as we left the woods, we came to a small stream and crossed over it on a railroad bridge. From then on, the area was open, flat country with an occasional farmhouse and barn along the way. We were never allowed on the roadway but always followed a path along back fences away from the houses.

Because of the heavy snow, we had been walking in single file since leaving the forest. After several more miles, I could see that we were approaching a rather large town that turned out to be Hoyerswerda. It had a population of roughly 8,000 and was 12 kilometers or about seven miles from our camp. Once in the town, we were halted in front of a large metal building. Apparently the town didn't plow its snow, because it was just as deep in town as it had been in the country we had just plowed through.

Several minutes later, the door of the metal building popped open and out stepped a most official-looking official. At least his bearing appeared official—not his clothes, though. I knew instantly I could never forget this character. He was short and skinny, sported a Hitler-type mustache and wore the most outlandish-looking checkered coat, which hung below his knees, that I'd ever seen. A homburg-type black hat, pulled down almost to his ears, covered his bald pate. He was an official of some kind or maybe the mayor's son-in-law, but he surely got our attention.

He carried a large oversized briefcase from which he pulled a sheaf of papers and proceeded to shuffle through them like some kind of confused idiot. Finally he said, "*Ja! Ja!*" as he evidently discovered the right page. Every day we subsequently worked in Hoyerswerda, we endured this same circus. We nicknamed this official Mortimer Snerd after the then-famous cartoon character. He would give our guards the orders for whatever details we were to do that day. Ol' Mort was good for a laugh a day.

Light, humorous moments were few and far between in our drab world of prison life, but we soon found ourselves looking forward to our meeting with the official job-giver each morning. His voice defied description. It was high-pitched, like a small child's. This, coupled with all his flamboyant gestures, kept us all amused. Of course, we dared not laugh aloud, but we fairly shook trying to contain ourselves.

Mortimer, as we all now called him, more or less jumped out of the door of the building on the first knock, as though he'd been standing just inside, waiting. He would run up to whomever was our lead guard, who was nearly always the little corporal we called Pops. Then, thrusting his arm in the air, the official job-giver would fire off a snappy, "*Heil Hitler.*"

In his early 50s, Pops had fought for Germany in World War I and had been badly wounded in both legs while serving with an artillery unit. As a result of the wounds, he had difficulty walking. His right leg slanted inward at a grotesque angle, forcing him to sort of hop along.

He was a jovial guy despite his infirmity, and his heart was definitely not in his job. Nor did he have any time for the Nazi regime of Hitler and frequently expressed this attitude. His disdain was most obvious whenever anyone greeted him with *"Heil Hitler."*

It was a comical scene to watch outlandish ol' Mortimer snap that salute in Pops' face, followed by his half-hearted response. Pops would raise his return salute half way up his chest and growl some inaudible curse. He was not a good Nazi.

After all the greetings were over, we split into three groups with each going in a different direction in the town. My first job assignment was at the ice pond, cutting big cakes of ice with an ice saw. I tried my best to stay upright on the ice while using the saw. But try as I might, I think I was on my knees about as often as I was standing.

The civilian in charge seemed disgusted with my work. He continually railed and cursed, partly in English and partly in German. I tried to act dumb and let him show me several times just what size he wanted these cakes to be. Finally, I cut them to his satisfaction. I could tell that the guard's temper was getting short, so I figured I'd pushed both him and the civilian as far as I dared this time.

This was a little game all of us would play during our entire captivity. Some days the game would work for me, and sometimes I would push just a bit too far and would suddenly end up on my butt or, at times, flat on my face in the snow. It was a dangerous little game, but it was one way we prisoners could fight back. Sort of a stalling ploy.

But look out when a guard's fuse was short. Sometimes he would explode into a rage and come at me, screaming and shoving that gun barrel in my gut. And sometimes he would pull back the hammer and threaten to blow my guts out—and not only mine. Lots of other men did the same thing I did. We'd stand our ground, hoping not to make a wrong move for fear he would get so nervous from rage that he would accidentally pull the trigger.

The guards were instructed not to shoot us unless we made an attempt to escape. I also think they had instructions to keep the chamber empty as a safeguard. They could quickly jack a shell into the chamber if the situation became desperate.

Games aside, though, standing on a slick sheet of ice trying to cut through 4 to 6 inches of solid ice with an unwieldy two-handed saw is a difficult task. The wind howled right through my thin clothing. And since I had no gloves, I had to stop frequently to try and warm my hand enough to hold onto the steel handles of the saw.

Each cake of ice we cut was supposed to weigh about 50 pounds. I had no idea what size of slab would weigh close to 50 pounds, but I quickly discovered that the first two slabs I cut were way too small. I had to push them aside and let the civilian boss man cut the next pieces to show me what dimensions he expected. Sure took me a long time and a lot of slabs to learn.

Once a slab was cut, a long pole with a hook on the end was used to coax the ice to one end of the pond where two of us would then hoist it onto a wagon. Trying to steer that damn chunk of ice in any direction was no easy task, forcing me a couple of times into knee-deep water to get the crazy thing to shore. I was already wet to my waist just from the splashing water to the point that my trousers were beginning to freeze from the stiff, blowing wind.

Two Holstein milk cows furnished the "horsepower" to pull the wagon, so we could only load about 10 cakes of ice per load. The small loads turned out to be a blessing; however, because when we arrived at the ice house (which was actually a brewery), we always received a reward. Four men would ride the ice wagon into town to unload. Upon seeing the decrepit condition we were in, the buxom *Frau* in charge would usually summon us to a small room. It resembled a kitchen and had a large porcelain sink, a cook stove, a table and a small heating stove.

There, the first time I made the trip, she bade us to sit down at the table and hurriedly exited the room, returning shortly with four large mugs of beer. A large pitcher of hot water sat on the top of the heating stove. She poured that hot water into the sink and placed the mugs of beer in the hot water for a few minutes. And presto! We each had a stein of warm beer.

We eagerly took huge gulps of the steaming brew. I felt a warm glow seep into my whole body almost immediately. The beer was a heavy, rather bitter drink; but by the time I had drained that last drop, I think I could've unloaded that wagon single-handed. I had never drunk hot beer before, but in this situation the results were good for the morale. It didn't take much beer to make us real mellow under the circumstances.

As I walked out of that room, I felt warm for the first time in months. Even my feet felt warm. Many mornings on our walk to work, a thin layer of ice would form between the soles of my shoes and the bottoms of my feet. This morning I think the warm brew even melted that layer of ice.

The woman, who I guessed to be in her early 70s, apparently was the owner of the brewery. She later confided to the guard that her husband had been killed on the Russian front where he was apparently sent with the German Brown shirts, and she was the only one left to run the business.

She motioned us through a door into a massive stone building in which we were to store the ice for use through the summer months. The wagon had been backed up to the door, and we headed in that direction to unload.

"Habens du nicht handschuh?" she asked.

"Nein," we said, muttering negatively to her question about us having no gloves.

With a disgusted frown on her face, she turned and went back to the office area. Shortly, she returned with an old ragged dress, which she cut in strips and handed to each of us. We quickly wrapped our hands with the strips. These and the hot brew made the handling the ice a much easier task.

In one corner of the building stood a huge pile of sawdust. She instructed us to spread the sawdust about 2 inches thick on the floor, place the ice cakes about 2 inches apart and then pack the sawdust in the cracks. This procedure took a goodly amount of time. The boss lady was very particular in the placement of each block and checked to be sure we tamped the sawdust in each chunk.

I spent the better part of two weeks on the ice-pond detail. The work at the pond was hard, cold work, using the heavy 6-foot-long ice saw. But just the anticipation of that big stone mug of hot beer at the brewery somehow helped me get through each long day.

As the ice pile grew toward the high ceiling, we used a long, hand-powered elevator to lift the cakes as we stair-stepped up to the top of the stack, packing each ice cake in sawdust. By going from pond to pond, we never ran out of ice before we'd filled the warehouse to the brim. The glove rags were actually not much help in the long run. They soon became soaking wet, which made our hands even colder. But we appreciated the old woman's caring about us, anyway.

On the morning of the third day, we were presented with a new set of gloves. Some brilliant German mind came up with this idea. These "gloves" were just an 8-to-9-inch-long piece of rubber, cut from an old inner tube. A hole had been cut into one side near the end, through which we would shove our thumb to hold it on our hand. The rubber surface was a tremendous help in controlling those slick cakes of ice.

Before this new invention, I would take my rag to the barracks each night to dry out. Now with this new glove, I was able to keep the rag from getting too wet, and it was a great help in keeping my hands drier and a little warmer. I left the new rubber gloves at the brewery at the end of the day.

I relished the time spent inside the ice house. Even though the place was cold, I was at least out of the biting cold, always-blowing wind. With a crew of four, we had little trouble sliding and lifting the 50-pound cakes of ice, and we could always spend a little extra time on our knees, tamping the sawdust. It was just another small way to resist the enemy, part of the POW creed.

My next job assignment turned into real, dirty work. After the daily ritual with Mortimer and his gyrations, about 10 of us were marched off to the far side of town, eventually arriving at a large brick building that appeared to be a hospital. As we rounded the corner, I could see another good-sized building being constructed of wood. This was to be used as an annex to the main hospital. A small crew was adding the finishing touches to the outside.

Our job was to dig the water and sewer lines from the building on out to the road to connect to the main water and sewer. A heavy cord was stretched from the building in the direction we were to dig. To do the job, we were issued shovels, picks, wedges and huge sledge hammers. After scrapping off the 2 feet of snow cover, we started trying to dig into the frozen ground. Progress was almost nil that day. Imagine attempting to penetrate nearly 18 inches of frozen ground, using a sledge hammer to pound long spike wedges to break up the ground in the dead of winter.

One of the work details had managed to relieve a backyard clothes-line of two heavy shirts. We ripped these apart, used the sleeves as gloves and wrapped our feet in strips of cloth. This thin protection did nothing to keep our hands warm and little to keep our hands from freezing to the spikes when one of us held the wedge while the other pounded with the sledge.

Hoyerswerda was situated on a broad, open plain. The wind howled from the north and east all the time. It never let up. The snow was light and powder-like, so that it seemed to be snowing all the time. Consequently, the man holding the wedge would be on his knee, in the snow, and every little movement kicked up puffs of blowing snow.

For the next week, I was assigned to the ditch detail. Progress was painfully slow—and painful as well—as we tried to break through the frost and then dig to a depth of 5 feet. Mortimer would usually stop by once or twice a day to check on the job, He'd walk around, muttering and pointing while one guard would just nod his head and repeat, "*Ja, ja.*"

Ol' Mortimer took great pleasure in talking with us, it seemed. Since we couldn't understand a word he said, we'd mimic the guard by shaking our head and repeating, "*Ja, ja.*" He always seemed satisfied with our work and would usually wave goodbye and spout words in his high-pitched, squeaky voice. While I was always glad to see him leave, he did add a little change of pace. And we would always quit work when he stopped to talk. His antics were always good for a few laughs, something we needed.

During the long days of hacking at the frozen ground on my hands and knees, there was a diversion of sorts. On frequent occasions, several exceptionally pretty, blonde-haired young women strolled past the job site on their way to the center of Hoyerswerda. They always stayed on the far side of the street, but they surely knew that all eyes were following their every move. We figured this out, because they seemed to slow down a bit as they came into view. The same group of three passed by every day; however, there must've been 15 or 20 young women, all told, that sashayed by during my time on the ditch detail.

On the third day, four young blonde-haired German soldiers sauntered up to where I was grubbing away on the 5-foot ditch. They appeared to be in their late teens or early 20s and were obviously SS to the core. Their display of arrogance gave them away. The civilians usually ignored us completely, so I was surprised to glance up and find these four soldiers peering down in the ditch at me.

They all spoke excellent English and immediately verified that I was an American. The questions then came thick and fast concerning my home life in America. Their voices were not intimidating in any way, so I took the opportunity to stop working and answered their questions, albeit sparingly. It seemed that they were only interested in America. They never mentioned the war or spouted Nazi dogma. Pops, the guard that day, finally moseyed over and joined in the conversation, using his best English words interspersed with German. He ignored the fact that I was not digging.

About that time, a couple of those blondes meandered by and exchanged greetings with the four soldiers. The conversation immediately swung from America to women. Although the women always wore long coats and heavy boots to ward off the cold wind and snow, I had begun to notice that some of them were in various stages of pregnancy and mentioned this to the soldiers.

They immediately launched into a wild tale about all those pregnant little blondes strolling by. According to the soldiers, a large apartment complex just three blocks down the street housed some 40 of these young women. All were pregnant or soon would be. These four young Nazis and several more, I learned, were nothing but young studs who were breeding the "true Aryan race." *Der Führer*, Adolf Hitler, continually bragged to the world of this fiendish creation I was hearing about as I stood in the ditch.

The Nazi soldiers continued to explain in great detail, their prowess with the ladies. I'll have to admit that I did derive enjoyment from watching the women go by. But the detailed stories from these studs failed to arouse any sexual desires in me in my half-starved condition. Pops' reaction was one of disbelief. He couldn't swallow the reports of all the sexual activity that the soldiers imparted to us. Hitler had been ranting for years that he was going to build the true Aryan race. Apparently this was how it was going to be accomplished.

Pops finally had heard enough and ordered the young Nazis on their way. The women continued their daily walks past us, and sometimes even some of the other young SS troopers came by. But none of them ever made an effort to stop again. I enjoyed the break from work, however brief, and would have listened all day, if Pops hadn't blown his stack and ordered the boys off. It was only three blocks from the work site to the "baby factory," but I never got the chance to observe it in person. My job was to dig ditches.

Each morning upon arriving at work, we would have to scoop out a trench full of snow. For some stupid reason, we had to lay the sewer tile and water pipe. I was sure happy to see the end of this detail. But then it was time to move on to the next one which would prove every bit as difficult. One thing I did miss from the ditch detail was the noonday break when we would retreat to a small shack to get warm.

Two German men, plus one of our "*Kriegies* "(American slang for *Kriegsgefangenen*, the German word for prisoners of war and what we called ourselves), were making beautiful steel stoves in the shack. The men used a charcoal- and coke-fired braiser to heat-treat the metal, and it was warm inside. We tried to soak up enough heat during our brief half-hour-or-so break to last the rest of the day. Those noondays were some of the few times I was ever warm during the entire winter.

We were usually treated to a tin cup of coffee but never any food. No matter. It was a chance to sit down, rest and admire the beautiful stoves as they were finished. The stoves were ornate and had colorful tile cemented over most of the outside. The stovemakers explained that the heavy tile helped hold the heat throughout the night. These stoves were unlike any I had ever seen. They were truly works of art, designed to enhance the decor of the homes they would heat. They looked expensive. Perhaps only the wealthy could afford them. I didn't know. But I did know that they were a far cry from the old, black potbellied stoves and cooking ranges I grew up around. These were masterpieces, lovingly constructed by master craftsmen.

And not only were the two *Ofenmacher*, or stove makers, masters at their trade, they were friendly characters, too. They were both in their late 60s and were not too keen on the new Third Reich. After a couple of days in their shop, they began to unwind a bit around us and quietly expressed their opinions concerning Hitler and the dreaded *Gestapo*.

The older one was the real character of the two. He sported a huge Kaiser Wilhelm handlebar mustache, the turned-up, pointed ends of which he kept heavily waxed. I enjoyed watching that mustache bounce as he talked. He looked like a famous old painting I'd seen somewhere.

Earlier, I had noticed a beautiful hand-carved pipe hanging on one wall. Pointing to it, I asked to see it up close. The mustachioed one gently took it down and handed it to me. It must have been carved from some type of ceramic or stoneware, but it amazed me that it was so light in weight.

While I was still holding the pipe he took out his tobacco tin—every German man seemed to carry a tobacco tin—and began smoothing the rough-grown shag into smaller pieces by rubbing it in the palms of his hands. He then took the pipe, filled the bowl, tamped it, lit it and closed the small lid over the bowl. The elaborate apparatus hung halfway down to his waist.

Leaning back into a big old wooden chair, he began puffing away and closed his eyes in what seemed to be perfect contentment. This would always be a pleasurable scene to remember. It was just like my grandpa did back home on the farm, especially after a filling noon meal before he went back out to the field.

I spent the next several days on the garbage detail. By far, this was the worst detail I'd been on at Hoyerswerda. We walked to the edge of town to a big open pit. There we raked the piles of garbage into a smooth surface after each wagon load arrived and attacked the big pile in between loads. Quite literally, there was a mountain of garbage, and the smell was overpowering, even in the cold of winter. I was glad I didn't have this detail in the heat of summer.

On this detail, we all learned a new trade that we called "scrounger" or "scavenger." We never found any bits or scraps of food, but we found treasures of another kind. Among our treasures were bits of string, newspapers and paper sacks. We brought all these finds back to the barracks. And from then on, we would wrap newspaper around our bodies and tie it with string as a buffer against the cold wind.

We tried to keep a small supply of paper and string hidden in the barracks. If any of this contraband had been discovered by the guards, no telling what would have happened to us. These things were all *"verboten."* The last month I was in Runddorf I had to resort to wrapping my feet in newspaper everyday to try to keep my feet a little warm. My one pair of socks had worn out and rotted away some time ago; my shoe soles were very thin with holes in each side of both shoes. I put extra layers of paper in the bottoms of the shoes each night for the next day's walk.

Our work details usually lasted for about a week or 10 days, then it was on to something else. Most of the time, Pops was assigned as guard on my work details. He was reserved, withdrawn and aloof, most of the time. It was hard to figure out just why he was so morose and uncommunicative. He seldom smiled and always kept pushing us to work harder and walk faster on the long trek back to the compound at night.

Those 12 kilometers got longer and longer. Many times darkness would overtake us as we plodded along through the snow in the big woods. The last five kilometers into camp seemed endless to our exhausted, starving bodies. And my days spent in Holland in muddy foxholes, wading through the canals and sleeping on the cold ground had brought on a condition known as chilled kidneys, which caused sudden, frequent and, at times, almost uncontrollable urination. Sometimes my trousers got wet, and not always from the rainy days and nights I spent in the land of the Dutch. It was a pretty bad situation that when I was continuously on the move or had to fight for survival that I didn't even have time to take a piss. This condition hounded me all during combat and throughout life in the *Stalags*.

The chilled-kidney syndrome followed me home and finally caused a prostrate infection that slowed my discharge and put me in the hospital for about four weeks at Brooks General Hospital in Fort Sam Houston, Texas.

After a few weeks of the putrid prison diet, the other men and I developed another nasty physical problem: that of frequent and loud explosions of stomach gas escaping from our bodies. Sometimes at night you could hear a fart so loud after we'd bunked down that at times I thought I was back in the front lines. These eruptions were odoriferous, to put it mildly—sometimes to the point of almost causing you to vomit.

Every morning, by the time we had walked about a mile on our way to Hoyerswerda to work, the exercise really had the gasses fired up. It got so bad that the guards distanced themselves from our ranks and walked several yards to the side of our column, all the time holding their noses and repeating, "*Scheizen in die Hosen.*" We'd grin from ear to ear, hold our noses and repeat the German words. From the sound and smell of some of the farts, due in great part to our diets of grains (mostly barley), it was entirely possible that we could have *Scheizen in die Hosen* any minute.

Of course, we would have to stop many times along the way to take a piss. We timed it so only one man had to go at a time; therefore, the guards became frustrated with the frequent stops. On some days they brought one column to a complete halt and insisted that we all urinate at the same time. But in our wily American way usually only one or two of us obliged. Then a few yards down the path the whole column had to halt again for the rest to answer nature's call.

After a few weeks of playing this game, the guards gave up, making us late for our work assignments on some days. This was just one of the few little ways that we could resist the bastards. And we always tried to do that or thought about how to get completely away from them.

It was during some of the darkest, most moonless nights that my mind would be racing, full of all kinds of temptations to escape. The thick trees overhung our narrow road so we seldom got a glimpse of either the sun during the day or any stars at night. We had discussed all sorts of wild ideas for escape during our evening sessions after supper. We usually concluded that our best chance would have to come at night, either from our barracks or during those long return hikes from Hoyerswerda after darkness fell.

Two guards usually walked in the rear of our column, while the other two placed themselves near the front. We had very little conversation during this trek. As a rule, we all kept our thoughts to ourselves. My thoughts, and I'm sure those of the other men, were always dreaming of home and food. We really had little to talk or joke about, anyway, and saved our discussions for after supper and before lights out. Then we mostly talked about life back in the States.

Despite old Pops' nature that we found difficult to figure out, he always, bless him, took our side in any confrontations with the civilians or problems with the bosses on our work details. His booming voice usually sent the culprit scurrying for cover, especially when he would swing his rifle at them in a menacing way.

At the same time, he also would not hesitate to shove the barrel into my gut during one of his tirades. He was a puzzle of a man to figure out. Some days I hardly knew he was around, always on the alert but keeping his distance from us. Other days he was an entirely different individual. In some instances, he would even carry on a conversation with some of us. On those good days, we would teach him a few words of English in exchange for common German words. This was a tremendous advantage for us as time went on; it helped us to understand what was expected of us on some of the more complex jobs. Mostly, however, we were given menial tasks that took a minimum of explanation or directions.

Pops seemed to soften a bit as the winter wore on. Trading words in both languages was part of the reason, I think. But I think he was aware of the worsening war situation in regard to Germany. He couldn't help but know that the Germans were losing badly and may have realized that he might end up needing our help. Yet he never once discussed the war or its progress with us, so we were always lacking in any substantive news of how things were in the outside world. I still had faith in my own American Army, however. It just had to defeat the Germans before I starved to death or was killed trying to escape.

In one of our discussions, escape was alluded to. Pops must have known we were always considering the possibility of being able to escape. We just hadn't talked about it with him.

"If I got an opportunity to run," I finally asked him one day, "would you shoot me in the back?"

As usual, we communicated in broken English with a few German words thrown in and lots of sign language.

"Of course, I would," he replied. "I would regret having to do so, but, you see, I would be shot if I did not fulfill my duty. Why should you needlessly waste your life, though? It would be simple to break away from this small *Stalag* some night."

He must have been reading my thoughts, because he mentioned the possibility of slipping out of line and into the dense woods on a dark-night walk from Hoyerswerda. But he also discussed the hazards we would face if we made any such attempt.

"Where would you go?" he asked. "You surely have seen the patrols on the roads and in the woods. And you know that all railroad and river bridges are heavily guarded. There are special 'kill zones' set up around all military-sensitive positions with orders to shoot anybody on sight for any intrusion. Dressed the way you men are and not speaking or understanding the language to any degree, you wouldn't get five kilometers before you were challenged.

"Use your brains. This war can't last forever, and when it ends, you can go home. In an escape attempt, you would have to have food or you would die in a few days in your present condition. And you are well aware by this time how hard it is to acquire food."

Pops' mention of food and kill zones put a quick damper on any thoughts I had of escape—for the present. I'd also noticed an increasing number of Hitler *Jugend* or Hitler Youth roaming around in town and out in the countryside. They all carried rifles and would relish the chance to shoot us first, without any questions. They were always shouting obscenities in our direction whenever they came within earshot of our work place.

Some would even walk toward us, weapon at the ready, hoping to anger or scare us into making a wrong move, before one of our guards would force them to back off. I had had some hairy times, especially while working in the hospital drainage ditch where we worked right along a main street. And on my last work detail, I would again confront the nasty Hitler *Jugend.*

From all of our conversations, I learned some interesting aspects about Pops' background. After fighting in World War I and being left crippled for life, he became bitter and disillusioned and left Germany in 1919 just after the war was over. Finally ending up in Argentina, he married a local woman and started a private business. Over the years, he and his wife had two sons and two daughters. The business was successful, and he bought a home and had money in the bank.

In early 1938, his sister had written him from Germany that their father was seriously ill and wished to see his eldest son one more time. So after an absence of 19 years, he returned to the homeland for a reunion with his father and sister. Two months after his arrival, his father died. Pops stayed on in Germany to settle the estate between his sister and him.

Germany was in turmoil with Adolf Hitler screaming threats at the whole world. After victory in World War I, the Allied countries had demanded, and received, reparations from the defeated Germany. As a result of the drain of payments, the country was in a deep depression. Many of its people were starving and many of the towns and cities in ruins. Germany was unable to raise enough food to feed its millions of hungry citizens. As a consequence, many fled the country, but those who remained became increasingly disillusioned and angry.

In early 1933, Hitler rose to power by cleverly manipulating the voting process. He arrived on the scene at an opportune time. Although he lacked a formal education, he was a brilliant speaker. Through fiery oratory and well-staged rallies, he was able to win the confidence of many of his countrymen—especially the youth. With his leadership, Germany once again became a first-rate power throughout the world. The people were so desperate they were ready to follow anyone who promised a better future.

Pops got caught in this resurgence of German power. After settling the family estate, he found the government wouldn't issue him a permit to leave Germany. He was still considered a citizen of the Third Reich. He was so desperate to return to Argentina and his family there that he made an attempt to flee on his own, only to be caught at the Swiss border and thrown into jail.

His jail term would be rescinded if he would agree to work in a factory, since most young, able-bodied men were already in the army. With Hitler gearing up for conquest, war clouds were gathering. Pops was ultimately drafted into the regular army but was too crippled up and was rather old for front-line combat. After several other duty stations, he ended up chasing prisoners at Runddorf. I think Pops felt he was a prisoner in his own land; thus, he harbored a hatred for Hitler.

I got to liking the old man and tried to do his bidding, thereby keeping him out of trouble. On one occasion late in my captivity, I was working in a crew cutting 9-meter logs in a dense woods close to Runddorf. By this time, we were all even weaker than ever from near starvation and were having a great deal of difficulty attempting to lift a big log to carry it out to a wagon on the road. The civilian boss that morning had been ranting at us to work harder.

"These Americans are all weaklings," he shouted at our guards.

Pops became livid with rage as he whirled around, faced the civilian and shouted in his face, "It's because these men are being starved. I have been to America. They feed their swine better food than these men are getting. They don't get enough food to eat to be strong. Now get out of here and leave us alone."

The man to whom this was directed was stunned at Pops' outburst but quickly turned on his heal and fled, daring not to look back as he left the forest.

9

Returning from Hoyerswerda at dusk one evening, we heard the roar of bombers low overhead. One look and I knew they were Russian and were headed in the direction of town, which we had just left. Then we heard the muffled sound of explosions back in Hoyerswerda.

"Hey," somebody said, "maybe there won't be anything left for us to do in town tomorrow."

"We'll probably have to clean up all the rubble," somebody else said.

And sure enough, we all ended up repairing railroad tracks that had been hit in the raid. This was heavy labor; but since the railroad was vital for movement of supplies, we worked alongside German troops. The repairs were finished by early afternoon, and we were allowed to return to Runddorf long before dark for once.

But as we finished putting the last rail in place, a small steam engine appeared from the southwest, pushing three boxcars ahead of it. I was helping with the final cleanup as they approached, and I quickly became aware that these boxcars were crammed with people. As the first car drew near, I could see a small child's face peering out through the small window at the end of the car. She was crying, her head jerking as she sobbed. I couldn't see the tears streaming down her cheeks or hear her sobs, but I saw and heard them in my mind. That sent chills through me.

At this time, none of us knew anything of the horrible death camps scattered throughout Germany. They were a well-kept secret. I had no idea that people going by inside the boxcars were Jews, headed for death in gas chambers and cremation in ovens. I just assumed they were more slaves rounded up for work in the German war factories. Later, we learned that the boxcars contained only women and children but didn't learn about the concentration camps until near the end of the war. The scene was bad enough, but I'm glad I didn't know their destination or fate as we watched them pass by our work detail.

How I longed for that Timberwolf wool uniform, especially the long wool overcoat. With the winter of 1944-45 being the most extreme winter ever recorded in Europe, the bitterly cold temperatures and inclement weather added much to our suffering. January and February were the coldest, snowiest and windiest of all. Considering the summery-type clothing we had to wear and these conditions, we had difficulty accomplishing a great deal of work in spite of the unending prodding and screaming directed at us. The tools were primitive, and most of the work details were unproductive as far as helping the German war machine—except the later jobs of building defensive positions in Runddorf.

But we got by the best we could, and the days dragged on without any variation in routine. Each morning we continued to be abruptly aroused by the banging on the bunks and the shouting of the guard. We hurriedly got dressed, lined up out in the cold morning and got counted two or three times. It seemed as though the guards couldn't count above 20. Of course, we weren't above shifting around a bit, just to confuse them.

Usually, though, we were in a hurry to down the cup of hot coffee and be on our way to keep from standing around in the snow. At least walking helped us to keep a little warmer. The winds must have whipped up every night because our path through the forest from the night before would be completely filled with snow every morning. Although the snow was light, it was still a grueling chore making a way through 2 feet of snow everyday. It got old. We were exhausted by the time we got to Hoyerswerda. That was nothing new; nothing much ever was new.

The first several weeks our return walk to camp was uneventful, too. Each man was searched upon passing through the second gate to our barracks. Any contraband found on us was confiscated amid the usual screams and threats of punishment for not following the rules. The only time we had contact with the *Kommander Führer* was each morning for a short briefing to remind us of those rules. He'd strut around, assuming the role of a tough sergeant, arrogantly shouting at us, threatening reprisals of dire consequences if we didn't perform our work satisfactorily or continued to bring in contraband. Each sentence would start in a low voice but would rise to a high, shrill pitch at the end.

He would pace up and down in front of us, arms flailing like a windmill gone berserk. We stood at rapt attention, staring about 2 feet over his head, trying to contain our laughter. After the first few days, we paid scant attention to his tirades—each day was a repeat of the one before. He never once appeared at any of our job sites and was seldom seen except at morning and evening lineups.

But one evening late in February after a particularly trying day scrambling over a frozen-ice pond and digging a bit in frozen earth, I was in the lead as we approached the *Stalag*. I'm sure I wasn't the only one looking forward to getting inside and soaking up a little warmth. At the main gate, I could see the *Kommander Führer*, hands behind his back, pacing vigorously back and forth, working himself up to the proper frame of mind to clobber us with a good chewing out.

We were rushed through the two gates, foregoing the usual quick body search for contraband, and were quickly brought to some semblance of attention. After a few seconds of eerie silence, the little corporal stopped pacing and abruptly whirled to face us from about six paces away. His hands were on his hips, his eyes blazing.

We usually grouped together according to our sleeping quarters, and I seemed to have emerged as the leader or spokesman for the 18 men in my side of the building. At least the *Kommander Führer* seemed to look at it that way. This was all too evident during this evening's diatribe.

"Have you not been receiving fair treatment?" the *Kommander Führer* asked, biting off each word and spitting it out in a raging guttural shout. "That will stop. Your work has not been equal to the requirements demanded of you; your work has been sloppy. You are slow to learn or do not make an honest attempt to understand what you are ordered to do."

He's figured us out all right, I thought, standing stiffly at attention with my eyes staring straight ahead. But I didn't want to give him any reason to do anything more drastic than shouting.

"Your production must increase immediately or you will find yourselves working longer hours and all day Sunday; your food ration will be cut. Do you understand?"

The last remark really had an impact on us. Our food had been getting worse in quality and less in quantity by the day anyway. And the scolding intensified. The *Kommander Führer* worked himself into such an emotional shouting frenzy that at one point he snatched his Lugar pistol from its holster, and charging toward me, shoved the pistol up under my nose, pushing my head back, and cocked the gun, all the while shouting obscenities and threatening to blow off the end of my nose.

"You must encourage the men to remember they have to work hard or else they will be shot," he said, shouting with his face close enough to mine that I could smell his sour breath and feel his spit spray my face as he spoke. He was trembling so much I feared his trigger finger would twitch hard enough to accidentally squeeze off a round.

The Sunday work day became longer that week. Our potato ration was cut in half for a whole week, and we missed those two potatoes at our daily meal. The soup was still watery, thin and fairly tasteless. Also, this was about the time when a noticeable taste took place in the bread. We got the same amount of black bread as usual, but the taste and texture were changing nearly every week.

On one of the weekly forays into Runddorf where we got our supply of bread, one of the men was quietly sauntering about the bakery and discovered the reason: Fine sawdust was being mixed into the bread dough to supplement the dwindling supply of available grain to make flour. Sometimes the taste came through as pine, sometimes oak or some other tree taste. Because it was food and we were always hungry, we ate the bread. But it played hell with our digestive systems.

During our evening discussion after supper around the table in the middle room the night the *Kommander Führer* pushed my nose back with his pistol, the men in my bunk area decided to work harder the next few days. A good report would calm the old boy down, the men thought, saving the end of my nose and getting our food allotment restored.

In spite of our resolve, however, this same scene would be played out numerous times during the next several weeks. On one occasion, the little corporal became so angry that he shot at my feet. I stood at rigid attention, staring straight ahead, showing no emotion whatsoever. That only tended to infuriate him even more, but I was at a loss as to how else to react. I had been chewed out a multitude of times previously, but he seemed completely out of control this time.

The snow continued to pile up, making our daily trip into Hoyerswerda all the more exhausting. By evening on the return trip, we more often than not had to break a new trail through the woods. Not enough food, not enough heat, not enough energy to produce what was demanded of us was all becoming overwhelming. By the middle of March, starvation was beginning to manifest itself within our ranks. My thoughts dwelled on food and happier days back in the States.

As we plodded along one evening, Abe, a short, wiry infantryman from the 28th Division, who was usually silent on these long walks to and from Hoyerswerda, suddenly turned to me and asked, "Charlie, have you ever eaten pancakes smothered with hot maple syrup? First, you let lotsa butter melt. Then you—"

"Shut up," I said, growling at him like a half-crazed animal, "or I'll throw you off the railroad bridge when we cross it."

He never said anything more. But a few minutes later after I'd realized I had lost my cool, I turned to say something cheerful to him and looked into a big, satisfied grin on his face. So I said nothing. He had come into the lines as a replacement just three days before he was slightly wounded and gathered up by the Nazis. He had celebrated his 19th birthday on a boxcar and was probably the youngest man in our camp. At this point, I was an old man at 22 years of age. In reality, I felt a lot older than that.

Under those conditions, our camp humor was somewhat bizarre. After we had finished eating that night, Harold, one of the two married prisoners among us, was writing a letter to his wife back in the States. He had written several letters to her over the weeks in camp, knowing damn well the Germans wouldn't let him send them. Even assuming that the letter actually got sent and that the censors didn't cut it all up, just what could he say that could possibly interest someone Stateside, I wondered. No one could comprehend the conditions we endured all day, every day.

But Harold usually ignored my queries regarding the content of his letters. Writing seemed to pump up his morale every time, so I knew the time and effort weren't wasted and hadn't mentioned the letters for a while.

"Charlie," Harold finally said from where he was perched on his top bunk scribbling like a maniac, "this will have to be my last letter to my wife."

"Why do you say that, Harold?" I asked. "You mad 'cause you're not getting any letter from her?"

"No," he said, looking quietly at the pencil in his hand. "It's just that I don't have any more lead in my stub of a pencil."

After a couple of minutes, he started laughing like a crazy man. I glanced across the small crowded bunkhouse to see him going through a frenzy of gyrations, trying to squeeze the last bit of lead from the pencil.

"D'ya wanna hear what I told my ol' lady, Charlie?" he asked through the funniest shit-eating grin I'd seen on anybody's face for a long time.

"Sure, let's hear it, if it's not too private."

"Well, I told her she had better get a good look at the floor, because when I get home, all she's going to see is ceiling! Love, Harold," he said and propelled that tiny bit of pencil at the pot-bellied stove. Still grinning, he lay back in his bunk and wished me a cheery, "Good night."

That bit of prison humor helped everybody relax, I think. It wasn't too long before, one by one, the steady breathing of sleep, plus the sound of snores, filled the bunkhouse. The little light went out. It was time to get our well-deserved rest, before another day and another work detail rolled around.

We were now working seven days a week because of our "previous poor performance," just as the *Kommander Führer* threatened we would. On this bitterly cold, windy day, I drew the dirtiest detail any man could have—cleaning out a sewer ditch on the outskirts of Hoyerswerda.

The houses were next to the road; the outhouses were in the rear, perched over the open ditch, which had become clogged with leaves, tree limbs and other trash. We were issue long-handled wooden rakes which were supposed to be long enough to reach across the smelly mess. Behind the ditch ran the railroad track. Beyond the track was the same setup of the ditch, outhouses and houses fronting the road.

Our eight-man detail had been split into two four-man units, with the other half across the tracks from us. The older civilian population generally stayed their distance from us, but we would be occasionally pestered by a wandering member of the Hitler *Jugend*. One was lurking in the area that day and picked a bad time to annoy us.

Two trains had already passed by noon, all full of civilians heading to we knew not where, although we had heard enough rumors by now of the horrible slave-labor camps. At a safe distance, this particular idiot had been hanging around our crew, trying out his limited English on us. We ignored him, hoping he would just go away. It didn't work.

Since we wouldn't respond to him, he wandered across the tracks to pester the other crew of American prisoners. They, too, ignored the youth until a third train arrived. This one had two boxcars. The fledgling Nazi broke the silence as he pointed to the boxcars and said, "*Juden*," gave a Bronx cheer and broke into a high-pitched, cackling laugh accompanied by taunting gestures toward the box cars full of Jews. That's when all hell broke loose.

From our vantage point, we could see the other four crew members engaged in a scuffle, but we couldn't see the Nazi. Then I heard Pops' booming voice, "*Auf mit Schnell! Raus! Raus!*" I looked over at Pops. He was hopping mad. The kid was running at top speed in the opposite direction.

That night after supper, we talked awhile as usual around the table. As a rule, there wasn't too much a of an exciting nature that occurred in our daily routine. But today was an exception. This little incident could have spelled disaster for Charley White, one of our guys who was definitely a hothead. He continually popped-off at anything and everything. This time it could have cost him his life, had he not been restrained by the other three men working with him in the sewer ditch.

We had been told many times since capture that any aggressive or violent action would be considered mutiny, subject to execution by firing squad as soon as possible. Charley's mighty temper had gotten the best of him, and he had charged the youth with the intent of throwing him into the slimy ditch. The melee was the result of the other three men trying to stop him.

Pops had been some distance away and hadn't witnessed the spark that ignited the uproar. After hearing the whole story, Pops vowed that the young Nazi would not be allowed near us again. Charley finally calmed down and began to realize the possible consequences of his actions. Then he broke into a cold sweat and got a severe case of the shakes. Pops promised to say nothing of the incident to any higher-ups.

Since the men on our crew were not involved, we calmly went back to our rakes. But this incident made for lively conversation around the table that night.

This detail continued for three more days without mishap. Three or four trains loaded with what we now assumed were more Jews sped by each day. Abe, the young infantryman who talked about pancakes and maple syrup, was staring into space as the last train of the day passed.

"Man's inhumanity to man," he said, muttering with tears streaming down his cheeks.

"Amen," I said, stammering as I picked up my rake and began clawing violently at the stinking mess in the ditch. Anything to alleviate some of my frustration and anger. Before I even joined the Army, I knew about all the slave-labor camps the Germans were using in their war plants. They were common knowledge and were widely reported in newspapers.

Abe glanced my way, grabbed his rake and tore into that canal like a young tiger.

With the ditch cleaned, I wondered what sort of job would be next on the list. The following morning was a carbon copy of all previous mornings as we approached a huge brick structure that had been a school. It was now being used to house sick and wounded soldiers from the Russian front. Since the building stood three stories high, it could only accommodate the walking-wounded or battle-fatigue cases.

Five soldiers came out to be our guards that day. We were herded into the building which, thankfully, was warm. As we stood in the main hall shuffling, stomping our feet and swinging our arms to start some circulation going after the cold walk, an open staff car arrived. A young German officer exited the car and entered the building, brushing the snow off of his greatcoat. We ceased our babbling and came to some semblance of attention.

The officer outlined our duties to the five guards. We were to work hard and fast. Anyone caught sloughing off would be severely dealt with immediately. We were free to roam the building in line with our work, but each exit would have a guard. If anyone attempted to leave the building without permission, the guards had orders to shoot to kill. Now we were to go to work.

But we stood fast, staring at the officer with vacant looks of incomprehension.

"*Verstehen sie Deutsche?*" the officer shouted.

Most gave a negative shake of the head. In exasperation, he turned to a corporal and ordered him to get some men to show these "*Dummkoph*" what was expected of them. He summoned about six soldiers from an adjoining room. We followed them into a room and watched as they started moving desks, chairs, books and bookcases. We goofed off until the officer suddenly entered the room, shouting at us to move.

We moved from room to room, carrying the items one by one to a large storage area in the basement. The going was slow. Some of the desks were heavy and cumbersome to move down the long flight of steps without a shred of help from the German soldiers. They soon left us to struggle by ourselves and went back to the room from which they were summoned.

Around noon, the officer was walking down the hall toward Fred, who was carrying a chair. He set the chair down and began pointing to his wide-open mouth with a finger and rubbing his stomach with the other hand, indicating to the officer what we all needed. That went over like a lead balloon. The officer stopped in his tracks as though he'd been slapped in the face, put his hands on his hips and started chewing out poor Fred.

"How dare a prisoner speak to an officer of the German army without permission?" he said, thundering, "You haven't done enough work yet to deserve any food."

Actually Fred had said nothing, merely gesturing with his hands. But the officer's tirade continued for a full five minutes while Freddie stood ramrod straight, visibly shaken by the outburst. Although he understood only a few words, he got the point. When the officer turned on his heel and disappeared, Fred meekly picked up his chair and headed for the basement.

I was headed up the same stairs and heard him muttering to himself. "Nice try, kid," I said as we passed. "They surely will feed us after a while, I hope."

Still shaking a bit, Fred said, "Yeah, maybe. But I'd like to empty an M1 in his gut."

We had about given up the idea of being fed when a soldier appeared in the doorway of one of the large rooms that we had previously cleaned out. Waving his arms, he shouted, "*Essen—kommen mit.*" He had to move out of the doorway at a fast clip to keep from being run over by the stampede of starved *Kriegies.* He knew he'd been as clearly understood as if he'd spoken in the King's own English and said, "Food—come with me."

But the food was hardly worth the scramble. A fat, scowling cook ladled out the watery mess with the exactness of a pharmacist dispensing a prescription. The pot full of soup barely went around with each man receiving only half a bowlful. The reason, I'm sure, was that there were already 30 to 40 wounded soldiers in the makeshift hospital, so the poor *Kriege* swine got what was left. We ate slowly, as if the bowl had been full to the brim, knowing that as soon as we finished, we'd be put back to work.

I continued to carry furniture for the rest of the day, but part of the crew unloaded supplies from a large truck. With a load of yellow turnips and sacks of barley, the crew unloading them managed to gorge themselves on small kohlrabi that just happened to fall out of the baskets as they were carried off of the truck under the watchful eyes of the two guards.

On my last trip down the long hallway, carrying a small desk, I saw Freddie stop and reach out to touch the lieutenant's greatcoat which was hanging outside his cubbyhole office. The four men on the food detail appeared from the storeroom at the same time and witnessed Freddie touching the coat, too.

"Why did you dare touch that officer's coat?" someone asked him and all of us echoed the question. "Haven't you had enough of his scoldings? If he had seen you, he would've had your hide for sure."

Freddie was beaming.

"That's the sixth louse I've put in his collar today," he said, barely able to contain himself. "I hope they multiply and eat him alive. If the lieutenant has no better way of getting rid of lice than we have, he'll be popping them between his thumb and nail for the rest of the war."

We couldn't help but share in Freddie's joy, chuckling to ourselves as we went back to work. We finished a bit early that day and had to stand around waiting for the other work crews to show up for the long walk back to Runddorf. I noticed some of the men in our crew were rather nervous. They stayed in one corner of the hall, huddled around Charley, the biggest and ugliest man in our compound.

It was a blessing that darkness fell just as we were leaving the hospital grounds. Charley was having difficulty walking at his normal gait. He seemed to waddle a bit from side to side, kind of unsteady on his feet. The guards paid little attention to Charley. With night falling rapidly, they were anxious to get back to the barracks.

Upon entering the second gate at the compound, the guard on duty waved us by without the usual body search. Tonight of all nights, it should have been obvious that some of us were trying to hide something. But we breezed right through and went on to the barracks without a hitch.

Once inside the barracks, we all congregated in the chow hall to see what had caused all the nervous excitement. The four men who had unloaded the truck told us about the daring plan they devised to steal some barley. To be caught stealing even a morsel of food from the German Army would result in dire consequences we dared not dwell on. But when a man is hungry as we all were, sometimes necessity blots out common sense. Or to put it in another way that I'd often heard, "Necessity is the mother of invention."

Charley was wearing two pair of trousers. So the plan called for him to tie the inner pair tightly around his ankles, creating a sack with the inner pair. On their last trip carrying sacks of barley into the pantry, the men poured handfuls of grain into his pants, being careful not to get to greedy and cause a noticeable bulge at the bottom of each leg. Each man also put a handful in his pockets.

At the schoolhouse, the storage area next to the kitchen was located at the far end of the big room which had a row of beds on each wall. The beds were occupied by wounded German soldiers. After subjecting each other to close scrutiny to see if anything unusual could be detected, the men decided to leave the room two at a time so they wouldn't attract too much attention. But Charley was so uptight that he insisted he go first and alone. He was going to walk down the aisle in a slow, casual manner, emulating the lazy attitude the Germans had come to expect from us *Kriegies.*

He started out in a slow, lackadaisical stroll; but by the time he reached the halfway point, he was nearly at a gallop as he exited through the door into the hallway. By that time, every eye on the long rows of cots was on Charley. We often wondered later what those wounded soldiers thought as he made such an unusual exit.

The other three *Kriegies* stood shaking in their boots, waiting for some reaction from the patients. But they all seemed to be still staring at the exit as the three made their way down the long aisle between the beds. No one ever gave them a second glance. Charley was in a state of near-collapse from the ordeal with the fear of being discovered. The other three were close behind.

After listening to this hair-raising episode back at the barracks, we untied the string around Charley's ankles and let the grain pour onto a piece of paper under his feet. Looking at that small pile of grain pouring over two feet that had not been washed for several months, I knew that in other times it would be enough to turn a man's stomach. But that night it was like pure gold to 36 half-starved *Kriegies.*

As the other men emptied their pockets, adding to the pile on the floor, we figured we must have at least two gallons of grain. While we admired our prize, the guard on duty stuck his head in the doorway and yelled, "*Zwei mann für die Küche.*" This meant the cook had the pot boiled, and our supper was ready for pickup. Two men for the kitchen, the guard had said.

We told the two men who headed out the door to ask the cook for a handful of extra salt in the pot. This request exploded into quite an argument before the cook finally got tired of arguing and grudgingly threw in the extra salt. And while the cook's attention was diverted during the salt-negotiation discussion, the other man managed to snitch two small onions, a delicacy that we'd never had before.

Meanwhile back at the barracks, we were stoking the fire in one stove with all the coal and wood we could scrounge between the two bunk rooms. Amazing what the prospect of a little extra food can do for a man, I thought. Instead of slouching around with sparse conversation or lying in our bunks waiting for the usual evening meal, we were yapping and laughing with each other over the events of the day.

By the time the black pot arrived and was placed on the stove top, we had managed a roaring fire—which was sure to use up our entire evening's allotment of coal. But we had to sacrifice the fuel for the stove, this time, for fuel for our stomachs. We poured in the barley, all of it, and using our spoon handles, diced the two small onions, including the sprouted and rotten ends, which were sure to give the soup just that much more flavor.

We sort of milled around the room, too excited to sit down while the pot came to a boil and the liquid absorbed the extra barley. Tonight's soup had seemed a little more watery than usual; but with the barley, we ended up with a rather thick gruel that would even heap up on a spoon. For the first time ever, each man had a full bowl; and with that added salt, the taste was much more palatable than anything we'd been fed in months. I couldn't actually taste the onions, but just the thought that they were there added to the taste.

In my mind, I had learned, each evening, to turn a watery bowl of soup, two or three small potatoes and a hunk of black bread into a delicious banquet. That's all there ever was, so I had to be content with it. Until tonight. This was the only night that I went to bed actually content with a full stomach instead of the gnawing pangs of hunger.

I fell asleep that night listening to the two men in the next bunk discussing their favorite foods and arguing whose favorite was the best. Sherman Williams, whose family owned and operated a chicken-and-egg farm in the far western United States, was pitted against Fred, who was from Kentucky. The last words I faintly remembered hearing as I drifted off into dreamland came from the Kentuckian.

"I'll agree chicken is good," he said. "But I still say frawg laigs is better'n chicken anytime."

Maybe it wasn't fried chicken or frog legs, but the full stomach surely helped me sleep. After spending a restful night dreaming of home, once more I was rudely awakened by the mean one beating on the soles of my feet and hollering, "*Aufstehen, Schweinehund! Raus mit dir!*" Get up, pigdog! Out with you! And so another day starts at Runddorf. This day, however, would prove to be a little better than some days past. Good memories today, not bad ones.

It was the custom of local farmers, on occasion, to hire some of the *Kriegies* for odd jobs around the farm. All of Germany's younger men were either in the Army or had been forced into factory jobs to keep production of weapons at a high peak. Consequently, the local farmers were without sufficient manpower to get all the farm chores completed. It was a fact, however, that most of the larger farmers had French prisoners living with and working for them.

The French were permitted by the German government to sign a parole card which allowed them to be assigned a job without the "benefit" of guards watching every move. These French prisoners were able to roam at will within a radius of 50 kilometers from their assigned post. All American and British subjects were not allowed this privilege but were subjected to barbed-wire enclosures or were heavily guarded when on work details outside the confines of the wire. So we had little opportunity for farm work.

My first such chance came when five of us were chosen to go to a small farm about four kilometers from the camp. Upon arrival, we were led to an extremely large barn. In the center of the barn sat a huge red piece of machinery mounted on four steel wheels. I had no idea what it was when I first saw it. But it turned out to be a thrashing machine, unlike any other I had ever seen back home on the farm.

The ends of the barn on each side of the thrasher were stacked to the roof with bundles of barley. An old iron, steam tractor was fired up in another shed and was pulled up in front of the thrasher and hooked to it by a long, side belt. Two men were assigned the task of feeding the bundles into the machine while two more were to rake and stack the straw as it came out the rear of the thrasher. The fifth man had to carry the sacks of barley to the farmhouse, up a long flight of stone steps to the granary. This was a difficult, back-breaking job for a healthy man—not anything for a weak *Kriegie* to tackle. So we each took a turn at carrying the grain sacks. I think that was the longest flight of steps I had ever climbed in my life.

It was hard work. But at least we were out of the cold wind, and the exercise helped keep me warm. Also, the creaky old machine coughed and quit sporadically, which enabled us to rest. It didn't take us long to discover that by "accidentally" throwing in an extra sheaf once in a while, the cranky old thing would sputter and choke up, causing the breakdown. Of course, we got a good chewing-out from the farmer and had to climb up into the machinery to unclog the mess. Our little sabotage slowed down the process, though, especially having to carry those heavy sacks. Any break from that was welcome.

At noontime, the farmer's *Frau* appeared, pulling a wagon with a pot of soup. The machinery shut down, and we eagerly gathered around the wagon like hungry wolves. It was a real treat to get a noon meal, and a home-cooked one at that. This was only the second lunch I'd had since arriving at the *Stalag*.

The soup, undoubtedly, was the best-tasting soup I had ever eaten. Like all the other soup we'd had, it still contained barley but no kohlrabi or rutabagas, the mainstays of stalag soup. The *Frau's* soup had real seasonings, plus a few chunks of meat and no potatoes. We each had two slices of *Roggenbrot* or the staple black rye bread.

To serve the soup, the *Frau* placed five bowls on a makeshift table and ladled out a full bowl of steaming broth for each of us. After finishing this, we each received an extra ladle for seconds when she drained the pot. We tried hard to watch our table manners and act as human beings instead of the animals we had become.

When we'd all finished the last delicious drop of soup in our bowls, we complimented the *Frau*, using our best German: "*Das war eine sehr gute Suppe.*" And it was very good soup. She seemed quite pleased and smiled for the first time. Then she gave us each a small 4-inch-square sandwich of *Kuchen Brot*, a white cake-like bread with a layer of some sort of cheese. It was the first white bread I'd had since I was captured. I ate the sandwich slowly in order to savor every bite. The farmer told us we had worked "*sehr gut*" that morning, and for a reward, we would each receive an apple. I couldn't remember the last time I had tasted an apple and looked forward to that treat with much anticipation. I could get used to eating as we had at lunch.

I drew the farm detail for the rest of the week. Although the work was hard, the soup, the sandwich and apple were rare treats and worth the labor. Our after-supper discussions at the barracks usually centered on the day's events, always seeking new ways to confuse the enemy with our feigned ignorance. We were always alert to any opportunity to increase our food intake, so we never hesitated to share our observations and scheming ways to pilfer food from our work assignments. I always returned from the farm detail with slight bulges in all my pockets.

10

During all my days in captivity, I had only one contact with the Red Cross, and that proved to be a complete disaster. Our 10-man detail was walking on the streets of Hoyerswerda one morning on the way to work when a small panel truck sped by us. It pulled to a stop about two blocks up the street. A man stepped out wearing a neat uniform, unlike anything I had seen in the German Army. He stopped a passing civilian and began a conversation. Obviously, the uniformed man was asking for directions, judging by the way he was using his arms to point in several directions.

As we approached, I could see a large red cross covering the whole side panel of the truck. Arched above the cross was lettered, "*Internationales Rotes Kreuz*," and the name of some town. My heartbeat increased rapidly with the thought that maybe he was looking for our *Stalag*. I had never seen, let alone received, any Red Cross parcels since capture—none of us had, for that matter.

Some Rhodesian soldiers were housed in a village several kilometers west of Runddorf. On the couple of occasions that we had contact with them, we'd been told that they received Red Cross parcels periodically, although the flow had decreased somewhat over the winter. We had often complained to the *Kommander Führer*, protesting the fact that we were not receiving any parcels. We also had informed him about the English *Kriegies*, whom we had seen on two occasions when they were brought into our work details from a small *Stalag* near a town whose name I could never pronounce or remember. These English *Kriegies* had told us they were receiving parcels on a regular basis. At least they got them frequently enough to help sustain life. Our lives were being drained from us, and no parcels ever came to Runddorf.

With a shrug of his shoulders, he always replied with the same lame excuse: "The Americans bomb all the trains bringing them in."

We knew this to be a lie, but what could we do about it?

Glancing over at the guard, who nodded and withdrew a few feet away and sat down on a row of steps, we all headed for the man by the white panel truck. He was indeed from Switzerland and was an inspector or liaison person for the International Red Cross. His assigned task was to visit the POW *Stalags* in this area of Germany and make a report to his headquarters. He spoke English with a British accent and seemed a bit puzzled at being suddenly surrounded by such a scroungy-looking group.

"You are Americans?" he asked in total disbelief.

I knew he was taking in our disreputable clothing, which was a mixture of several nationalities, with a sprinkling of civilian clothes that had been light-fingered here and there, mainly from clothes lines, and our looks. Among our group, there was not one item of clothing that was of American origin. And the Germans always shaved the heads of their political prisoners, which certainly contrasted to our long, matted hair and beards. No wonder he was skeptical.

"Yes, we're Americans," we answered in a resounding chorus.

Roy Pineyon stepped forward and said, "We would like to start getting some food parcels; because if we don't, some of us are soon going to die of malnutrition. We can't steal enough to stay alive. These people don't have it for us to steal."

The man reached into the front seat of the van to retrieve a brown briefcase. "I'm convinced you're Americans," he said, pulling a sheaf of papers from the briefcase. "Where is your camp located?"

Roy told him and gave him precise directions to the *Stalag* and to Runddorf.

Leafing through his sheaf of papers, the Red Cross inspector kept shaking his head. "I can't find it here," he said, continuing to shuffle through the stack. "Oh, yes. Here it is. Runddorf, *Arbeitskommando*, 36 men, American."

He stuffed the papers back into the briefcase and laid it back on the seat before continuing. "I'll see if I can get a representative to visit your *Stalag* to assess your needs. You must understand, with our enormous workload and with yours being a small *Stalag* . . ." his voice trailed off. He took a deep breath, paused and shrugged his shoulders as if to indicate this was a satisfactory solution to our situation.

I think he quickly realized that this was not going to fly. I'm sure he could feel the anger and resentment building as first one man, then another vented his anger.

"Just wait 'til I get home," one man said, muttering.

"*If* you get home," another man said, correcting him.

"Be quiet," I said, shouting and then looked the Red Cross man squarely in the eye when I continued. "I don't mean to be disrespectful, sir, but by the time your representative arrives 'to assess' our situation, some of these men may not be alive. What you see here is the strongest of our camp. Some of the others have to be helped to their feet each morning; some are becoming incoherent with slurred speech from their near-starved condition. My own father was treasurer of one whole county back in Illinois, busting his butt to raise money for the Red Cross, yet you can't help us when we really need help."

Others started spouting off, too, soon drowning me out completely. The man, by then visibly shaken, reached into his pocket and pulled out a pack of cigarettes. A pack of Camels! He fumbled around, opening the fresh pack, and stuck one in his mouth. After lighting the cigarette, he started to return the pack to his pocket. But he wasn't fast enough. The pack was plucked out of his hand and quickly passed around to anyone who wanted a smoke. I didn't smoke, but I took one and stuck it in my pocket for future bargaining power. That cigarette was more than I'd received from the Red Cross so far. And you could be guaranteed that I was taking one.

I wasn't able to get a hold of many cigarettes; but when the opportunity presented itself, I didn't hesitate. It was sometimes possible to steal them from a work area. My one lucky find came at a most unlikely time and place. During a clean-up job near a factory, I was scrounging for some coal from a small pile at the rear of a house when an old man and woman came bursting out the door screaming insults at me, a lowly thief. The guard nearby stepped in and made me empty my pockets onto the ground. Then he turned away. We always got a good chewing out from the guards when we got caught, but they knew that we always shared a few chunks of coal with them. The ranting and threats or promises of punishment when the culprit was returned to the *Stalag* usually satisfied the civilian.

The guards' coal supply was rationed just as ours was, so any extra was a blessing for them. Occasionally, we would get a rifle slammed across the back for emphasis but not as vicious as during the times the guard himself was angry. He would feign anger to show the civilian that duty was being done in protecting the property.

The old man then bent over to retrieve the briquettes of coal and in doing so a full package of American cigarettes fell from his shirt pocket. He was so anxious to get the coal that he didn't notice the pack on the ground. I had hit the jackpot. I was able to snatch up the cigarettes, plus I still had four briquettes of coal hidden in my waistband. That one package of smokes helped me sustain life for a full week. Anyone wanting a smoke was willing to pay dearly in food for the privilege. I was amazed at the value some men placed on the lowly cigarette.

It was even more amazing when I watched them smoke a cigarette after not having one for a long time. I'd actually laugh at them sometimes when a man would light up and take a long drag on the cigarette. He'd hold his breath for a while, then exhale and start coughing, his eyes watering and half fall down from weakness. What a price to pay for a cigarette, I thought. I never could understand it.

One day on a detail in Hoyerswerda, I stole a full pack of American cigarettes from the desk drawer of a German officer. He was out of the room, and I was supposed to be bringing some new furniture into his office. Had he discovered the cigarettes missing while we were still at work in the building, I'm sure the guilty party would have been shot immediately. Later, I was able to trade each cigarette for a bit of extra food from one of the guards. The Germans loved American cigarettes. And these cigarettes helped me to survive the last few weeks in Runddorf when our already meager rations were cut in half.

"Made in America for Americans," someone in the rear said, muttering as he crumpled the empty Camel pack and threw it to the ground.

"I'll see what I can do for your *Stalag*," the Red Cross man said nervously. "I really must go now."

As he retreated into the panel truck, the cursing rose in volume and intensity with each man venting his wrath at the Red Cross. "If I ever get back home, I'll tear up every Red Cross donation poster I see," one man said, making a promise that we all felt along with the profanity.

Tensions remained high all that day and carried over into a lively discussion after evening chow. Our morale was given a huge boost after the brief and rather nasty encounter with the Red Cross worker. We were greatly enthused by thinking perhaps there would be some improvement in our living conditions. Wishful thinking, I knew. Had we objectively analyzed the response the man gave us, we would have realized the probability of ever receiving any Red Cross help was hopeless. We were grasping at straws. The positive aura enveloped us for a few days, though. But it eventually faded as each day became, again, just like the day before. No hope. Other than some venting of hostility and a catharsis of sorts, nothing came of our visit with the Red Cross inspector and our discussion. No Red Cross representative ever appeared at Runddorf. Nor did we see any semblance of a food parcel. So much for promises.

I had had no contact with the Red Cross since arriving in Europe. I never got far enough to the rear from front-line combat to ever meet any of the coffee-and-donut women of Red Cross fame. Even my contacts in England after the war gave me a sour opinion of the American Red Cross. My best results were with the Salvation Army canteens and the English St. John's Society.

So we continued to be isolated from the outside world at Runddorf.

Those with whom we ever had any contact spouted the propaganda from the Nazi radio.

My parents didn't know if I was alive or dead, only that I had been reported missing in action on 23 November 1944. I had written one postcard on 2 December 1944. It was actually a pre-printed card on which I could only state my condition and name. And I was able to write two barely legible short letters on the last days of January and February 1945. These letters, however, did not reach my folks until after the war in Europe had ended. The Army did finally inform my mother and father of an address at Mühlberg, Germany, where they could write me, but her letters were all returned, marked undeliverable.

The German military put such harsh restrictions on what we could and couldn't say that the only news would be the fact that I was still alive and able to write. An attempt in December 1944 to write my folks was returned to me in several pieces, resulting from the censor cutting out more than half of the letter. When it was returned to me, I received the letter and a stern lecture on what I was allowed to put in all future letters.

Thoughts of escape were always visiting me even though I knew it would be nearly impossible. One of the men on the other side of the barracks was determined to make a break, though. He talked of nothing else until it became an obsession with him. Our occasional contacts with the French prisoners and other conscripted prisoners working in our area had cemented the idea of escape for him. From them, he learned they would help him slip through the French Underground network to Dresden and then on to Allied lines.

As the plan progressed, he was supplied with a French uniform. He was a Cajun named Bob Debord from Louisiana and spoke fluent French. He was the only man in the group who would have any chance, since no one else was the least bit familiar with the language. It was a risky proposition, but he was determined.

"I would rather take my chances with the French Underground," he said, "than stay here and starve to death or end up being shot because of my attitude. I just can't stand any more barbed wire."

By the look in his eyes, I knew he was dead serious, and I immediately agreed to do anything to help. But I wasn't taken into the confidence of the five men who actually engineered the plan.

Many nights we would be called to the dining room and forced to take all our clothes and shoes out of the barracks and hang them on a numbered peg in the supply building about 50 yards from our quarters. This occurred at bedtime with the theory that without clothing, an escape in the extremely cold temperatures would be next to impossible. And we made the 100-yard round trip through the snow, mud and water barefooted and in our underwear.

Occasionally, we were able to steal an extra pair of trousers or a shirt from an unguarded clothes line; but under our working conditions, they became tattered and worn, too. The guards, of course, knew we were master thieves. So about every three weeks, we would be rousted out at 0200 hours to stand at attention for 30-40 minutes while the guards trashed our sleeping quarters looking for contraband of any type. As a result, if you managed to requisition a shirt, you wore it. Stealing a pair of shoes was next to impossible. Nearly everyone finally ended up with one extra shirt and trousers. But no shoes could ever be located, and two pairs couldn't have been kept long, anyway.

Nothing was usually found in the search, but it took the rest of the morning to make our quarters habitable again. These night searches were just another form of harassment to let us know who was in charge, not much different than forcing us to hang our clothes on a peg 50 yards away. If a man was ever to make an escape attempt, then, he had to pick a night when we got to sleep with all of our clothes.

During the next two weeks, the French Underground gave Bob a code name of Frenchy, a French uniform and a roughly drawn escape plan, pinpointing a farm where some 26 French laborers worked and were housed. The farm was located about six kilometers from our front gate and near the edge of the big forest we trekked through each day on our way to Hoyerswerda. He would have to travel at night through the woods, avoiding patrols, especially those dreaded Hitler *Jugend* bastards. With a French uniform and his excellent command of the language, he might be able to pull it off.

The plans were hush-hush. Because there was always the possibility that a chance slip-of-the-tongue could give away the plan, only the initial five men were to be in on the final operation. I knew nothing of any of the details of how these five men were going to stage the actual escape until it was over. This is how it would play out on a dark, stormy night: It would be useless to cut through the fence surrounding our barracks. The sentry would notice it on his rounds and sound the alarm. But the perimeter fence surrounding the whole camp was far enough away that on a dark night it would not be noticed until daylight. By then, it was hoped that our man would be safe among the French at the farm.

The first obstacle, the fence around the barracks, could be surmounted by two of the long benches in our dining room. If one of the long benches was laid across the two fences, a man could then be hoisted up and crawl across, drop down on the other side and head for the outer perimeter fence, cut it and then slip into the woods. The issue of wire cutters was soon solved with the discovery that one of the men had stolen a pair while working on the hospital project in town. He agreed to relinquish them, even though he wasn't to be a part of the final plans.

In rehearsing the sequence for escape, the original five men discovered it would be difficult to manhandle two long benches without the support of a sixth man. So they reluctantly approached Charley, who was still the biggest and strongest among us. He was eager to help with the benches or any way he could, thus the plan was set in motion.

Complete darkness was imperative, but Mother Nature was not cooperating. Although the nights were extremely cold and snow still lingered on the ground, the moon rose every evening for nearly a week, putting added tension and frustration on the escape planners.

Even though the rest of us weren't involved initially in the escape plans, tension was building, and we all sensed something was in the wind. But nobody asked questions.

The day started off as a normal work day in Hoyerswerda. By noon, a heavy line of storm clouds was moving slowly toward us. The rains started two hours before quitting time and continued as we trudged home at dusk, soaking wet and shivering from the cold winds. No moon tonight, I thought. It'll be dark and overcast. By now, I was fairly certain this would be the night and already knew who was going over the fence because Bob wanted to escape so badly. I said nothing to him, although I worked beside him all day. Oh, I tried a few jokes or witty sayings to help ease the strain, but all my efforts fell on deaf ears. He was in a world of his own that day—beyond the fence and Runddorf.

The rain continued. We all retired to our bunks before 9 p.m. I was restless as I lay on my bunk, thoughts racing through my mind. This is the night. Say they are successful in getting Bob over the fence. What will be the consequences? Will the Germans carry out their threat to shoot 10 prisoners for each escapee? Rumors had filtered down about the massacre of 50 British airmen shot in retaliation for an aborted tunnel escape in which only two men successfully reached Allied lines. The rest were recaptured and subjected to even more brutal treatment. Not a pleasant thought.

I was quickly brought back to reality by the sudden commotion coming from the next room. I left my rickety bunk in such a rush that I thought it was going to come down around my ears. Everyone rushed into the next room to witness frantic activity at the window overlooking the fence. Then I heard shouting and cussing coming from the front of the barracks as the men rushed through the front door to witness a fight in progress between two *Kriegies.*

All the shouting had aroused the guards from their billets, and they rushed to the melee, some half-dressed, and the rest trying to get into uniform while running. The *Kommander Führer* came boiling out of headquarters, shirtless, with his hat crammed down over his bald pate at a comical angle. I knew nothing about anything being staged as a means of drawing attention away from the back window and started out to watch the fight but turned toward the window instead. Someone hollered for help in getting a bench through the window and raised up over the wire fence. I was there to give a hand. That done, the foot of the second bench was then lifted up over the inward protruding wire and touched the end of the first bench resting across the top.

My hunch about the night had proven correct, and I saw Bob being hoisted to the shoulders of two men and scramble up the bench. He lost no time crawling over, and I heard a thud as he hit the ground on the far side. I was fearful that he might injure an ankle or leg in the ten-feet drop, but evidently he landed okay.

"Thanks, men," he said in farewell.

The disturbance out front had attracted Old Bones, the 6-foot-6 rawboned, mean-spirited Polish or Serbian guard we knew was pulling duty that night. (We called him both because most of us didn't know the difference.) So Bob would have no trouble cutting his way through the perimeter fence undetected.

This fight, this diversion, had to look genuine since it was the key to the success of the escape plan. And it worked to perfection. The guards seemed to enjoy the fact that we were fighting among ourselves—the turmoil would keep our morale at a low key. All the guard and the *Kriegies* had gathered around, some egging-on the combatants. Our men would get in the way of the guards who were trying to separate the men.

Meanwhile, back at the window, four men were still outside the building trying to retrieve the two benches from the 10-foot-high fence. The men were sweating profusely, partly from exertion but mostly from the prospect of Old Bones appearing around the corner and opening up with his rifle. This would have been sure death because of the short range from the end of the building and all four men being bunched together in a small space.

As the benches came down, they were shoved through the open

window. I guess I was a bit startled at all the activity. Someone finally jarred me awake by shouting, "Take it, damnit," and shoved the bench in my lap, nearly knocking me over backwards. The fight out front had been broken up. So we knew we had to get the guys inside at once and close and shutter the window.

Luckily, the only casualty of the big altercation was a huge swelling rising on the forehead of one of the men when the second bench came tumbling down out of control. In attempting to bring down the top bench by bouncing it on the wire, it almost bounced over on the far side of the wire, giving us all a bad scare. With sheer luck, the men were able to bounce it toward the barracks which resulted in the bump on the head when the weight was so heavy the man lost control.

By this time, we could hear the shrill voice of the *Kommander Führer* chewing the hell out of the two fighters. From the way things looked, the fight had been a convincing one. One man had a bloody nose. Both were a bit bruised and dirty from rolling on the muddy ground. With a final outburst, the *Kommander Führer* ordered everyone to bed. The Polish guard returned to walking his post, seemingly without any hint of the gigantic struggle that had occurred just behind the barracks.

I still couldn't relax enough to sleep, even though I was exhausted from handling those benches. My mind was racing with dire thoughts about the escape, and I was dreading the arrival of dawn.

Fear made its appearance completely at early light when all hell broke loose as we prepared to head out for our work detail. As usual, we lined up in our two columns and had our coffee. The first detail of 18 men and three guards, including the Pole, headed for the gate to work in Hoyerswerda. The remaining 16 men were to go to Runddorf with the other three guards. Counting the two men who were kitchen helpers and always stayed in camp, the total was always 36 men in camp.

As the Hoyerswerda detail reached the gate, the little corporal in charge of the Runddorf detail began shouting that we had too many men, that he only had 15 men. Pops counted and recounted his men, always arriving at 18. Back we went to be lined up for another count. This time a roster was produced, and the official roll was called. Everyone answered "Here" to his name. Midway through, Bob's name was called and someone in the rear rank muttered, "Here," and they continued on down the roll. When the final name was answered, "Here," Pops turned toward the gate and called for his detail to follow. Again the little corporal stopped him and started counting. He wound up with 33.

Abruptly the guards' manners changed, and they started snarling at us and at each other. One of them ran to the *Kommander Führer's* office and started pounding on his door. We were held strictly at attention, and as our name was called, we took two steps forward to form in another rank. When Bob's name was called and no one stepped forward, they finally knew who was missing. Two guards ran into the barracks and two more fanned out into every corner of the compound.

With only four small buildings and no vegetation, the search was soon over. The *Kommander Führer* came running out red-faced, hastily buttoning his tunic. Then he apparently remembered that he had forgotten his hat, wheeled and ran back to get it. He had evidently phoned his unit commander in Runddorf, reporting his missing prisoner, because he soon arrived with a full detail of soldiers.

The unit commander interrogated each man in the usual German manner of shouts and threats to do bodily harm if we were not forthright in answering his questions. Each man swore he'd been outside watching the fight and knew nothing of Bob's disappearance. The two men involved in the fight came under extreme scrutiny and questioning. But their physical appearance finally convinced the commander that the fight had been legitimate. Their bruises were quite evident.

Finally, the conclusion was reached that Bob had seized upon the opportunity during the scuffle and had just vanished. No further questions were asked as to how he had managed or if he had had any help from any of his fellow prisoners. The blame was placed entirely on the Pole since the prisoner had escaped on his watch.

Upon hearing this verdict, the Pole simply went wild, wading into our ranks with his rifle and viciously striking every man within reach. Several men were knocked to the ground, and he was battering the rest before he could be restrained by the other guards. They had been taken by surprise at his sudden outburst and were slow to react, giving the crazed Pole time to roam up and down our ranks. I received a butt stroke to my back, just below my left shoulder blade, that severely bruised or cracked three ribs and sent me flying on my face in the mud and snow.

I was quite shocked by his sudden rage. But since we were all at rigid attention during the questioning, none of us had any time to react. Some men were bleeding from head wounds; others were holding an arm or clutching their side or stomach. I was slow to rise, fearing he might decide to unload his rifle into our ranks. He was 6 feet 6 inches of bone and muscle, and it took four or five guards to finally subdue him. The Pole was placed under arrest and marched down the road toward Runddorf surrounded by the full detail of soldiers.

Meanwhile, we stood at attention half the morning while the unit commander and our little *Kommander Führer* discussed the morning's events and what form our punishment would take. Apparently satisfied that he had solved the mystery of the missing prisoner and that the appropriate punishment would be dished out to us, the commander finally left the *Stalag*.

Then the storm erupted. The *Kommander Führer* turned to us, pacing up and down our ranks, hands folded behind his back and raged at us. He had been thoroughly chewed out for being lax in his command. The duty guard would possibly be court-martialed and, if convicted, shot for dereliction of duty. From now on, the *Kommander Führer* said, the rules and regulations would be obeyed without exception. All privileges would immediately be terminated.

Privileges? I thought, wondering what privileges we had that could be taken away.

On and on he paced the length of our ranks, ranting almost out of control while the guards glared at us, the hostility showing in their eyes. From this day forward when we left the front gate, we would speak to no one, not even each other, for the entire day. Speak only if spoken to by one of the guards became the order of the day—forever. After a few more choice words, he wheeled around and disappeared into his headquarters.

For once, I was ready to head out to Hoyerswerda. The eerie silence was deafening, but that suited me just fine that day. I was having difficulty taking a breath without an excruciating pain shooting through my rib cage. That evening back at the barracks, we took stock of our injuries at the hands of the crazed Pole that morning. Nearly every man had been hit directly or by a glancing blow from the guard's flailing rifle. A large welt had raised up on my back, surrounded by a 6-inch, round bruise. I couldn't determine if my ribs were cracked, but I surely was in a lot of pain trying to breath.

After that, we worked every Sunday, leaving the *Stalag* before sunrise and returning after dark. The guards had turned extremely abusive toward us, screaming and cussing at us continuously and always pushing us to do more work. We dared not try to steal any food or coal now: We were thoroughly searched every night at the main gate. Food was becoming scarce even for the civilian population. And our rations were cut down to less than a full bowl of soup, two and sometimes no potatoes and one less loaf of bread per day to divide among us.

The long hours plus the shortened rations were having a devastating effect on us, taking an even greater toll than we thought possible. The guards were beginning to tire of the routine and realized the futility of trying to make us work harder. We just couldn't do it. We even chanced uttering a few words to another *Kriegie*—out of earshot of a guard, of course.

Although we had suffered mightily for Bob's escape, no one ever uttered a word of blame against him. We tried to lift our morale with the thought that he was safely threading his way through the French

Underground, and maybe he was in Dresden by now where he would be safely hidden until the Americans arrived. Those thoughts helped me through the days and weeks following his escape.

I didn't know anything about his actual fate until I chanced seeing him at a hospital in Rheims, France. There he told me his story:

The pitch black darkness had been a blessing in the actual escape; but when he entered the forest, he became disoriented and blundered onto a lane. He'd been successful in crossing the main road after waiting and listening for patrols but thought the narrow lane through the timber would be safe. Anyway, he was thankful not to be walking into any more trees in the dark.

He was making slow progress up the lane, attempting to regain his bearings by trying to use the map furnished him by the French. He said he progressed no more than 100 yards up the lane when he was blinded by a light shining squarely in his eyes. Two Hitler Jugen *on night patrol had heard him coming and waited until he got near enough to put a light on him. He was dressed in the French uniform and tried his French-worker routine on these boys. But they didn't buy it and turned him over to the local constabulary in Hoyerswerda.*

Bob was severely beaten about the head and shoulders and would undoubtedly lose his right eye. He had received no medical attention for his injuries until he was repatriated back to American lines after the end of the war. Instead, he was sent to a special prison for escaped prisoners. The conditions there were much worse than at Runddorf. The lack of medical attention was the cause of the loss of his right eye.

I spent several minutes with Bob, listening to his story, before I was moved on to Camp Lucky Strike, France. I'm glad I didn't know his story while I was still in Runddorf, for the thought of him making it to Freedom was a good morale booster for the rest of us at a time when we had little else.

He asked about how things went in Runddorf, but I never told him of the resulting beatings we all endured the morning after he left or of the crackdown by the Kommander Führer *and the guards. I felt he'd suffered more than I had and wished him luck in regaining his eye-*

sight in the right eye. Then I turned and left. A couple of tears rolled down my cheeks as I went out the door.

11

Every two weeks the *Kommander Führer* would call out two men for the trip into Runddorf to replenish the food supplies for the entire camp, including the guards. "Red," an obvious nickname for a prisoner who had red hair, and I were chosen early one morning to make the bi-monthly trip. This was the first time I'd been put on this particular detail, and I was eagerly looking forward to an easier-than-normal day.

As we were leaving the *Stalag*, I noticed the *Kommander Führer* walking along behind us with a jaunty spring in his step. "Ol' Baldy's in a jovial mood today," I whispered to Red.

"Yeah," Red said, replying in a whisper so we wouldn't be overheard. "According to Carl (the German-speaking informant), Ol' Baldy's wife is coming in tomorrow for a visit. Hope that improves his damn attitude for a few days."

We pulled a little red wagon toward the Runddorf Army Contingent Headquarters. There we received a sack of barley to be taken to a mill to be ground into flour. Pulling a small wagon containing a large sack of grain became a chore by the time we'd covered the more than five kilometers to the mill, then back to the bakery in Runddorf to trade for our bread ration.

But during the long walk that day, Red and I talked about the man he'd mentioned earlier. Carl bunked next to me in my side of the barracks but was reclusive and spoke sparingly during our evening discussions. I had attempted to befriend him since no one else paid much attention to him. But I guess maybe that's how he wanted it. The one time I did talk much with him I was able to learn a little about his family and his life in the States.

Carl said the confinement was beginning to bear heavily on his mind, and he felt he was slipping into severe depression. One evening, he was more fearful than I'd ever seen him. He went over the events of that particular morning and how they had affected him. We'd been roused extra early and hardly had any time to get our clothes on before we were called out to line up. As I joined the men in the lineup, I could sense that something was different; I'm sure all the men could, too. Even the guards, including Ol' Bones who had pulled guard duty patrolling the perimeter all night, were standing at rigid attention. Bones looked exhausted, but he was as ramrod straight as the rest.

We had stood at attention in the snow and cold of the early morning for at least 10 minutes when the door opened to the *Kommander Führer's* office opened. Out stepped a man, small in stature, dressed in black civilian clothes, wearing small, thick eyeglasses and carrying a briefcase. Ol' Baldy was close behind him.

The man Baldy was following was the epitome of arrogance. I didn't know who he was, but I knew he had to be some powerful German government official. His manner fairly oozed of pomposity as he approached our lineup. Withdrawing a few official-looking papers from the briefcase, he handed them to *Kommander Führer*, whose hands were shaking so much I doubted he would be able to read what was on them.

After taking a long look at the documents in his hands, the *Kommander Führer* took a deep breath and launched into his usual tirade about all the "lazy, stupid American *Schweinhunden.*" He informed us that from now on we would work longer hours to accomplish the goals set forth by the German government or face dire consequences.

"From this day on, there will be no talking at any time of the day," he said, puffing up and delivering more of the menacing threats we'd all heard many times before. "Your rations will be cut in half for the next week.

God, I thought again. With the meager food we're receiving now, that means we'll have to make a more concentrated effort to steal more or slowly starve to death.

The bug-eyed man in black seemed pleased with Ol' Baldy's forceful display. I observed a slight smile on his face and could see a glint through those nearly inch-thick glasses. He was trained to show no emotion. Just another of Hitler's stooges, I thought.

More shuffling of papers took place between the visitor and Ol' Baldy while we stood shivering in the snow. Even the guards were rolling their eyes at us, signaling that they'd had enough of this farce, too. When at last the two retreated to the *Kommander Führer's* office, the cook's men hurriedly ran up with our morning's coffee. Our guards were visibly shaken and were extremely cranky the rest of the day.

Later, in a hoarse whisper, Carl told me more about his family. He was born in Germany in 1923 of Jewish parents. The family had migrated to the United States in 1937 when Hitler had just started his persecution of the Jews. Two years later in early 1939, Carl's father returned to his homeland in an attempt to bring his aging father to safety in the United States. The trip was made in spite of the ugly rumors that Hitler was luring many native-born Germans back to the Fatherland on one pretext or another, then refusing them visas to leave.

Carl's parents had applied for U.S. citizenship, and the family had agonized over the risks if his father returned to Germany. But the pull to see the old man and to unite him with the family in America was great enough to take the risk, or so Carl's father thought.

But the family never heard from him again. So when the United States entered World War II, Carl enlisted in the infantry with the hope of serving in Germany and perhaps learning of his father's fate.

"Well, I served in Germany," Carl said, "but not quite the way I wanted to. I had hoped to survive the war and then volunteer to serve with occupation forces to search for my father."

Ruminating more, Carl related that shortly after he had celebrated his 19th birthday, a letter had arrived from a distant relative in Germany, stating that his father and his grandfather had attempted to flee the country by going to Italy but had been caught and thrown into

Charlie Dukes

I carried these pictures of my parents throughout the war and continue to do so to this day.

My father, Russell Dukes

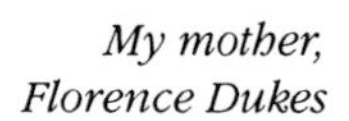

My mother, Florence Dukes

Photograph courtesy of Mr. and Mrs. David Schneck

The letters, "POW," mark the roof of the barracks at Stalag *XIIA to protect it from Allied air attacks.*

CLASS OF SERVICE

This is a full-rate Telegram or Cablegram unless its deferred character is indicated by a suitable symbol above or preceding the address.

WESTERN UNION

A. N. WILLIAMS
PRESIDENT

1201

SYMBOLS
DL = Day Letter
NL = Night Letter
LC = Deferred Cable
NLT = Cable Night Letter
Ship Radiogram

(11)

The filing time shown in the date line on telegrams and day letters is STANDARD TIME at point of origin. Time of receipt is STANDARD TIME at point of destination

C240 20 GOVT=WUX WASHINGTON DC 29 737P

RUSSELL F DUKES=

45 MAY 28 PM 7 14

225 SOUTH WALNUT ST GEORGETOWN ILL (RTE FQ FONE)=

THE SECRETARY OF WAR DESIRES ME TO INFORM YOU THAT YOUR SON PVT DUKES C W RETURNED TO MILITARY CONTROL=

J A ULIO THE ADJUTANT GENERAL.

2401

RSD

718P

The long-awaited telegram to my family.

15 WORD FREE SENDER COMPOSITION PRIORITY MESSAGE

To: MRS FLORENCE DUKES
(Full name of addressee)

225 SOUTH WALNUT STREET
(Street and number)

GEORGETOWN, ILLINOIS
(City or Town) (State)

INSTRUCTIONS
One message only to next of kin in US from each Recovered American Military Personnel. PRINT message, including address and signature, in BLOCK LETTERS. Message, exclusive of address and signature, will be 15 words, one word above each of the 15 lines provided below.

PASSED BY U.S. ARMY EXAMINER

MOM AM BACK IN YANK
HANDS SO PLEASE DONT WORRY
ON MY WAY HOME SOON

CHARLES DUKES
(Full name of Sender)

DO NOT FOLD THIS FORM

15 304102
(Army Serial Number)

Because of the large number of messages filed by liberated American military personnel, the overload was sent by air to Washington, D.C., and mailed from there. That's how the above message to my mother was sent.

prison. Germany and Italy had a secret pact to return all German Nationals caught anywhere in Italy. The letter was brief, Carl said, but his grandfather had died in prison, and the relative had no knowledge of the father's whereabouts.

Many of the political prisoners could be released from prison by signing a parole and work in a war factory under strict surveillance. The letter from Carl's relative evidently had traveled through an underground network since, according to the date, it had been written more than 30 days prior to receipt. And that was the extent of his information regarding his father. Being an American prisoner of the Germans, Carl would probably be forced to return to the United States upon repatriation and have no opportunity to search for his father.

Shortly after our arrival in Runddorf, we had been visited by the *Gestapo*, the dreaded German police. It had been during our first week there, and we didn't realize at the time who the visitor was until days later. The mere mention of the word *"Gestapo"* sent every German into fits of panic. The *Gestapo* had complete and absolute power over life and death in the Third Reich. So the man had stayed out of sight, but the *Kommander Führer* had engaged each of us in a friendly conversation in a veiled attempt to probe our family backgrounds.

Little did we know at the time that they were looking for any Jewish men among us. Even a Jewish-sounding name meant intense interrogation. If there was any question, the suspect would be yanked out and put in a much tougher prison and would eventually share the same fate as the women and children we'd seen on the trains.

Many immigrant families coming to America legally changed their last name to a more common American name. As I recall, Carl Weiss' father had the foresight to do the same and changed the family name to White, so Carl's name was as ordinary as Smith or Jones. But I called him Weiss. He was berated by the Kommander Führer *at the encouragement of the visiting* Gestapo *because his family left Germany and did not return to fight for the Third Reich as did all good Germans.*

Carl had confided in me at length of his family travails. At this point, he broke down and through barely audible sobs he said, "I am still afraid that I might have let slip some minor clue that would bring the *Gestapo* back to me. It scares me to my bones."

I thought about all of this as Red and I talked, but I never said anything about what Carl had told me. I never told anyone that he was Jewish; although as the days dragged on, I began to mistrust him a bit. He was our liaison with the enemy. During late March and early April, he seemed to spend more and more evening hours at the *Kommander Führer's* office. I knew Baldy had him over, listening to the news and translating what the newscaster on BBC had to say, but I was equally sure that they listened to the propaganda spewed out by Herr Göbbels.

Too many times Carl had told of the glowing picture of progress of the war from the German viewpoint. Either he was beginning to swallow Göbbels' line or he was trying to placate the boss man. But even the Krauts were beginning to disbelieve some of the stuff put out by their own propaganda machine as the wounded began to filter back from the fighting fronts with an entirely different story. Who could not believe them? They bore the scars that told the truth. And refugees from the bombed-out cities in Czechoslovakia and Poland were streaming west, fearful of Russian vengeance as the German army faced defeat in one sector after another.

The first clue I had that he was in the *Kommander Führer's* favor was evident the night Carl took only a few spoons of soup and gave the rest to me. He said he didn't feel well. I ate the soup without doubting his reason. A few days later, however, I observed that he seemed to be getting around better than the rest of us, was steadier on his feet and even looked to be gaining a few pounds. On reduced rations? I thought. He must be getting extra food during his night-time forays at headquarters.

Carl had reported to us that Göbbels always ended his broadcasts by announcing an exciting event such as the development of a new and faster plane, the availability of self-propelled rockets, which actually did exist before my capture, and anything else to keep his audience. Posters were plastered on posts and tree trunks everywhere, spouting aspects from his speeches about Germany.

My suspicions about Carl paying too much attention to those speeches were confirmed the evening he burst into the barracks as we were preparing to hit the sack.

"They're bombing New York City," Carl said, shouting the news he'd just heard from listening to the nightly broadcasts in *Kommander Führer's* office.

We were stunned and shocked at that announcement. Precious little news of the outside world had filtered into our midst since November. And after hearing all the horror stories about the fiasco in the Ardennes at the Battle of the Bulge, we knew anything could be possible.

"Who's bombing New York City?" I asked quietly after regaining my composure. "The draft dodgers or the war-plant strikers?"

"Well, uh, no, I don't know. They didn't actually say who."

About that time, several of the guys let fly with both barrels.

"You'd better not get too chummy with that short, fat, little bastard," somebody said, "or some of us will turn you in for collaborating with the enemy when we get back home."

"Man, don't listen to that garbage," somebody else said. "Just try to absorb what you hear on BBC."

From that day on, Carl was noticeably quiet and visited the *Kommander Führer's* office with decreasing regularity. He seldom told us what he'd heard on the radio, and we didn't ask. So we continued to be isolated from the progress of the war on any front. Nothing we could do about it anyway.

The day-long trip to the granary, then on to the mill and finally to the bakery was made about every two weeks. One particular trip we had heard about earlier became quite an ordeal for the two *Kriegies* picked for the detail. On a previous trip, they had scouted out the bakery with the intent of stealing a couple of extra loaves that had no sawdust. The men had quite a story about the day's events.

The bakery was a two-story building with an office, some bake ovens and a toilet on the ground floor. When freshly baked, the outer crust of the loaf was hard, but the inside needed three or four weeks to dry out. The second floor was used as the drying room. Bread hung in long rows the entire length of the room. Some loaves were on racks, but most loaves were hung on a hook so air could circulate all around them. Each row was dated so the baker knew when the bread had sufficiently dried out and was ready for consumption.

An open stairway was outside the building, near the entrance to the toilet. We always had to carry the bread down that long stairway to our little red wagon. The plan the two *Kriegies* had was simple: When the men loaded the wagon, they stood at the bottom of the stairs while the *Kommander Führer* and the baker went inside to sign the paperwork. As soon as the door closed, one man ran up the stairs, grabbed the first two loaves near the door and hurled them down to his buddy waiting by the wagon. Then Ed, the man at the top of the stairway, came running down himself.

But he didn't realize until it was too late that he had grabbed from what had just been baked that day and that the loaves were hot. The only solution was to grab the round 12-inch loaves and dash into the toilet to finish out their plan. Both men then shoved them inside the front of their shirts, hunching over and buttoning their overcoats in an effort to hide the bulge. They emerged from the toilet at the same time the officer emerged from the bakery. Without so much as a glance, Ol' Baldy ordered them to grab the wagon and head for the *Stalag*.

Had he paid much attention, it would have been obvious that the two *Kriegies* were acting strangely, all huddled over and sweating profusely from the hot bread. They set a speed record returning to camp that trip because the hot bread was literally burning their bare chests, dropped the wagon off at the kitchen and took off fairly running for the barracks. My own work crew arrived back from Hoyerswerda a few minutes later, and my first instinct was that they both had a 104-degree fever. They were both still red-faced and sweaty.

When they told us the story, we were all laughing with them about their caper—despite the large burned circle on each of their bare chests. We had extra bread that evening; but without having gone through the drying process, it was soft and gooey inside. And the taste was poor. So much for thievery.

With the *Kommander Führer's* wife arriving the next morning from Dresden for a short visit, his mind was not exactly on our little trip to the bakery for bread. So Red and I were able to carry on our conversation most of the trip into Runddorf and back. We hadn't tried to steal any bread, but we enjoyed the opportunity to talk at length. I'm sure Ol' Baldy was lost in his own thoughts and wasn't giving us a second thought.

Frau Mueller arrived on the early train from Dresden, dressed in her finest. We didn't have to work that Sunday, so we were all just sitting around the barracks waiting to get a glimpse of her.

"Here they come," someone yelled and we all mad a mad dash for the door.

The weather had improved somewhat; the sun was shining and the snow was melting a little. We had little to get excited about in our dreary surroundings, so the *Frau's* visit was a pleasant distraction from the ordinary. This was an event that rather tugged at our hearts, even thought we had no love for the Bald One. It rekindled memories of home and furloughs, where we hoped we would once again be experiencing the excitement of reunions with our loved ones.

A few tears were actually shed as we took in the scene of this couple, hands tightly clasped approaching the camp. They were jabbering to each other like little kids filled with the excitement of a new discovery. The *Kommander Führer* was pulling the little red wagon that contained one small suitcase of his wife's belongings.

Frau Mueller stayed four or five days, keeping close to her husband's room and venturing out only for short walks with him during the day when we were out on work assignments. So we didn't see much of her. But the morning she was to leave, a guard chose Freddie to accompany them to pull the wagon. She was taking several extra items, ones Ol' Baldy was evidently sending home.

Freddie described an emotional farewell at the train station.

They would never see each other again. Later, I would personally witness Ol' Baldy's death at the hands of the Russians. And with the bombing of Dresden a few days after her departure, she may have suffered the same fate.

A few days after *Frau* Mueller's visit, I had sacked out early one night. I was awakened when my bunk started to shake, and I was afraid it was going to collapse. We had robbed all the bunks for firewood so many times that I had to be careful every night when I climbed into my bunk. Now it was still shaking. What was going on? I wondered. It was dark as night in our barracks from the blackout shades. It couldn't be morning. No one was beating on the soles of my feet. No one was shouting, "*Aufstehen! Raus! Raus!*," the normal signal for morning.

I ran headlong for the door for two reasons. First, I wanted to find out what was happening; second, my stomach was in turmoil from the vile-tasting soup from earlier that evening. I was headed for the door as fast as I could go as my stomach was preparing to reject my supper.

At first, we heard a muted rumbling in the southwest, toward the city of Dresden. The earth began to shake, and I feared we were in the middle of an earthquake. Then we saw the glow in the sky. At the same time, I thought the barracks was going to collapse from the shaking and rumbling. The shutters were banging from the thunderous roar of hundreds of bombers as they roared overhead, clawing for altitude and circling back west to return to their bases.

A few seconds later, the sky was aglow with a purplish red color, and I could feel the vibrations from the bombardment as the formations continued to roar overhead. By now, of course, everyone was awake and had poured outside to witness the view above.

"They're bombing Dresden," someone yelled.

"Give 'em hell," someone else shouted.

All this commotion knocked the sick feeling right out of me, and

I joined with my fellow *Kriegies* in back slapping and gales of laughter. The guard walking the perimeter even came over to the fence and joined in the celebration. He knew that the end of the war was near and that maybe he would end up as *our* prisoner, especially if the Americans got to us first.

The bombing of Dresden continued into the early morning hours and all day and all night for the next few days. The glow from the fires could be seen for several days after the bombing stopped.

The Americans and the British bombed Dresden night and day for four days, using fragmentation and incendiary bombs. The heat from the incendiary bombs was so intense that it created a firestorm that literally consumed the oxygen in the air, suffocating the civilians from lack of oxygen before the fire consumed them. An estimated 140,000 people perished.

Some of the civilians we were working with had relatives in Dresden, and they became quite understandably hostile. Their attitude caused us some concern for our own safety. We all feared retaliation of some sort because Dresden was really not of any military significance. It was a beautiful city, now destroyed for no apparent reason except to destroy German morale. And it was the home of *Frau* Mueller, who had visited her husband only a few days ago.

12

Finally the weather began to improve. The snow was virtually gone. In its place was a quagmire of mud. So now I drew a farm detail in the mud rather than on the streets of Hoyerswerda. But the prospects of good food were worth the sacrifice, and I didn't complain. A small shed had collapsed because of all the heavy and wet snow. With the snow gone, now was the first time the farmer could get near the shed. Our eight-man crew was to dismantle the mess, clean the boards and stack the good lumber. The foundation was constructed of cobblestones which we also restacked near the lumber.

The day was sunny, and though the work was tedious, I was really enjoying the spring-like weather. More vapor trails from high flying bombers were evident, all heading northeast. Rumors had the targets as Chemnitz (off to the southwest) and Cottbus (to the northeast), two cities with heavy concentrations of chemical and petrol plants. The bomber formations were usually so high that I could only catch a glimpse when the sun reflected off the shiny fuselage.

About noon, the farmer appeared and started screaming at us and at the guard. We weren't working hard enough. At one time, he'd had six French prisoners working on his farm, he said, but the government had taken them away from him and replaced them with a dumb Polish girl to help his wife around the homestead. I shot a sideways glance at Kap, our Polish-born prisoner, at the farmer's words berating one of Kap's countrymen. His eyes blazed, but he said nothing as the farmer walked away.

The Polish girl arrived pulling a small wagon with some watery cabbage soup that was nothing to write home about. Kap, in a low voice, started speaking rapidly to her in Polish. She caught her breath, looked startled and then began answering his questions. The conversation was rapid fire for several minutes, abruptly coming to a halt when the farmer started back from the house.

She ventured a weak smile as she left our midst and turned toward the house. We never saw her again. After we had gathered in a circle to eat our soup, Kap related what he had learned.

"She was 16 years old when she was brought here in a labor-force roundup," he said. "She has been on this farm for nearly five years and has no idea what happened to the rest of her family. Says she might hang herself if things don't get better soon or if Germany wins the war; says she has been abused by the farmer, and her treatment has been very bad most of the time.

It was only too clear what the girl had meant. My guess was that she had been molested. But who was to know? And who could do anything about it?

The farmer arrived on the scene, shouting again. But suddenly our attention was diverted to a strange howling sound coming from the sky. We quickly located the source: an American plane in rapid descent, flames shooting from both engines. I recognized it as a B-24 bomber.

This time the farmer panicked and headed back for the house. He dove into a bomb shelter near the back door while we stood watching the drama being played out in the sky. The pilot was struggling to stay aloft as long as possible, but they were a long way from their base.

"Why in God's name don't they bail out?" I asked nobody in particular as we watched helplessly. "They're going to wait too long and the plane will explode. They'll all be killed."

Just then, three figures emerged from the belly of the plane. The first man appeared to be lifeless, tumbling end over end. His chute never opened. The second chute opened immediately upon leaving the plane, but the body hung loose and floppy in the chute. The third man dropped for several seconds before his chute blossomed barely a hundred feet above a group of trees about a kilometer from us. The plane continued on for several kilometers to the south before crashing in a giant plume of smoke and flame.

We had stopped work, first because we didn't know but what the plane might come crashing down on us; and secondly, we were anxious about the condition of the downed fliers and what might happen to them. In a short time, five or six men appeared from the woods, each carrying a club or a pitchfork and prodding one American flier. Apparently the other two were either dead or too wounded to walk out of the woods. Or for all we knew, they could've been finished off by these captors. Most civilians had a burning hatred for the Air Corps which had bombed their cities and towns. Now, the civilians were heading for Hoyerswerda to turn the flier over to the military.

It was near quitting time. Ironhead, our guard for the day, motioned us toward Hoyerswerda where we would link up with the other work crews and head for the *Stalag*. He seemed interested in the downed flier, so we had no problem intercepting the men and the flier on the road.

Upon seeing a German Army guard, the civilians were eager to turn the American over to him. As they were detailing their gallant deed to Ironhead, another *Kriegie* and I moved toward the airman. He was still more or less in a state of shock from his ordeal and was still shaking noticeably as we approached him. I'm sure our unkempt appearance did nothing to relieve his mind, but we weren't wearing German uniforms.

"It's okay, Major," I said, speaking up quickly in an attempt to put him at ease. "You can relax now. You won't be harmed."

He brightened up right away when he heard English. He had a couple of tears in his tunic, had lost his hat and had a noticeable lump on his forehead that was bleeding slightly. Otherwise, he seemed uninjured.

"I'm an American soldier," I said, "a prisoner of war, just like you are now."

The civilians who'd brought the flier this far headed back toward the woods, rejoicing in their good deed for the Fatherland. We turned toward town and began clueing the flier in on what he might expect from his captors. He would be interrogated and then sent on to a

Stalag somewhere. The major pulled out a pack of Camels and gave each of us a cigarette.

Again, although I didn't smoke, I always took one when it was offered. Cigarettes were better than gold, the best trading material there was and worth just as much to the guards; cigarettes were the medium of exchange throughout the war. A man couldn't have too many for bartering when things got really tough. If we'd have been receiving Red Cross parcels, we would have had those little packs of three or four cigarettes. But since the Red Cross never found us at Runddorf, it was our tough luck.

The downed flier did find us at Runddorf. He had been turned over to the military, but was brought into our *Stalag* about 30 minutes after we arrived from Hoyerswerda. The German military was not prepared to handle war prisoners of any kind, but the military commanders didn't want to put him in the local jail with civilians, either. So he was brought to Runddorf by two soldiers for safekeeping overnight. He would surely be moved to a larger *Luftwaffe Stalag* the next day. He was pleased to be staying with us after the hostile environment of the local soldiers in town.

Supper arrived in our barracks about the same time he did. We asked for an extra bowl, ladled out his meager portion to match ours and gave him a chunk of bread. The chatter died down as we began eating our soup and bread. We knew we could talk with the major after chow. But no one seemed to notice that the major was not eagerly attacking his supper. That was our habit because of our continual hunger.

"What kind is it?" he asked, lifting his spoon and letting a spoonful of the watery liquid fall back into the bowl.

"Why, this is the specialty of the house, Major," someone said, jokingly. "This place is famous for its watery cabbage and rutabaga soup. Sorta grows on you, particularly when you don't have anything else."

He looked at the soup with a critical eye, tasted a spoonful and quickly put his spoon down. Then he took a nibble of bread. "Is this all you fellows have to eat?" he asked with a look of disbelief, staring at the food in front of him like a sick cow.

"That's it, except for two potatoes that we always save to eat after the soup," somebody said. "What you see is what we get, Major. Once a day."

"Well, I've heard rumors," the major said, "but I just passed it off as propaganda."

"Better eat it now, Major," I said, looking at him across the table. "It will prevent 'Bang's Disease.'"

Everyone had a good chuckle from the explanation of "Bang's Disease," an ailment common to all POWs who were on the same diet as we were fed.

"It'll keep your backbone from bangin' against your ribs," two or three men said in unison.

The major didn't seem to be amused at our prison humor.

"You eat everything placed before you," I said, trying to explain the facts of prison life, "because you never know where the next meal will come from. This is our only food for the day. In the mornings before we leave for work, we receive a tin cup of hot coffee, if you can call it that. No other food for the rest of the day. Sometimes we might get a little soup at noon, depending on the job site."

The major, poor man, was staring at me as though he didn't want to believe what he was hearing. After a few seconds, he picked up his spoon and started eating the soup. By the look on his face, you could tell that it wasn't his usual fare back at the air base. He finished most of it and then ate one of the potatoes after carefully peeling it. We dared not waste a morsel and always ate peel and all.

Half the night was spent talking, or rather listening, to him talk. He'd been overseas less than two months, so we caught up on what was going on stateside. God, it was good to hear about America from an American. He said the war was going in favor of the Allies and was sure it would be over in a few more weeks or maybe a month or two at most. He told us the names of some new songs that had been written or that had become popular since we left civilization. One of the songs was "Don't Fence Me In." What irony! Here we were, fenced in by the enemy and unable get out. A good POW song, for sure. He said several movies all about the war were being shown in movie theaters now.

"Hey," I said, "when or if I get home, maybe I'll learn all about the big battles in Europe. I'll go see all these new movies.'

"Yeah, Charlie," Bill Curry said, "your last battle might have been the 'big one' that broke the back of the great German *Wehrmacht* and go down in history as decisive."

This brought a hearty laugh from the guys. The major didn't seem to understand our distorted brand of prison humor and just looked at us while we laughed. He was flying out of Italy. His squadron was a member of the 15th Army Air Corps based in North Africa. Their objective in this aborted flight was a chemical plant at Cottbus, Germany, several miles north and east of our *Stalag*.

They had run into heavy flak on their approach to the target and had had to jettison their bomb load before reaching the assigned area in order to maintain altitude. The damage to the plane was greater than the pilot and co-pilot thought, and the plane was rapidly losing altitude. The major made the order to bail out; the co-pilot refused, saying he would rather stay with the plane and try to survive a crash landing. Wishing him luck, the major made his way to the rear of the plane to be sure the crew bailed out. He found only two men, both bloody and badly wounded. After a quick assessment of the damage, he assumed that the rest of the crew was either dead or had been blown out of the plane by the force of the winds through a large hole in the fuselage.

"I was amazed at how that plane could still hold together and stay in the air," he said, a bit incredulously. "We were in a steep gliding descent, but at least not in a tailspin, going straight down. This gave only precious seconds for us to bail out. I dragged one of the men over to the gaping hole in the side of the plane, put his hand on the D-ring (the ring pulled to open a parachute) and told him to pull it as soon as I shoved him out. He never heard me; he was dead when he hit the ground.

"The second man staggered over to me, and I put his hand on the D-ring and gave him a push out. His parachute did open, but he either died when he hit the ground or those German civilians finished him off before they found me. I don't know; I was right behind him. But I went through the trees and hit the ground pretty hard, momentarily knocking me out."

When he came to, the major said he was staring down the barrel of his own sidearm, surrounded by the German civilians. They all carried a club and/or a pitchfork and were a bit unfriendly. In some cases, the locals would severely beat the downed airmen before turning them over to the military. The major had been lucky that we were so close to where he had landed.

He choked up at this point, thinking of his crew that didn't come out of it alive. We all grew quiet, all of us lost in our own thoughts of good buddies lost in battle. After a few minutes of prayer-like silence, someone changed the subject, and we continued talking long after the lights went out.

Before we left for work the next morning, we made sure the major got his tin cup of coffee and that he still had that one little potato in his pocket. We took turns shaking his hand and wishing him luck, then left him standing rather forlorn in front of our barracks.

By the time we returned that evening, he had been picked up. He was gone—somewhere. The major was a good man, and his presence in camp gave us a much-needed boost in morale.

As the weather began to warm up, so did the attitude of the guards. Both the Americans and the Russians were putting the squeeze on Germany, and the realization that the war could end shortly was beginning to tell on everybody. We had talked to a wounded German soldier the previous day, and he informed us the Russians were about 50 kilometers east of Hoyerswerda. They had been dug in for the last month or two but were bringing in supplies and fresh troops for a spring offensive. The soldier had been wounded the week before during a minor skirmish across the Czech border.

Crews still went to Hoyerswerda, but some of our men were working in Runddorf. The main gang there went to the forest to cut timber. We had two-man crosscut saws to fell the trees and then cut them into 9-meter logs. These tall pine trees had been hand planted and were in perfect rows about 20 meters apart.

Starting at the edge, we felled the trees into the roadway in perfect lines. Then we had to lift the logs into a wagon to be hauled into Runddorf. We started this work around the middle of April. The effort it took us to lift a log showed just how weak we all were by now. It took three times the manpower to lift one log than it would have taken healthy men, so the progress was slow. It was so slow and so bad, in fact, that the next morning we had help. But it came in the form of a platoon of Hitler *Jugend*. These cocky little bastards prepared to make life miserable for us *Kriegies* for the duration of the job.

As they came marching down the road singing their Nazi songs, we knew immediately that we were in for a rough day. Although the weather was still a bit nippy, they stripped bare to the waist to show off their manhood. And they lost no time in taunting us, showing off and pointing to the one "Lightning S" tattoo on the inside of their upper left arms, the true mark of the youth organization. This was the beginning for them. Soon they could add the second Lightning S and become full-fledged SS troopers.

The order of the day was to pair a *Jugend* and a *Kriegie* on the crosscut saw, forcing us to try to keep up with their frantic sawing. After a couple of hours, our men started dropping to the ground from sheer exhaustion. I was assigned to a three-man crew carrying the logs to load the wagons. We would slip a short limb under the log and then lift it to the crook of our arms for transporting out to the road. It was the same deal as the sawing detail: Us on one side, them on the other.

As we headed out of the woods, these cocky little squirts would break into song. Picking up the pace, they compelled us to keep in step—or else. To add to our misery, on a certain phrase in the song—

all German words, of course—they would hoist their side of the log and roll it against our arms, sometimes forcing us nearly to our knees to keep from being crushed under the weight of the log. We were never sure when this was going to happen, so we were constantly on the alert. My upper arms were cut and scraped and would bear the scars of the days spent working with the glorious Hitler *Jugend* for as long as I lived.

By the end of each day in the woods, I was barely able to make it back to the compound. All of us on this detail were getting weaker by the day. These young punks were thoroughly brainwashed in the Nazi doctrine. Although they refrained from any physical attacks on us, they constantly taunted and verbally threatened us. They persevered in their attempts to provoke us into retaliating.

But we knew what was good for us. In spite of our intense dislike for the punks, we kept our heads. None of us *Kriegies* had any control over the situation, so we had to accept it and control ourselves for the duration of this job.

The anger continued to build in my mind during the time I was imprisoned, though, because I was unable to vent this anger on my captors. This pent-up frustration was with me long after I returned to the States. And it stayed with me after I was finally discharged. Now, more than 50 years later and in my mid-70s, it is still a part of my make-up and is something I'll undoubtedly take to my grave.

After working a full week in the woods, I was near total exhaustion. I could barely get my supper down before falling into my bunk and into a sleeping state of near collapse. Every once in a while I wondered where those logs, cut in nine meter lengths, were going and for what they were going to be used. But I dismissed these idle thoughts. What did it matter to me? I wondered.

Well, it did matter to me. The next week I saw those logs again. In Runddorf. We had to dig trenches more than halfway across the main road, in the railroad tunnel. Then we hoisted the logs upright into the trenches three abreast and tamped dirt around them, thus building two strong, solid walls extending from each side of the tunnel. A narrow gap was left for civilians and troops to walk through, but the barrier of walls would prevent tanks and heavy trucks from passing through.

Actually, this type of work was against the Articles of War from the Geneva Convention: We were building tank traps. But the Russians were fast approaching, and the Germans were pressing everyone into the construction of defenses.

For the next two weeks, I dug foxholes setting up an MLR on the eastern outskirts of Runddorf. I spent several days digging a huge trench stretching for miles along the edge of town and in front of the foxholes. Change was in the air. For the first time, I worked alongside German civilians and soldiers. And the next few days I worked in Runddorf, I worked alongside civilians, regular *Wehrmacht* soldiers and, of course, those little Nazi bastards who were always harassing us. Most of the regular soldiers were cordial.

While there was little communication with them, the atmosphere was friendly, and I could lower my defenses and relax a bit. On occasion, an older *Frau* would gradually work closer to me to say something. The stock words were always the same: "I'm not Nazi." Never in those final days of contact with civilians and soldiers did any admit their allegiance to the Nazi doctrine.

One afternoon I was pulled off the ditch to dig more foxholes in the defensive line. I was to dig two holes at the edge of a stand of trees. As I started to dig, a rabbit came barreling past me and dove into his burrow. I quickly moved the foxhole a few feet and started digging frantically, hoping to dig that sucker out. The mere thought of fresh meat gave me a surprise surge of energy, and the dirt flew.

A couple of feet down I caught him trying to wriggle out. One karate chop to the back of the head, and I had my prize. I ducked down in the hole and twisted the animal in half, shoved the rear half into the front of my shirt, blood, guts and all and tossed the other part to Roy, who stuffed it into his shirt. We were both a gooey mess by the time we reached camp that night.

But we were going to have cooked rabbit for supper. We skinned out both parts, then started scrounging for coal and wood. Since the weather had warmed up, the Jerries had cut our coal ration. So we had to resort to bunk wood again to make a good fire. Actually, we had already robbed our bunk beds of so much wood that they had become quite rickety. Mine was so wobbly, I was almost afraid to sleep on it.

A beat-up old tin can that we used for cooking whenever we had a little extra stolen food was the pot. I filled it with water, ripped apart the hindquarters of the rabbit, added it to the water and placed it on top of the pot-bellied stove to cook. Either we ran out of fire or our hunger got the best of us, because we feasted on half-cooked rabbit that night. We ate liver, heart, lungs and even part of the entrails. Of course, dividing up that little guy into so many portions didn't exactly constitute a feast for any of us, but a taste satisfied us a little. Meat was a difficult commodity for us to come by, and I went to bed that night without a gnawing hunger in my stomach.

The next morning I heard, for the first time, the roar of artillery on the Russian front, signaling the start of their spring offensive. While on a short break at midday, I heard an eerie sound—one I'd never heard before. Looking skyward, I saw a plane appear suddenly over the treetops, guns blazing. He was strafing the town and flying at an amazing speed. I was witnessing my first jet aircraft, a Russian ME-109. I stared in awe as he made four more passes over the town at lightning speed.

On our way through town after work, we picked up our other crew of eight and headed to the *Stalag*, chattering like idiots at the day's events. We were relieved to find that none of our men had been hit by the strafing, although the gunfire had killed and wounded several civilians caught in the open streets by the sudden appearance of the plane. This was just the first of several strafing attacks on Runddorf, apparently to shake the morale of the townspeople. There was nothing of strategic value in the whole area.

That day was the first indication to me that the Russians were on the move. This gave me a shot of adrenaline, but it also brought thoughts of my future in Russian hands. We had heard so many rumors of the brutality of the Russian soldiers that I was feeling a little apprehensive, too.

The next day while taking a short break from the shovel, I stood leaning against a tall pine. My eyes were closed and I was deep in thought, very nearly asleep. I felt something touch my arm lightly. Opening my eyes to see what had touched me, I was face to face with a pretty young blonde-haired girl who looked to be about 18 years old. She was standing behind a tree, out of sight of a guard who was about 30 feet away. I edged around the tree, and she handed me a small sandwich, smiled and motioned for me to eat it.

As hungry as I was, I was hesitant about accepting the food from this lovely civilian who was probably not eating much better than I was. I knew they were all suffering a severe shortage of food because we hadn't been able to steal anything for the past week or two. The sources seemed to dry up, and there just wasn't enough food to go around.

But the girl kept shoving the sandwich into my hand. Finally, with my mouth watering, my sense of guilt dissolved and extreme hunger overpowered me. I wolfed it down in two bites. The next instant I was on my knees. I'd been so engrossed with the sight of a pretty girl up close that I'd failed to hear the approach of the guard. He'd walked up behind me and lashed out with the blacksnake whip most of the guards carried to keep prisoners in line. He caught me across the backs of my legs, and the sudden pain forced me down on my knees.

I picked myself up as quickly as I could. By then, the girl had disappeared, and I never saw her again during the rest of my days on the ditch. Picking up my shovel and going back to work, I knew I could do nothing else. But I hoped she wasn't punished for fraternizing with a prisoner. The whipping raised long red welts across the backs of my legs and were extremely painful when my pantlegs rubbed against them. The pain lasted four or five days, although the welts didn't disappear for three weeks.

Elements of the Hermann Göring SS Division had moved into the area to supervise the defenses being constructed along the entire front. I recognized the unique cuff title worn on the lower left sleeve of all SS troops. This told me I was in for some rough days. I had exchanged a few nasty words with an SS captain two days earlier and knew I was being watched more closely than the other *Kriegies.*

My second confrontation with the SS captain nearly cost me my life.

Roy Pineyon, one of the men on my side of the barracks, was a short, wiry man from hill country in North Carolina. Like the rest of us, he was getting progressively weaker. Before being captured in November 1944, he'd spent many days in continuous combat with the 28th "Bloody Bucket" Division. He was suffering from battle fatigue and tended to act strangely at times. Because of his condition, I felt a bit sorry for him and tried to help him out all I could when out on work detail. And as somewhat of a leader of the 18 men in my bunk section, Roy sort of looked to me for guidance in certain situations.

He occupied the top bunk next to me, and every night he always said a prayer before climbing into bed. He prayed for his family back home and for his buddies in the *Stalag*. The prayer always ended with these words: "If the fleas, lice and bedbugs will please excuse me, I will come to bed with them now." Those who were within earshot would smile at this humor, but Roy was dead serious. No one ever commented or laughed at his remark.

Some evenings we sat around and had a little contest to see who could catch and smash the most lice in the shortest period of time. It was amazing how fast those little devils were. They hid deep in the seams of our clothing and in our hair and beards. We always tried to keep a constant chatter that didn't amount to a damn. It just kept us from getting stir-crazy during the dark, cold evening hours. Otherwise, we had no resources available to us to relieve the boredom and thoughts of home in the bunk room.

Our own guards had begun to slough off and weren't constantly pushing us to do more work. But the SS troopers were always pestering us. One morning we had gone to Hoyerswerda to build a tank trap under another railroad bridge. The SS troopers were already at work when we arrived. The orders were to have it finished by noon because the Russians had started their offensive and were headed this way.

I was so weak that I was stumbling over clods of dirt, but still the Germans compelled me to carry logs. Roy had fallen down near the trench and was having difficulty getting up. By now we were all so weak that we were truly a pitiful sight and just were not able to do the work demanded of us. The captain walked over and actually kicked Roy backwards into the hole. I went over to help him out, muttering a few choice words at the captain.

Initially, I didn't realize that he was within earshot, nor did I realize that he understood some of the foul words I was throwing his way. He had spoken only German all the time I had worked with his crew, so I just thought he knew little or no English. I guess you could say that my mind wasn't always functioning normally of late, or I would have known that all SS troopers could speak fluent English, since they were well-trained and intelligent men.

I pulled Roy from the ditch and turned around to go back to my digging when all of a sudden the captain was screaming at me, using every filthy word in the English language. On instinct, I whirled around and found myself staring at a bayonet barely inches from my gut. I took a quick glance at his face. At that moment my body was completely consumed with fear. He was in a rage, eyes blazing with hatred and shouting that I had insulted an officer of the German Republic. He started at me with a long thrust of the rifle. Instinctively again, thanks to hours and hours of bayonet training at Fort Carson, Colorado, I went into a crouch and deflected the bayonet to one side with my bare hands.

This only infuriated him more, and he came at me again. And again, I was able to evade his thrust. I could really see no way out of this situation, but I was determined to defend myself as long as I could. I hoped cooler heads would eventually step in and stop this maniac before he killed me on the spot.

Then I heard one of our guards shouting as he ran up to the captain. I relaxed for an instant and glanced toward Pops who was coming to my rescue. And that's all I remember until I woke up, stretched out on the cold ground. The instant I glanced away towards Pops, the captain had straightened up and slammed a butt stroke to the left side of my face, knocking me cold. The force of the blow nearly tore my head off, broke my jaw in two places and knocked out four jaw teeth. I finished the rest of that day on the ground, spitting out teeth and blood.

The walk back to the *Stalag* that night was a complete blur. I remembered nothing. My comrades had to practically carry me several kilometers and put me on my bunk, for which I will be eternally grateful. I was allowed to lay on my bunk the whole next day. But the following day, I was rousted out and put back in the forest, a ways from the SS troopers, thank God. I still had to work with those detestable, youthful Nazi bastards.

From then on, until we made our escape from Runddorf, I had a rag stuffed in my mouth to cover the exposed roots of my missing jaw teeth. Although I was in constant pain for several days, no medical aid was forthcoming from my captors. With my jaw clamped shut, I became known as the Silent Indian. I took the rag from my mouth only at the evening meal to slurp my soup. I mashed my two potatoes so I wouldn't have to chew them. The bread I could eat only after it had soaked in the soup for a while. I could relieve the pain a bit by lying on my back, so I spent as many non-waking hours as possible in bed.

Of course, I should have known when to keep my mouth shut. But because I had no recourse but to absorb the captain's abusive tirade, I guess the anger just got the best of me. However, I paid dearly for my outburst.

13

The sounds of artillery fire from the east and northeast were becoming more frequent. The road was filled with troops moving to the front and the wounded returning. Hoyerswerda had been bombed and strafed several days in a row, we learned.

Still in agony from my sore jaw, I sacked out when I could. I was so weak by now that I could hardly pick up a shovel of dirt, let alone toss it out of the ditch. And according to the Geneva Convention on war conduct, prisoners weren't supposed to be working at the kinds of jobs that built defenses for the enemy. That's about all we had been doing the last few weeks. I'd been doing as little as possible to help them all along, but now I was doing even less now because of my condition.

The next morning the strange sounds of rattling chains, creaking wagon wheels and shuffling feet woke me. Hurrying to the window, I flung open the blackout shutters, and the sight before my eyes took me back home to Illinois, watching a Western movie. The road was filled with covered wagons, reminiscent of the Western migration in America, except that these wagons were using cow power instead of horsepower. All the horses in Germany had long ago been relegated to the army, leaving only Holstein milk cows for pulling power.

Wagons were crammed to overflowing with personal belongings. The wagons were so full, in fact, that no one except the driver was able to ride. The civilian population, consisting of old men, women and small children, was plodding along as if in a daze. Most were pulling small loaded wagons or pushing perambulators.

This wasn't a spring picnic. The kids weren't running and playing along the roadside. One little boy immediately caught my attention. He appeared to be 8 or 10 years old and wore a torn white shirt and baggy pants, at least two sizes too big for him. His shoes didn't match, and he wore only one sock. He trudged along wearily, as though each step would be his last. He'd crumple into a heap, fall back a little, then he would jog a few steps and grab hold of his mother's long skirt.

She seemed to pay scant attention to him. My heart went out to that little tyke. He was suffering through no fault of his own; he was just one of millions of noncombatants who were bearing the brunt of this brutal war. These refugees were fleeing from the Russians. I didn't know where they were going, and I doubted that they did, either. But the string of refugees stretched as far as the eye could see. Some of them apparently had been on the move for more than two weeks, according to some of the refugees our guards talked to along in front of the *Stalag*.

Their movement signaled that the Russian offensive was in full gear now. Sprinkled in among these long lines were several *Wehrmacht* soldiers, some in full uniform, some wearing mostly civilian garb but all carrying their rifles. These stragglers and our lack of food kept us holed up in our billets for fear some crazy Kraut would shoot us as escaped prisoners. These soldiers were mostly deserters and not front-line troops, anyway. With our physical appearance and their low morale, a possible explosive situation existed for us.

On several occasions, shots were fired into our compound. A couple ricocheted off our pot-bellied stove. We dared not stick our heads out the door. We asked our guard for one or two rifles for defense, but they were afraid we might shoot them and make a break for it. So they refused

The sporadic firing increased in intensity each day as more deserters came by. We were under siege with no way of protecting ourselves. As a result, we spent a great deal of time lying flat on the floor as the bullets whistled through the walls. Luckily no one got hit, but there were a lot of close calls from ricochets and flying wood splinters.

On the second day, my poor old bunk took two hits on one post, and the whole double-decker collapsed in a heap. I had hit the deck as soon as I heard the *Schmeisser* open up. The bunk landed across my legs, leaving several cuts and bruises. Everybody was laughing as they pulled the bunk off of me.

Carl, who slept in the bunk below me, kept chiding me, "I told you that you'd taken too many boards from our bunk. Now look. Kaput! Now we sleep on the floor."

"Maybe we won't be around here long enough to sleep," I said, getting up off of the floor, "especially if that SS group stays around, because I'm leaving."

By now our situation was deteriorating rapidly. For the past three days, our diet consisted of only a half a bowl of the thin, watery soup—no potatoes, no bread. We didn't dare venture outside the confines of our camp to scrounge for food. We had, however, done our last day on work details at the camp, it seemed.

Finally, on the fourth morning, the *Kommander Führer* set out for Runddorf near mid-morning with four *Kriegies* pulling the small red wagon in hopes of finding some rations. Two extra guards accompanied them for protection. I held out little hope of them finding any food, considering the fact that the entire German population was already on a starvation diet. They certainly wouldn't want to share with their enemies.

Yet he did have some measure of success. It was past noon when they returned with a wooden barrel half full of almost rotten kraut and a few stringy mangel-wurzels, a large coarse yellow to reddish orange beet grown exclusively as food for cattle. After taking the barrel to the kitchen, one of the returning *Kriegies* told us what was in the barrel.

"I wish I hadn't looked into the barrel," he said with a sick look on his face. "There's some green scum on the kraut. I suppose the German soldiers wouldn't eat it, so they gave it to us. They're either going to poison us or starve us to death."

We got the usual watery soup that evening, prepared with some of the kraut. At first, we were wary of eating the stuff. But as we tasted it, our unrelenting hunger took over and we wolfed it down. Nobody died that night.

Next day the *Kommander Führer* went back into town to forage for more food. This time he found a sack half full of small potatoes. Supper for the next three evenings consisted of a small chunk of bread and two potatoes per man. We couldn't survive long on this ration, but we still couldn't leave the compound for fear of reprisals from the civilians and the stragglers from the Russian front. So we stayed inside, lying around on what was left of the bunks and on the floor, keeping doors and windows closed.

Everybody knew we were in dire straits and had to make a decision. If we stayed in the *Stalag*, we would run the risk of being killed by the retreating Germans; if we made a run for it, we would be at the mercy of both the army and the civilians. Should we take the big risk of waiting for the Russians to come through? We really had no idea about how long that would take. Food was nonexistent at this point.

Soon we would be unable to walk out under our own power. Several of the men were already beyond the power of rational thinking. Some were unable to rise from their bunks without a helping hand. They were unsteady on their feet, as though they were drunk or drugged. A couple of them were becoming incoherent and sort of babbled when spoken to. Severe malnutrition, plus the manual work were expected to perform were taking their not-so-subtle toll. Whatever we did, we knew we had to decide now and all stay together for our own safety.

Just after dark, though, the door suddenly burst open. Six of our guards, including *Kommander Führer*, crowded through the door. By their sudden, unannounced appearance, we knew something quite out of the ordinary was up.

Old Baldy was brief and to the point. His headquarters unit in Runddorf had pulled out, leaving him with no orders and no food. He was now acting on his own and made it plain that he and the other guards wanted no part of the Russian barbarians who were now situated on the other side of Hoyerswerda, headed in our direction. The other seven guards had shed their uniforms and quietly slipped away during the first sign of darkness, blending in with the hordes of refugees streaming past the *Stalag*.

Baldy then made us a proposition. The American lines were now southwest of Dresden, somewhere near the Elbe River. He would be in charge and march us through the countryside. The German soldiers would pay no attention to Germans herding a group of prisoners. He would try to find a way through German lines at the front, which shouldn't be too difficult since there were so few soldiers left. Then he and the other guards would turn their weapons over to us, and we could surrender the six of them to the Americans.

He paused briefly to let his proposal sink in. Then, as our interpreter guided us through it, Baldy began to explain our alternative.

"We can leave you here to meet the Russians," he said quietly. "They're sure to arrive in a day or two. But, consider this, whether you speak English or German, they won't understand you. Since you men are all young, they'll think you're German soldiers who have shed your uniforms to fool them into believing you are just civilians. They are barbarians, uneducated and brutal. They will probably shoot all of you on sight. Just think, in 24 hours you could all be with your American Army."

Old Baldy stood nervously watching as we quickly huddled to make a decision. The main sticking point seemed to be whether he could maneuver us through the German army at the main front lines. It was obvious that he and the guards were leaving, with or without us, so we made a quick decision to accept his proposal. Granted, it was a way to protect their own skins by giving them safe passage. But it afforded us the same. So why not?

I was in favor of going to the Americans, even with the risk involved. I could definitely understand the *Kommander Führer's* rationale concerning the Ruskies. Had we all been in American uniforms, I believe our chances of survival would have been good; but from what I'd heard, I didn't trust the Russians, either.

The *Kommander Führer* was pleased with our decision.

"Soon I will be your prisoner," he said, undoubtedly feeling that his chances of survival were better with us than without us. "We must leave before dawn tomorrow. We will travel on back roads, avoiding all army units, and will stay in a small village tomorrow night. Then we will try to cross the lines the next night. Take only what you can carry. To travel light is to travel fast. Be ready to go early. Good night."

He and the other guards turned and disappeared out the door and into the night. A hushed silence descended upon us with the full realization of what had just transpired. We all became unglued and started jabbering like idiots again. Gaunt scarecrows laughed and slapped each other on the back with a renewed sense of life.

God! It will be good to eat again, I thought. Even the despised K rations will taste like steak.

Few slept the rest of the night—the night before we were to head for Freedom. The prospect of leaving this God-forsaken place and the intermittent firing at our barracks kept us revved up. No problem taking only what I could carry. My entire belongings consisted of a blanket, a bowl, a spoon, a beat-up old tin cup and the clothes on my back.

The sole of my right shoe did present one minor problem, though. Long ago, I had been obliged to cut slits in the sides of my shoes in order to accommodate my "new" pair of socks (newspaper wrappings). The bottoms of my shoes were so thin that I felt as though I were walking barefooted. I had resorted to using two loops of wire, which I slipped over the toe of my right shoe, to keep the sole from completely separating from the shoe. I even carried two spare wire loops in case one would break or slip off. But in spite of all this, these old GI shoes were still better than the wooden shoes most of the men had to wear. Those things were killers.

I couldn't sleep, either. My bunk had collapsed several days before, so I sat around the table with most of the other men, talking of better days ahead—and waiting.

We were excited at the prospect of leaving this miserable barracks, even though we were somewhat apprehensive of what might lie ahead. At the barracks, we did have a semblance of stability in living with a roof over our heads. No food, though. The kitchen was bare, so we would be forced to take chances on finding food along the route. If we could just reach the American lines all in one piece, we'd have it made. And we were willing to take any and all chances to do so.

For the first part of our journey, we would have to depend on the six guards who had elected to go with us. They knew the direction to take, they would carry the rifles to protect us from any stray German forces, and we would still appear to be their prisoners. After that, they had our assurance that we would vouch for their safety once we reached American lines.

Regardless of what the guards did, however, we were determined to take the risk of running into German soldiers who could shoot us on sight as escaped prisoners. We thought our appearance should be good cover. We were such a horrible, rag-tag-looking sight that we were pretty sure everyone would avoid us. In fact, we were counting on it. Our clothes were in such filthy, ragged condition that we didn't think anyone would give us a second glance. No one had even a fragment of an American uniform.

During the last two weeks in camp, the condition of our clothing and our physical health had deteriorated to an alarming degree. For much of this time, we had not been allowed outside the fence because of the many German soldiers and Hitler *Jugend* who were retreating from the Russians. For much of the night, we debated whether we were strong enough to travel. We knew that two of the men were unable to move much under their own power, and we could only travel as fast as the slowest man.

So before we left, we persuaded the guards to help us rig up a wagon. All the wagons had been pressed into serving the army, but the guards scrounged a small two-wheeled cart that had a tongue and wooden sides. The cart was used to haul our two comrades. We managed several pieces of rope—enough for a four-horse hitch. With four men on the tongue and two or three to push, we were ready to roll before daylight. We were on the way without the faintest idea of where we were nor where the Elbe River was located.

Dawn caught us a mile or so west of Runddorf.

The first obstacle on our journey almost proved to be our undoing. Because all the roads were clogged with a continuous stream of refugees fleeing west from Czechoslovakia and Poland, we weren't able to travel on any road. Wagons, livestock, people, baby buggies piled high with personal belongings, occasional army vehicles—you name it, and it was there on the roads. We were compelled to go across fields, ditches, fences and other obstacles, all the while struggling with the cart.

By noon or what we figured to be noon, we had made little progress. We did manage to grub for a bit of food as we crossed the fields. At an abandoned farmhouse, we found a handful of small potatoes and a loaf of exceptionally stale black bread. Whatever we found, we ate on the move, afraid to stop moving for fear if we ever sat down, we wouldn't get back up.

The cart was proving to be quite a hindrance in our trek, because after a few hours of travel, two more men had to be added to the load and slowed us down even more. Several others were just barely able to walk. Some needed to hang onto the sides of the cart for stability. Still we were fortunate that we were a small group, out away from the roads.

At every encounter with German soldiers who would just as soon shoot us as mess with us when they found out we were Americans, our guards took quite a risk. In those confrontations, the officers allowed us to pass and be on our way. But it was a different scene when the encounters were with individual remnants of renegade soldiers and civilians. These times were scary.

The civilians could only berate us and threaten us with a club or their fists—their weapons had been confiscated by a Hitler decree years before; the renegade soldiers, though, got nasty and attempted to strike us with their rifles. Several times our guards had to physically restrain the soldiers and threaten to shoot them. The soldiers, seeing that our guards were well-armed, ceased their resistance, and we proceeded on our way, drawing big sighs of relief. On the whole, the civilians were subdued and cowering, and we passed unnoticed. War had certainly taken its toll on these people for many years. They had lost everything and were as sorry a looking bunch as we were at the time.

More of a threat than meeting soldiers and civilians were the Russian planes. These jets were continuously strafing the roads, having a field day shooting at anything that moved and forcing people into the ditches and the surrounding fields. The carnage along the roads and fields resulting from this random strafing was horrendous. And I had witnessed plenty of death and destruction by this time. Roads were littered with dead and dying people, mostly the elderly but also many children. By this time, our minds were so callused and subdued that we seldom paid attention to the slaughter occurring around us. Our only thoughts were on our own survival. We stooped so low as to look for food among the dead bodies of both German soldiers and civilians whenever we crossed a road.

Early in combat and especially since becoming a *Kriegie*, I learned to never make eye contact with anyone. On the first day away from the camp, I forgot that lesson once and was haunted by what I saw long afterwards. All of us were really struggling to get the cart over a fence, through a rather deep ditch and over the roadway. During this struggle, I became entangled in the wire fence and fell headlong into the ditch. I wasn't hurt, but as I lay sprawled in the bottom of the ditch, I heard a pitiful moan or a cry for help. I instinctively hurried to my feet and found myself staring up at an old gray-haired gentleman, sitting along the road at the edge of the ditch.

As it had several times before, my mind was playing tricks on me. Looking into the eyes of that old man, I was swiftly whisked back home, and I was staring at my grandfather. I "saw" the same slight build, gray hair and mustache and haunting blue eyes of my grandfather. For several seconds, I stood motionless in shock, transfixed by the similarities between this old man and Grandpa.

It was then that I became aware of his situation. The old man was cradling a frail-looking old woman in his arms, and the tears were streaming down his cheeks. She was covered with blood, her eyes were closed and she was not moving. One quick glance told me she was dead. But there I stood, powerless to do a thing to help the old gentleman—so frightened, so aimless, so alone.

He probably had once been the pillar of a family now torn asunder by the war. As with my Grandpa, the old man was the strong one, the one Grandma always looked to and depended on as did all their children through the years. The old man was a victim of this horrible war. He did all he could for as long as he could to shield his wife from the horrors thrust upon them. But the situation became overwhelming for them after being uprooted from their home and family.

Now all he could do for his beloved wife was cradle her lifeless form in his protective arms to ward off any more harm to her. It was as if these two were my own flesh and blood. Grandpa used to say, "All that's between men and heaven are the few white hairs left on my head." So it seemed to be with this old man.

I had to look away from his pleading eyes and completely lost it. I climbed out of the ditch, tears streaming down my own cheeks. Never had I felt so hopeless as I did at that moment. So much for eye contact.

When I returned home some months later, I made a quick trip to see my old gray-haired grandpa. I hugged him and cried like a baby. I'm sure he often wondered about my sudden burst of tenderness. I never told him. But that scene, back in that ditch in eastern Germany near the end of the war, has popped up in my nightmares many, many times. I usually wake, crying.

We struggled unbelievably, from dawn until dark, that first day on the road. But just the thought of freedom, food and a warm bed kept us on the move. Several times that day, we had to hit the dirt when the Russian MIGs came screaming overhead. They usually went after a larger concentration of civilians. So when we heard one coming, we would instinctively scatter to present a smaller target.

Because of our poor condition, we didn't go far that first day. We just had too many obstacles to overcome since we couldn't travel the roads. Late afternoon found us hobbling into a farmyard that had a large barn where we could rest and sleep a little before pushing on. The *Kommander Führer* informed the farmer of our intentions and ignored his protests while we pumped his well nearly dry for drinking water.

This farm was devoid of animals, although there was plenty of evidence there had once been chickens, ducks and hogs. But the Master Race had preceded us and had cleaned the place of everything edible. We did find a scroungy, bony old horse staring from a stall in one corner of the barn. I looked the nag over closely with thoughts of roasted meat dancing in my brain. With a second look in its woefully sad eyes, though, I wilted and relented. The horse didn't have enough meat left on its scrawny bones to feed us more than a bite or two apiece, anyway. Besides that, we didn't have the luxury of time or the energy to butcher it.

By mere chance, someone uncovered a small pocket of potatoes the farmer evidently thought he had hidden well. We found a rusty old feed trough hanging on a wall, scrubbed it out as best we could, filled the tank with water, poured all the potatoes in it and prepared to build a fire for boiling those little devils.

Then we began a frantic search for fuel. No coal could be found anywhere. So we decided to use some of the boards from the buildings. Nails screeched and boards cracked as we pulled them off of an empty grain bin. Soon we had a roaring fire and soon after that we had boiled potatoes, our only food for that day. We had just barely enough potatoes to afford each man a good treat.

We were now a united group of men, prisoners and guards alike, whose goal was to survive in an extremely hostile environment. The animosity that had previously built up against the guards in prison camp had begun to soften. We all realized that we needed each other in order to reach the Elbe River, which meant Freedom for us all.

As darkness approached, we snuffed out the fire. Nobody wanted to chance burning the barn down around us while we slept. We all sacked out on the barn floor. I wrapped myself in my beautiful baby blue blanket and dreamed of home.

By dawn, we were again on our way, fortified only by our determination and those few potatoes from the night before. As the day wore on, the men became weaker and weaker until we were obliged to head for the nearest small village to seek cover and forage for food. We had been avoiding all villages, fearful of running into hostile civilians. Now we cautiously slipped into the edge of this town, a few at a time, trying not to create any commotion.

Evidently, we thought, the civilian population had fled upon hearing rumors of the Russian advance. At least we found no one nearby but could see evidence of the strafing attacks. Otherwise, the town seemed quiet and untouched by war. We later learned that the townspeople were in hiding. And more people drifted in from the east with the continuous flow of refugees from the Russian front. Some days there were very few; some days there were many.

Now, we quickly searched a large brick structure on the edge of town. It appeared to have been a schoolhouse. It was completely deserted. After assurances that we were completely alone, we turned to the task of helping those too weak to help themselves. A few men scattered, looking for food and blankets, and we all prepared to settle in for the night. A small sign over the front entrance to the building said, "Rosenthal, Germany."

Rosenthal was stuck in a small valley with low hills on two sides. We had approached from the east and walked down the hill into the schoolyard, which was at the rear of the building. We were never able to secure any sort of map of the area, so we still had no idea where we were or how far it still was to the Elbe River and the American lines. Likewise, we had no idea how far we had traveled during the day. But considering our physical condition and being encumbered by the cart, we knew it wasn't possible to have covered many miles.

Left to our own initiative by the guards, our foraging crew returned with blankets and food. Somehow three or four chickens had gotten away from the chicken coop and been left behind for the two former POWs to find for our supper. With undue risk, we built a small fire inside one room of the schoolhouse. That evening we put a steel basket on the fire and had roasted chicken. This was the first real meat I'd tasted in nearly eight months. A taste of that single rabbit didn't count. And the occasional blood sausage (ground-up barley with warm horse blood poured over it) and the horse meat we had a couple of times on Sundays in Runddorf when a horse had died in our vicinity didn't qualify as meat in my book. What a feast we had that evening! We dined on chicken, potatoes, bread and marmalade and even drank some rather foul-tasting German schnapps that really cleaned out the pipes. Somebody had found two small bottles to share.

With full bellies and a little schnapps, it didn't take us long to collapse into a deep sleep. Life like this wasn't going to take much getting used to for us.

At daylight, we were abruptly awakened by gun fire, the clatter of hoofs and a great deal of shouting in a language I'd never heard before. We were fearful of the commotion. It was taking place outside in the courtyard at the back of the school. So we had little time to prepare for anything. The door was smashed open and in burst a group of short, stocky Mongolian-looking creatures. Their clothes appeared to be Russian, although they were by no means a very neat, complete uniformed group. The lone recognizable feature was the red star appearing on their caps. This alone signified that they were, indeed, Russians.

They carried an assortment of rifles and pistols, some of rather ancient origin. We later called them Cossacks because they were on horses. But initially and when we were able to carefully confront them, we deemed them to be Mongolians by their appearance. They were shouting and gesturing to us to move quickly out into the courtyard, waving their weapons like crazy idiots. One of our group who spoke Polish began trying to carry on a conversation with the man who seemed to be the leader of the group.

After an exchange of a few words, he abruptly shouted for order and at the same time grabbed our interpreter in a big bear hug. This action left the interpreter gasping for breath.

"Amerikanski, Amerikanski," the leader kept shouting as he continued to squeeze our man into semi-consciousness. He bear-hugged each of us, in turn, leaving us all staggering around and trying to catch our breath.

Man, that Mongol was strong. He had arms like a gorilla.

Out came a bottle to be passed around for a friendly swig. After that bear hug and a swig of vodka, we were practically falling to our knees. Then we were ushered out into the courtyard where we were greeted with more hugs and shouts of *"Amerikanski! Dobra!"* More bottles magically appeared for us to drink from, but this time we merely touched our lips to them and remarked how good—*dobra*—the stuff was before quickly passing the bottles back. Some of us were still staggering from the first round of hugs and vodka. We could see Cossacks running around like crazy banshees, so we never knew how many were in town. But by the way the village was shot up, there must have been more than 100 men and ponies.

The Russians then made a search of every room in the building. The German guards had found their own quarters and had not even joined in on our feast the evening before. The guards undoubtedly realized long before any of us Americans did that they were in for capture or death. We had heard more rumors—true or not—of the brutality of the advancing Russian troops. We were just not sure how well we would be accepted by our Russian allies. They were unpredictable in most situations, I later found. But I have no doubt that the German guards' fears were a bit worse than our own and knew exactly what their fate would be if the Russians caught them.

In all the confusion, we had nearly forgotten about the guards—until we heard a commotion at the far end of the building. Evidently the Germans had barricaded themselves in one room and were putting up quite a firefight against the Cossacks. The firing subsided. A few more minutes passed before our six German guards were herded out into the yard. With much shouting and pointing by the Mongols, we finally got the point: They were handing us their rifles to shoot the Germans. We refused. The Mongols became quite angry with us, causing a few anxious moments for us while they quarreled among themselves. Were they going to shoot us first and then kill the guards? I wondered.

Their leader finally came to a decision. The Germans were hustled over and lined up against the wall of the toilet. They knew what was coming and looked at us with pleading eyes. They had taken the risk of getting us past German soldiers and hostile civilians with the hope of also reaching American lines where they would have a better chance of survival. We had given them our word that we would help them for their help in return. But now we could do nothing. It really hurt us to see them lined up, waiting for the bullets to cut them down.

And I think most of us showed our sadness at the way things had turned out. The sympathetic feelings among the men for those six Germans was amazing. Memories of their recent past treatment of us seemed to melt away. Compassion enveloped me as I thought it did the others who had to stand and watch what was about to happen. They were human beings, after all. It was so odd that five months of anger and hatred could vanish so quickly. But they had homes and families somewhere, the same as we did. Someone waited for their return which now would never be.

I could see the sadness in their eyes. Most of the guards were crying softly and turning away from the Cossacks so as to not show the tears. After all, these were Germans, the enemy we had been fighting. We should have been exuberant. But the Russian allies cared nothing for their lives and set about to carry out the executions.

We were forced to stand and watch as these wild men gleefully prepared to shoot the unarmed old men. Tears were streaming down my cheeks as I forced myself to look into Pops' eyes, knowing the situation was beyond my control. Maybe we should have left Runddorf a few days sooner, I thought, and we could have gotten a bit closer to the Elbe River. Maybe then the guards would have been able to get us through the German lines to safety. Pure speculation, I knew, but I was trying to cover my sadness for the cruel way Pops was about to die.

Then, unceremoniously, the Cossacks shot the guards, one by one, right in front of our eyes.

I guess we were supposed to be jubilant and thank the Cossacks for saving us from the enemy. Little did they realize that those six guards were our safety net in reaching American lines. Without their presence, we were now escaped prisoners behind enemy lines subject to being shot on sight.

14

The Russians seemed to be a disorganized group with little leadership. We kept trying to get information from them regarding the whereabouts of the rest of the main Russian force. Their leader seemed to have no more of an idea than we did. He would wave his arms and point eastward. Later, we learned that these Cossacks were miles ahead of the main Russian army. These men who had found us were actually reconnaissance troops, roaming miles behind enemy lines and wreaking havoc in the German rear areas. We witnessed some of their handiwork soon after they rode out of town.

Before they rode away, though, we stood together in the center of the courtyard trying to communicate with them near the small, rectangular, concrete building where the German guards had been shot. I was standing near one side of the building which was the school toilet, trying to understand some of the yakking of three or four of the Cossacks. My participation in the conversation consisted of nodding my head and saying, "*Dobra*," over and over. This tactic was getting me nowhere. Then I heard the unmistakable rumble of a tank.

A Tiger tank peeked up over the hill to my right and immediately swept the entire area with 50-caliber machine-gun fire. Two or three of the Cossacks standing in front of me were instantly cut down. I had a split second to seek cover. I dived head-first through the small, open window of the toilet. Fortunately, I wasn't injured; but it was a messy, smelly landing.

The tank continued to sweep the area with its 50s. Then, without warning, it withdrew just as quickly as it had appeared without throwing any cannon fire at us. No sooner had the tank withdrawn than several Cossacks seemingly came out of nowhere. They were leading their small horses, ponies actually, and jumped on them and rode away, leaving three dead comrades behind. Most of the ponies had a crude saddle, some no saddle at all. It was a strange sight as they rode away with the soldiers' legs nearly dragging the ground.

At this point, we decided we had better take stock of our situation. We fanned out through the area, checking for any civilian occupants, food, blankets and clothing. We had advanced no more than 200 yards down the village street when we discovered an array of bodies lying in the street. The most shocking scene was the sight of three women, stripped of their clothing, hanging from a utility pole.

Evidently the Cossacks had ridden into town at earliest light and savaged the whole area while we were in deep slumber. They could have entered the village from any direction. We happened to be discovered on their way out of town. The entire area seemed to be completely deserted of human inhabitants now. The only sign of life now were some chickens and a penned-up hog.

While we stood there taking in the situation, we knew more decisions had to be made. We were now in a singularly precarious position, in a no-man's-land where we were subject to being shot by the Germans as escaped prisoners. And God only knew what attitude the Russians might have toward us. Nobody could tell we were Americans with our long, shaggy beards and a hodge-podge of tattered clothing. Our meager contact with the Russians had only increased one of our fears: They seemed to shoot first and then investigate their targets.

Since the alternatives seemed hopeless, we decided to stay put for the time being. If we moved on toward the Elbe River, we would somehow have to infiltrate the German lines. How many days' walk was it to the American lines? Would we have enough physical strength to make it without food? These were questions we didn't have answers for, and we still didn't know where we were going.

Scavenging for food had now become almost impossible. The German Army was confiscating all food and animals for its own battlefield kitchens. The land was being stripped of all edibles. Nothing was left for the poor civilians. They existed the best they could after the army plundered their food supply. And it was hard telling how long the roads would remain clogged with refuges fleeing to the west. They seemed to be everywhere, reinforcing all the brutal things we had been hearing about the Russians. Whole villages were fleeing en masse.

So we immediately set about the task of gathering any and all food we could find in the village. Because the stream of refugees had started through the village and would be never-ending, we had to get what food we could find quickly and take it to the schoolhouse. The refugees undoubtedly had exhausted any food supply they had started out with. Refugees from Poland and Czechoslovakia, and even eastern Germany, had been on the road for weeks. They were having to live off of the land for survival, too.

Even though I was worse off, physically, than most of these displaced persons, it still tugged at my heart to witness this human exodus. It was so difficult to ignore the children. I had plopped down along the road with my back against a tree, gazing at the passing civilians. My mind was wavering again. I thought by concentrating on the moving crowd that maybe I could collect my thoughts. But when I would try to recall an incident that happened at home or at college, I could never seem to really sort it all out. I just couldn't concentrate on one subject long enough.

It was then that I noticed a young, frail mother with a suitcase in one hand and a box tied up with rope in the other hand. Tied to her left wrist was a short length of rope that fastened to the wrist of a small girl at the other end. The girl was having a difficult time keeping up with the woman. She would stumble sometimes and be nearly on her knees. When she would fall back so far, the rope would yank her along. The little girl was pretty and had blonde hair. Her dress was torn and dirty. But what I noticed most was that her eyes had an unblinking, blank stare, as if she were blind to her surroundings. Undoubtedly the trauma all these people were living through daily just numbed her senses.

I smiled, waved to her and voiced a cheery greeting. But she showed absolutely no recognition or emotion back to me. All she had was that blank stare as she continued to stagger along, trying to keep up with her momma.

A small boy trailed along behind them on his spindly legs that looked too frail to carry even a body of his small stature. I wondered how long they had been on the road, probably traveling night and day, stopping only when sheer exhaustion forced the family to rest.

These were the hordes of innocent victims of war who were suffering and dying without ever knowing why. War is bad enough for the men fighting it; but in a country ravaged by war, it is the civilian population that does much of the suffering. These displaced persons or DPs had no destination, so they would never know when they arrived. Their only intent was to put as much distance as possible between themselves and the oncoming Russians. This, the result of the great, uncaring leaders of the world who glory in the art of war. I knew that those spindly little legs and a thousand others would walk through my mind many times over, causing me to have many a restless, sleepless night if I ever got out of this place alive.

The other men were scattered around, thinking their own private thoughts or talking quietly with each other. I had had enough of watching the passing parade and retreated inside the schoolhouse to regain my composure. Sitting inside at a school desk a few minutes later, my head buried in my hands, I heard soft footsteps approaching. When I looked up, I saw a pleasant-looking young woman walking toward me. After determining that I was an American, she introduced herself as the daughter of the headmaster of the school. She spoke English with a heavy accent, explaining that she had taught English in a school in Dresden before it closed.

Then she had returned to Rosenthal to her mother and father who had not only taught at the school but also lived in the back two rooms of the building. By the look on her face and her halting speech, I could tell she was quite apprehensive. She trembled as she sought for words.

"The Russian soldiers don't treat women as I've heard they do, do they?" she asked, haltingly. "They *are* civilized human beings, aren't they?"

I sat stunned by her questions and especially by the haunting look in her eyes. Where has she been? I wondered. Hasn't she seen some of what they had done to the women in this village? How can I answer questions like that. I wanted to tell her exactly what I thought from things I'd seen that morning, but I knew my answers would only increase her fears. If she didn't already know the truth, though, I thought for her own protection she should know it.

"If I were you," I said, "I wouldn't be here whey they come back. You had better hide. Or better still, try to make it to the American-controlled sector. We can do nothing ourselves to protect you."

Some of the other men heard us talking and sort of filtered in to join our conversation. After they heard her situation, they were all in agreement that what I had told her was the right thing for her to do. She said she would leave that night, joining the other refugees who were streaming through town. I was truly relieved to find that she would head for safety. I could only imagine her fate if she stayed around when the bulk of the Russian army arrived in a few days. But I could only hope she would make it to American lines.

Rumors continued to run rampant from every angle. We knew the Russians were not too far behind us; we could plainly hear the sound of their artillery and knew it was growing closer every day. Sometimes we also could hear the faint sound of artillery coming from the west. We knew that *that* had to be American. And every time we heard the rumbling of artillery drifting in from the west, I could feel a sense of exhilaration. With the sound getting louder, the prospects that the Americans were coming in buoyed me up. It meant better days ahead. But we still did not have the faintest idea how far we were from the Elbe. We had been told the Elbe was as far as the Americans would come.

With the death of our little German boss, *Kommander Führer,* and the rest of his men earlier in the day, we were still fearful of trying to go through German lines. The guards had skillfully kept us from being shot after we left Runddorf. Anytime we had met German soldiers, the guards had always answered that we were being transferred to another prison. I don't know what prison they were talking about, but the bluff had worked with the German troops we had met and got us through some scary contacts.

Because we had lost the edge afforded us by the guards, we felt that our best chance for survival was to stay put and take our chances with the Russians. After all, we reasoned, they were our allies. What few we had come in contact with had praised the Americans for all the help given to their country. We would keep ourselves out of sight during daylight hours and forage for food at night. Most of the time, we would be ignored as just more refugees. But there was always the chance that some German soldier had discarded his uniform and blended in with the civilian population. Still a soldier of the Third Reich, he would no doubt take great joy in killing an American soldier.

Since all the guns had been confiscated by Hitler some years before the war, we had little to fear from the general population. Still knives and machetes were visible on occasion. Luckily, those streaming through were mostly old men and women. The most they could do was to yell and berate us with threats.

"Here they come," someone shouted.

I immediately hit the floor of the schoolhouse and crawled over to a small window that faced the east. The scene curdled my blood. About 300 yards away, the field was literally alive with hundreds of men walking toward us. What a motley-looking crew to be called an army, I thought. Very few had a complete uniform. All had on high-topped walking boots and a mixture of clothing similar to some that we were wearing. A few had buttoned-up tunics. Every man wore a field cap bearing a red star. Russians. No doubt about that.

Most of them carried a rifle of dubious origin; some had sidearms; and a few were merely armed with a long sword or machete-like knife. All had a red armband about four inches wide around the left arm, just above the elbow. Later, we learned that many of these men were released prisoners pressed into service, still wearing their ragged prison garb. They were a mixed group of racial origin: white European types, Orientals, Tartars and a mixture of other races I had never before seen in any of the prison camps.

They were a wild-looking bunch, jabbering away in several languages that none of us had ever heard before. They seemed to congregate in small groups, speaking to each other in their native tongue or dialect. Although many of them probably couldn't speak much Russian, they all seemed to at least understand it. We couldn't understand anybody.

The obvious leader of this rag-tag army was the only man dressed in full uniform. He was more than 6 feet tall and towered over his men, most of whom were short, squatty people. He had a military bearing and had complete command of his men. But he spoke a regional dialect that our Polish-born buddy could not interpret. Then a big, bear-like soldier came pushing his way to the front of the group surrounding us.

"I heard there were Americans here," he said in a booming voice with an American accent. "Where are they?"

"Right here," about a dozen voices answered him.

"I grew up in New York City," he said, standing before us. "I came back home to Russia in 1937 and decided to stay."

He told us his name, but all those foreign names sounded the same to us. So we called him "Ivan," after Ivan the Terrible, just as we did all the Russians. He talked with some of our men from New York and assured the captain that we were Americans. With his arrival on the scene and assurance of our nationality, the tensions eased considerably. Still many of the group continued to eye us cautiously, especially the Oriental-looking men.

It was difficult for us to relax in their presence. Ivan, however, continued to talk with us, interpreting for the captain. Through Ivan, the captain informed us that we could go with them or stay and wait for the headquarters units that were following and should be arriving in two or three days. They would see to it that we were returned to the Americans. The captain and his men were not heading toward the Elbe River but were cleaning out pockets of German resistance in the area.

We were not interested in getting close to any more combat, so we all elected to stay in Rosenthal for now. Ivan concurred in this decision, telling us that it would be foolish for us to attempt to make it to the Elbe on our own. We were actually behind the German lines while in Rosenthal. Any advance by the Russians would surely push the Germans right through our area. He knew as we did that the Germans and the Russians would both fire at us on sight.

"The town is yours," Ivan said. "Take what you want from the townspeople and tolerate no resistance."

That was easy for him to say, harder for us to do. We had no armed means of protection, and we were in hostile territory.

"Do what you can," he said, shrugging at our predicament. "We do not take prisoners. We are constantly on the move and have no means of caring for them."

Ivan and the captain then gave us some red cloth and told us to make red armbands and to wear them on our left arms at all times. This would, they said, at least keep the trigger-happy Russians from shooting us without first finding out who we were.

So much for the Russian side, I thought. But what if we awoke one morning to find the town full of German soldiers? The red armbands would certainly put us in immediate danger. We had heard rumors of German elements holed-up in pockets all around the area. The presence of this band of Russians only reinforced the rumors.

In fact, this group was moving out to attack a pocket just a few kilometers directly south of Rosenthal. If we headed out, we would be moving in that same direction. We had some doubts about whether the red armband would be sufficient to ensure the chances of any Russian asking first before firing at us.

Someone came up with the idea of having Ivan copy the word, "AMERICAN," in Russian for us. We could then copy it in big letters and hand that to a Russian if he had a gun stuck in any of our ribs. Ivan immediately complied but was laughing quite hard as he did. His hilarity became apparent when he handed over the word he had written for us.

"Most of them can't read anyway," he said, still laughing.

Maybe that was a big joke for him, but for us it only added to our already precarious situation in no man's land. We did, however, secure some heavy paper and some red paint in the storeroom of the schoolhouse to make a large sign saying, "*Amerikanski*" for every man in the group. These signs were primitive but with much pointing and repetition we thought we would be able to get the point across to most of the Russians. We were going to need everything possible for identification if we were to stay alive with them.

They left in the same manner in which they had arrived—a ragtag group walking out across the fields with no semblance of military order. Ivan bade us farewell as they left on a mission to wipe out a company of SS troopers who were well entrenched in the woods some two kilometers away. You had to wonder how these Russians could ever exist as a unified force. Rogue bands of Ruskies seemed to be everywhere, some with a leader, some with no apparent leadership. This and the fact that there seemed to be no main front made these groups exceptionally dangerous.

As they were leaving, I noticed some of the Russians had rounded up a band of townspeople. They were carrying the bodies of our guards up the hill to be buried. We had neglected to mention that a band of Cossacks had been in town at dawn that day, even though Ivan had questioned us about all the damaged houses. We had not had time to roam much outside of our safe schoolhouse, so we were as shocked as our visitors to see the damage inflicted by the Cossacks. We had seen several bodies lying grotesquely in the street and the four or five houses that were ablaze.

But a second look showed doors kicked in, windows smashed and a general trashing of the entire town. They must have had more men in their group than we saw at our quarters or else they were in town earlier than we thought. It had been plenty dark when we first heard the gunfire and the clatter of hoofs. At any rate, those Cossacks were certainly thorough in their destructive capabilities.

As soon at the band of Russians headed out to battle, eight or nine of our men who didn't want to sleep on the hard floor of the schoolhouse started out for town to look for a softer bed. I was content to remain with the largest group for protection. Roaming in small groups could invite trouble, I thought, particularly with German soldiers so close to town.

Some of the more friendly townspeople had warned us about seeing several SS sneaking into town at night, foraging for food. So we were aware of the possibility of their presence before Ivan told us where the Russians were headed. But we would make it a point to be careful in our nighttime forays, fearful of any confrontation. We had heard sporadic gunfire from the moment we had left the *Stalag* in Runddorf. The war was going on around us all the time. Rosenthal was quiet when we arrived, but we could hear gunfire in the distance nearly all the time and had heard it the night before. We had heard a lot of gunfire from the general area of the dug-in German force after the Russians left us. Now we knew there were more Russians roaming around, too.

These roving bands put an additional strain on our chances for survival. None of them understood a word of English. So far we'd been able to compromise all chance meetings by using two words, *"Amerikanski"* and "*Dobra.*" Our heads also got a good workout engaging in much nodding with our attempt to be understood. This sometimes became a side show but seemed to break the initial hostility with people who were supposed to be our allies.

At the first light of day the next morning, I was rudely awakened by the glare of a flashlight in my face and a gun shoved against my head. After the initial shock, relief flooded over me when I determined these men were Russians, not Germans. As dangerous as those rag-tag looters were, we still felt safer with the Russians than with any

German troops. The greatest fear I had was coming out of a deep sleep, swinging or making some quick movement. A reaction of that sort might startle them into shooting first, then asking questions.

These Russians kept moving west in small groups, and we would undoubtedly see more of them before the war was over. They seemed to have no direct front line as in the American front. They passed many pockets of German infantry. Often the more disciplined German troops would surround and annihilate these small bands of Russians who seemed many times to be without leadership or any sense of purpose except just wandering and looting.

I began to realize that maybe my unkempt appearance was the one saving grace that was keeping me alive. From then on, I made no attempt to improve my looks, either by combing my hair or trimming my heavy beard. After seven months, why bother anyway? I thought. This meant, however, that I would still be home to my friends, the lice. No amount of water or washing seemed to faze them.

The members of our group that left the schoolhouse found accommodations in the small hotel in the center of Rosenthal while the main group continued to hole up in the school. We continued to hold daily discussions on strategy. Nothing changed our minds about our best chance for survival being to stay put and hope and pray that hostilities would cease sometime soon. The booming of artillery was getting closer from the Russian side, but we heard little from the American side. We were still smack in the middle.

The men in town lucked out in a big way. The woman who owned the hotel was still there and willingly welcomed the Americans after she was assured that they meant her no harm. They persuaded her that with their presence in the hotel, the Russians would leave her alone. She said she would cook for our whole crew. All she had in her kitchen, however, was some flour, a loaf of bread, a few small potatoes and some salt and pepper. We hadn't had any salt and pepper for months.

In our foraging for food, we had noted that a couple of small chicken pens also held a huge white sow. Given our state of near starvation, we simply walked into the hen house and took the chickens. The owner just stood there and watched us, doing nothing to stop us.

The Russians had put fear into the inhabitants to the point that we were allowed to roam at will and take what we wanted. Most of the villagers would retreat into their homes upon our approach. They quickly realized that we meant no bodily harm to them. We were only seeking food. We also added to our wardrobes, acquiring some neater fitting garments that also helped ward off the colder nighttime temperatures.

On the third morning in Rosenthal, we heard a knock on the schoolhouse door. We were extremely jumpy at every little sound. But a knock on the door suggested friend, not foe. The Russians would always bust in the door, guns ready. Since this was a light, sensitive knock, we answered right away. The German man we'd seen at the chicken pens stood on the step.

He was extremely nervous and started blurting something out in German at such a rapid-fire clip that we had no chance of understanding him. Finally, we slowed him down enough that we could get the gist of what he was saying. The huge white sow we'd seen was in the pen back at his house. His family was very hungry, but the Russians had already spotted the hog and had told him that if he butchered it, they would kill his family and him.

What he was wanting us to do was to kill the old sow and butcher it. He explained that if the Americans killed it, the Russians would not kill him—at least this sounded logical to him. I wasn't so sure. All he wanted was part of the meat for his family; we could have the rest. With the Russians, he knew he would get nothing.

The Russian army lived entirely off the land as they advanced, taking all livestock and food. Russian trucks would haul in fresh troops and would haul back loot of every description. They cleaned out furniture, tools and anything that wasn't nailed down. Undoubtedly, the occupation troops would later take all that was nailed down, too. The Russians seldom ever buried the German dead, leaving that chore to the civilian population. Only when the civilian population completely cleared out did the Russians attend to the dead.

Listening to the German civilian's proposition made me even more aware of the desperate situation these people were in now. The hog was the man's last and only source of food. His share would probably last only a few days. Today, he would have food. Tomorrow—

We had a rough time killing that old sow. She was huge, mean and cantankerous. It took several blows to the head with a big ax to bring her down. Then someone was finally able to stick a big butcher knife into her throat to finish her off and bleed her. Since no one in our group had ever butchered a hog before, the task of gutting and skinning such a large hog was almost an insurmountable task. But when you're hungry as we were, nothing is insurmountable. That includes killing, skinning and butchering a big old sow that probably weighed nearly 500 pounds.

After we'd finished butchering and cutting up the meat, we shared it with the owner's family and gave several pieces to the woman—besides what she cooked for us—who owned the hotel. With some of my teeth knocked out, I pulverized the pork as best I could but was unable to eat little of the tough meat. I felt I needed the meat for strength, though, and struggled the best that I could.

Although we ate sparingly that night, several men still got deathly sick from eating too much pork. For the first time, we fully realized just what havoc a starvation diet can wreak on a man's stomach. It was a delicious meal, but I nonetheless swore off pork for many months. As good as the pork tasted while I was eating it, I kept thinking how much better it would be with white bread, real butter, a vegetable and a green salad. I had forgotten what real bread and butter tasted like. Nevertheless, I was eating much better now since we'd left Runddorf only a few days ago. While I was eating better and gaining a little strength, though, my despondency was growing to the point that I was having difficulty talking with my buddies, the other men in our group. Would it ever end? I wondered.

I didn't sleep well that night, either. My stomach was puffed up, and I had difficulty getting my breath. I was too full. Isn't that something? I thought. I've been hungry and wanted a good bed for months. And now that I've got something to eat and a bed, I'm miserable. I'd requisitioned a small single mattress that certainly beat sleeping on a hard wood floor. I even had a fluffy feather comforter to tuck under my chin. When I'd gotten the mattress and comforter, I'd thought if this is anything like what Heaven is like, I'm there. Now I wasn't so sure.

Sometime during the night, I was rudely shaken awake. I opened my eyes to the blinding light of a flashlight in my face. Three or four Russian soldiers were staring down at me with their rifles about two feet away, pointed directly at my head. God, I thought, how many of these sudden confrontations at all hours can a man survive without some trigger-happy Ruskie squeezing off a shot before a man has a chance to respond?

On the occasions that I was accosted by small groups of Russians roaming at will behind the front lines, I relied on being calm and would slowly point to my red armband, my dogtags and, of course, use my fluent mastery of the two Russian words in my vocabulary. Now I methodically repeated "*Amerikanski*" several times, slowly pointing to my red armband and all the while staring at the dark figures behind the flashlight.

These encounters were becoming more frequent, and I feared my luck might run out tonight. I could barely see the faces. It seemed like several seconds before I noticed any semblance of recognition. Just those cold, dark staring eyes. Only when they lowered their rifles did I dare take a breath. I can certainly understand what a condemned convict feels like when he gets a stay of execution. This was the third time I had had a close brush with certain death in only a few hours. And it was sure to occur many more times during my stay with the Russians. The average Russian was scary enough on nights like this one. I could only imagine the really close calls that would come from those who were stupid drunk on vodka.

The Russian front was so fluid that you could never determine whether you were in front or behind their lines. Many groups of

Russians roamed at will without leadership or control of any kind. These groups were the bands that pillaged, raped and killed indiscriminately. And these groups were what we feared. They had no control and were mostly ignorant.

15

Rumors persisted that German SS troopers had been spotted at night on the outskirts of the village. Some of the locals had apparently talked with them and reported that the soldiers were amazed that there were no Russians in town. This information sent our skins crawling. We prepared to move out quickly at the next report of any sighting of the Germans.

The next morning, our fifth day in Rosenthal, we were up early. As a result of a little rest and better food, everyone had regained some strength. But we still had no maps and no idea how far it was to the Elbe and American lines—we had only the direction.

An eerie silence seemed to hang over the whole town that morning. Things didn't feel right to us. Being combat-wise men, we quickened our pace of preparations for departure and moved out of the schoolhouse. We had accumulated no extra food that we could take and only had one blanket each and the clothes on our backs. Heading for the center of town, we dodged and weaved as though we were in a front-line firefight. We scooted from house to house, always in the rear of the structure to avoid the open street. Just before we reached the hotel where the other men were staying, all hell broke loose.

The early-morning stillness exploded as machine-gun fire raked the houses, shattering windows and bouncing off the brick walls of the hotel. I hit the dirt and crawled into the nearest house. Making my way to a window, I stuck my head barely above the sill. My heart skipped a beat or two as I recognized the source of the firing.

"Germans," I said, shouting to the others who had taken cover wherever they could. "Let's get the hell out of here fast."

The machine gun was set up openly on the play area behind the schoolhouse. How lucky can we be? I wondered when I spotted the machine gun. We just left that spot no more than 10 minutes ago. They had to have been moving into the edge of town at the very moment we decided to leave.

As the machine gun continued to rake the whole area on our side of the road, my next observation confirmed my worst fears. German soldiers were firing and running from one point of concealment to another. Then came the whistle of incoming artillery and the whomp of the shells exploding all around us. A direct hit completely demolished the house next to where we were hiding. The Germans were mounting a full-scale attack on the town, apparently after the Americans who were reported to be in Rosenthal. I guess the Germans didn't realize that we were without weapons.

We scrambled out of the back door, across a small courtyard and into the rear of the hotel. The building was two stories tall and constructed of solid brick. Although the east wall was pockmarked by the machine-gun and small-arms fire, the building was still solid. Several houses were now burning around town.

Just as we joined the other men in the front lobby of the hotel, the firing began to slack off. Then abruptly it stopped. Cautiously peering out the front windows, we saw a beautiful sight: The civilians of the town were walking down the street, heading for the other end of town and away from the firing. They poured out of the houses—men, women and children. Many were waving white flags made from everything from pillowcases to large white sheets. I had no idea that there were that many civilians still left in the village. Obviously they had been hiding during the four or five days since we arrived because we had seen very few.

Some of our men were already in the "parade," and we were quick to mingle, although somewhat apprehensive about the attitude of these villagers toward our presence. But joining this stream was our only chance of survival because we knew the German soldiers would surely shoot us on sight. A few locals told us that the only reason for the assault was "to kill those Americans in town." Naturally, this didn't endear us to the people of Rosenthal.

The German soldiers were apparently the small platoon of SS troopers that the Russians had first told us about that had been holed up and surrounded by the Russians two kilometers south of town. And these were the same Germans that had been sighted nearly every night around the outskirts of town. They must have broken out of the pocket, escaped the Russians and were now attacking Rosenthal when they thought that the few Russian stragglers who had been in and out of town every day had left. For us to be caught in town at this point would be certain death.

We tried to infiltrate the column in twos and threes to avoid attracting the attention of the German soldiers who were advancing behind the column of refugees. Because of our appearance, we didn't look any different than most of the civilians. Some of us had found better clothing, but we still had our matted, dirty hair and beards and were still a motley crew.

A few civilians hurled a little hostility and some angry threats our way. But we ignored them and moved quickly up through the column to the front, putting distance between us and the advancing Germans. Then the firing picked up again, and bullets would occasionally whine overhead. The artillery rounds started again, too. All the firing seemed to be avoiding the main road full of people, though. I hoped the soldiers hadn't had time to spot any of us in the crowd and zero in on the street.

As we walked along, we were continually eyeing either side of the column to see if any of the soldiers were paralleling us. Nobody saw any. In their haste and fright of getting away from the shooting, people tended to ignore us after the first few minutes. That was good. We hadn't exactly endeared ourselves to them during our stay in their village. Our fear was that if we came across some soldiers, we would be singled out in the crowd, denounced and shot immediately.

When we began moving out of the range of the firing, the crowd grew more sullen and began casting dark and angry looks at us. It could only be a matter of time until the civilians felt they were far enough away from the shooting to feel safe enough to attack us themselves.

At the edge of the village, the road turned sharply to the right, and we were suddenly in a large wooded area. As the column continued on up the road, our lead man quietly slipped from the column into the thick trees and bushes. He called out to each of us as we passed by. A big, rotund German man stepped out of the column, cursing and shaking his fist at us. It was to the point that I thought we'd have a real problem with some of the civilian men.

But cooler heads prevailed, and he was frantically jerked back into the line by several women who were anxious to keep moving. He finally rejoined his friends but kept looking back menacingly and cursing loudly as he retreated. Once again we'd avoided another hassle that could have become quite ugly and also would have attracted the soldiers. And we surely didn't need that. By this time, we were around the bend in the road and out of sight of the advancing troops.

"Now what?" someone asked.

After taking a quick check to see that everyone was present, the decision was made to go deeper into the thick woods and then decide our next move. We knew we had to swiftly put distance between us, the hostile civilians and the advancing German soldiers. The woods were so thick that we almost lost each other in the underbrush. But we planned to move deeper into the woods for a mile or so in case the Germans decided to continue looking for us. Everybody knew that and kept moving.

Thank God for the forest, I thought. It'll give us a chance to slip out of sight of any patrols that may have been sent out. But what now? Our situation had been growing more dangerous and more desperate as the days continued. Having lost our one good chance of making it safely to American lines, we now found ourselves complete outcasts, subject to rough treatment or even death from both the Germans and the Russians. The red armbands surely helped when meeting any Russians but would be sudden death if we were confronted by a German soldier before we had time to rip off and hide that piece of red cloth.

We had gone less than a quarter of a mile from the edge of the woods when I suddenly realized that I was staring down the muzzle of a large machine gun. I soon saw the reason it appeared to be so large. It was mounted on two big iron wheels about three feet in diameter so it could be pulled by men and spun around into firing position in a matter of seconds. I looked to the right, then to the left. Every tree seemed to have a Russian behind it; each Russian was pointing his rifle at us.

It was such a sudden encounter that we were frozen, stone-like. The only man among us who spoke any semblance of Russian moved forward quickly, talking loud and fast. He jabbered in Russian, all the while pointing to the red armband he was wearing and indicating that all of us, sweeping his arms toward us, were also wearing the red armband.

For what seemed like an eternity, not one of us moved. The Russians stood staring at us without any indication of comprehension. Finally, a soldier standing at the rear of the big machine gun turned and ran back into the woods. I was terrified standing there, not making the slightest movement and having to stare into that big weapon and about 20 or so rifles that were pointing in our direction.

Abruptly, three officers appeared from where the Russian had run into the dense woods. After listening to our man who had been born in Poland speak furiously and nonstop while pointing to his left arm and the red armband, one of the officers shouted a command. The rifles slowly lowered. Our man, our ticket out of the woods, never knew if his brand of Russian was of the right dialect until the soldiers started to relax their weapons.

"This is beginning to get old," someone in the rear ranks said, murmuring quietly but loudly enough for us to hear. "We belong to neither side, and everyone keeps sticking a gun in our face. How long can our luck hold out before one of these confrontations ends in our slaughter?"

Those were my sentiments exactly, but I didn't think this was the time to be voicing them. It was difficult to estimate the size of the

Russian force because of the thick foliage, but it seemed to be a relatively small group, maybe 30 men. I never knew the makeup of any of the Russian army components. They had been fighting for many days, and their ranks were thinned out as a result of casualties. It wasn't a well-defined unit. It consisted of several different uniforms and partial uniforms, probably containing some repatriated from local prison camps.

"Shut up," somebody else said, muttering my thoughts. "We don't need negative thoughts in this situation."

I heard more grumbling as the men began to relax and regain normal breathing. The officers were pleased with our report of the Germans being in the village. Supposedly, these Russians had been chasing the same German troops for several days, but they would never stay in a place for any prolonged period of time—always pulling back and moving on. Maybe this time the Russians had them cornered and immediately prepared for battle.

This might prove to be interesting, I thought. At least we'll be behind the lines for a change instead of always in the middle.

The woods came to life with the roar of trucks. Every truck was an American Studebaker, towing American 105 howitzers and with rocket launchers mounted over the cab. I had never seen a rocket launcher before. It was something new, an entirely new weapon added to the arsenal since I left combat back in November.

As the heavy stuff moved out toward the village, the infantry fell in behind. We decided to witness this skirmish and fell in behind the last of the infantry. The Russians positioned the four trucks carrying the rocket launchers about 75 yards apart on the very fringe of the woods but out of view of the German soldiers. I could see them walking around sort of nonchalantly or lounging in the doorways of houses and other buildings. Apparently they figured they had cleaned the town of all resistance and were savoring their victory. From what I could determine, they had failed to set up any observation posts or to send out any patrols—things that normal combat units do for security.

But I soon turned my attention and became engrossed in the procedures of loading, aiming and arming those rockets. They had to have been about 3 feet long and were shoved into the long tubes. Wires were attached to each rocket, then to some sort of electrical firing system. The order to fire was soon given and, "whoosh," they were off. The launchers were quickly reloaded and another salvo fired. Some of the rockets were incendiary, and several of the houses immediately caught fire and burned furiously. Other rockets were high-explosive anti-personnel rockets, spewing steel shrapnel in all directions. Several more rounds were fired. But after the initial impact, smoke obscured the entire area.

The gentle "whoosh" of the rockets gave little warning to the German soldiers. They were caught completely off guard. The first salvo wiped out every visible soldier who was not under some kind of cover. The enemy didn't get that few seconds of warning as was the case with artillery fire where the initial detonation of the firing mechanism sends you scurrying for cover. No advance warning preceded the rockets.

Even above the din of the exploding rockets, I could hear the screams and shouts of the Germans. Those who survived the first shower of lead shouted orders and quickly took up defensive positions or scurried out of town. Before the last of the rockets were fired, the Russian infantry was already rushing into the village. The fighting lasted about two hours. We all sat back and watched the whole operation from a safe haven in the woods. It was even relaxing in that we felt safe from the prospects of recapture by the German forces. Supposedly we were with our allies, too.

Some of the Russian infantry soon returned with a few German prisoners. The rest had been killed or had fled into the fields at the other end of Rosenthal. The town was now deserted and burning fiercely from rocket fire. What was not already on fire when the Russians entered was quickly set ablaze by the soldiers before they returned to the woods.

We retreated into the woods along with the trucks and the soldiers.

All we hoped for now was something to eat and maybe a good night's sleep without the interruptions we had been getting the past four or five nights in Rosenthal. It wasn't long before I spotted a field kitchen set up in a small clearing. Stepping up our pace, we all headed for it and got a bowl of soup. It was hot and nourishing and not half bad. I could almost feel my strength returning and sat leaning against a big pine tree, really relaxed for the first time in many, many days.

The soldiers were friendly and crowded around us as we enjoyed the soup. Our lone interpreter was kept busy trying to answer their questions and getting answers to our questions. It was a rather comical scene with arms waving, several Russians talking at once, all crowding around the interpreter who was trying to sort out different dialects in order to give them some satisfaction.

We learned of their customary strategy when approaching these small villages. They would surround the town with artillery pieces and rocket launchers. Then they would send a lone, unarmed soldier into the center of town, carrying a white flag. If he wasn't shot on sight and someone confirmed the presence of German soldiers, the Russian would tell them to lay down their arms and surrender. If they did, he would lead them out of town.

The Russians would allow him just so much time for the Germans to decide to surrender. If they refused and the lone soldier didn't return, the Russians promptly burned the town down around them, civilians and all. Most of the towns surrendered, according to those who had volunteered on occasion to carry the white flag. We wondered—but didn't ask—how they got the volunteer to "volunteer."

After a time, we joined the main force gathered in a large clearing, deeper into the forest. These men were definitely well-disciplined, regular army troops. They all wore complete uniforms, and their weapons and other gear were clean and well cared for. For the first time, I felt safe and relaxed around these Allies.

The troops seemed appreciative for all the weapons that the United States had supplied. Every heavy weaponry that I saw was American, although the smaller arms were mostly Russian with an occasional confiscated German rifle or sidearm thrown in. The one big machine gun was an American 50-caliber mounted on an old wagon axle for easy transport.

A large fire was burning, and we all settled back in sheer exhaustion. As darkness settled in, we could see the glow of the fires in Rosenthal on the horizon south of us. My fate—our fate—would have been sealed by now had we stayed there. Our luck was still holding, but the future still looked a bit gloomy unless we reached the American lines soon. The Russians wouldn't let us move with them. They kept insisting that we head east, further behind their lines, for safety. Their headquarters groups, they said, would take care of us and see that we were transferred back to the American Army.

But since the war was still raging all around us, we didn't see how we were going to know exactly where the Russian rear was located. No definite front line seemed to exist. We later learned that the Germans were on three sides of us during most of our stay in Rosenthal.

With darkness setting in early in the heavy forest, we were ready to settle in for some rest and, we hoped, some sleep. Tomorrow would be time enough to decide where to go from here. That sleep, however, was not to be had for quite sometime yet. Guitars, mandolins, accordions and a varied assortment of other odd, stringed instruments were brought out by the Russians for an evening of entertainment.

The music started almost immediately, and it was surprisingly good music. It had a good, fast tempo. Then the vodka started being passed around. Soon the night air was filled with robust singing and shouting as the vodka began to take effect. It became difficult to distinguish between what was supposed to be singing and what sounded like shouting. After a while, it all began to sound the same.

And it didn't take long for them to get really wound up. That's when the dancing started. When a particularly fast tempo was played, they would shriek, jump into the air with arms folded across their chests and settle into that half-sitting, crouched position that was considered their national dance. They raced around the fire in that cramped position, kicking out their legs and singing as they went. I could never understand how they kept their balance and didn't pitch backward into the fire. Nearly all took their turn gyrating around and around with never a collision.

During the whole show, the vodka kept making the rounds. After my first swig, I would just put the bottle to my lips and fake it. My stomach was in no shape to handle that fire water. That one big swallow was enough to put me into a feeling of paradise, blotting out some of the shenanigans going on in front of me.

Just then, one of our men started singing "Dark Eyes" in English in a clear, melodious voice. The vodka could conceivably have helped improve his vocal chords; he surely could sing. The musicians instantly picked up on the song, and every Russian in the circle was grinning like a Cheshire cat. I remembered the song as being popular back in the States, but I didn't realize that it was a popular Russian folk song.

The fact that we were singing one of their native songs put us in a most favorable light for the rest of the night. That meant, of course, that the vodka flowed even more freely. The show must have lasted past midnight, but with the vodka and the excitement of the day, I didn't last that long. Despite the noise, I was soon floating in dreamland.

Before daylight the next morning, I was aroused by the rustling of men moving and the sound of motors on the big Studebaker trucks. We lined up for a cup of scalding, weak tea and a slice of black bread with some kind of greasy topping of a tasteless nature. We ate it without hesitation, not knowing where our next meal would come from.

An officer warned us against trying to make it to the Elbe on our own. He suggested, instead, that we return to Hoyerswerda, explaining that it was a headquarters town where we would have a better chance of being repatriated back to the Americans than trying to make it on our own. With a wave of his hand, he bade us farewell, and the entire Russian force moved out to hunt for more Germans, leaving us to decide our next move. Our decision was unanimous to head east for Hoyerswerda.

Skirting the still-smoldering ruins of Rosenthal, we hiked cross country for a few hours and came to a highway. We decided to walk down the center of it and be visible. Surprising troops in the middle of a forest was a dangerous pastime. We thought we should have a better chance just nonchalantly walking along in a non-military fashion.

We passed many graves scattered along this roadway. Some had a crude cross made from splintered boards or tree limbs but always with a small piece of red cloth visible on Russian graves. Those unmarked mounds of earth, we surmised, contained German dead. The Russians just buried their comrades where they fell, disregarding local cemeteries. These graves were grim reminders of the running gun battles being played out all over this part of Germany.

The first night, we sacked out in an abandoned farmhouse. We made a long, but fruitless search for food. Finding none, we finally lay down on the cold, hard wooden floor and quickly fell asleep from sheer exhaustion. It had been a long, tiresome day with only a cup of tea and a slice of bread. It was another cold night, sleeping in our clothes without blankets, which had been left behind in Rosenthal. The house had been gutted by advancing Russians. It had no windows or doors; however, the night was slightly warmer than the previous night, spent on the ground, lying around a fire that died out during the night and left us shivering by morning.

Arriving in Hoyerswerda the next afternoon, the first thing that caught my attention was the group of dirty, disheveled German soldiers, still in uniform, guarded by Russian soldiers. The Germans were at work clearing the streets of rubble from the many bombed-out buildings. The town was a shambles, and I found it difficult to picture the town as it was when I spent so much time working in it.

No one seemed to pay us much heed as we walked to the center of town looking for the headquarters that was supposed to be here. We approached the building that had been the city headquarters. It was now draped in red banners and had large pictures of Stalin and two or three Russian generals prominently displayed. These pictures must have been 20-feet square. They were hung from the second-story window sills.

As we neared the front of the building, we were stopped by a uniformed guard. We attempted with little success to explain that we were Americans and were seeking the headquarters commander for help in getting to the American lines along the Elbe River. Finally, he disappeared inside and another Russian greeted us. This time it was a large, buxom, blonde Russian woman. She was dressed in full uniform and made quite an imposing figure. But she also spoke few words of English. She led us down the main street for about four blocks to a large house that was to be our sleeping quarters until they decided what to do with us. She also gave us a paper that would admit us to the mess hall, two blocks back up the street. As soon as she was out of sight, we headed for the mess hall.

The two guards at the mess hall looked at us suspiciously for several seconds. One of them read and reread our pass, counted us at least three times and finally allowed us to pass into the mess hall. It was the usual fare during our time with the Russians: soup and bread. Both were tasty but not nearly enough to satisfy our hunger. With no food for the past two days of travel and no seconds, we went away hungry after hastily eating.

Our quarters were in a big two-story house with all the windows intact. And we each had a bed with a mattress after scrounging in abandoned houses to secure the mattresses. Hoyerswerda was practically deserted, so no one bothered us as we carried the feather ticks, one by one, into our quarters. It was the first *real* bed and mattress since October in Holland when I was invited to spend the night with the Dutch family in Breda.

Breakfast the next morning was the usual chunk of black bread and bitter tea. The German coffee in Runddorf tasted better. We spent the days roaming around Hoyerswerda, visiting the places where we had worked. No one paid a bit of attention to us, and we found no inhabitants we had worked for or with. The only activity was the multitude of German POWs cleaning up the rubble, and a continuous string of trucks and artillery pieces heading for the front.

The days had slipped by without us having any knowledge regarding the progress of the war. As far as we knew, it was still raging between Hoyerswerda and the Elbe. And we were unable to obtain any information on the conduct of the war or what the Russians intended to do with our group. Again, we were in limbo with no assurances that we would ever be repatriated to American lines. We certainly weren't regaining any of our strength on the meager rations from the mess hall. We still got only one meal a day, and there was no way to supplement this diet. The food pantries were bare; the only food available to all inhabitants left in town was at the Russian-controlled mess hall.

Our sole source of information was, once again, rumors, none of which could be confirmed. On our sixth day in town, we talked to a truck driver who indicated we should go to a town called Zagan, in Poland. This was the site of a large POW camp where the Russians were gathering up people of all nationalities and shipping them to their native countries. He said he had made several trips to Zagan and noticed long lines of people at the gate to the camp. Skeptical, we listened intently to his story.

Again, decisions had to be made. Some of us wanted to stay put while others were bored and tired of the monotony. Finally, about ten of the men decided to try for Zagan, even though the driver estimated it to be about 100 miles to the northeast. Just farther away from American lines, I thought. So I elected to stay with the remaining 20-some men for the time being. During the night, we quietly stole enough bicycles to outfit those leaving. Then before daylight, with feather ticks tied on the rear of the bikes, those ten men slipped out of town, heading in the direction of Zagan.

Of the 36 original POWs with me in Runddorf, one had escaped and three had become ill and left the Stalag, *leaving us with 32 when we finally left. I never saw any of those men again until some 40 years later at our first Runddorf Reunion in the States. The men all had made it home.*

Nobody said anything about the missing men, but the situation in Hoyerswerda was rapidly deteriorating. The food was inadequate, and the Russians were becoming more hostile toward us. I could sense a sudden change in their attitude, and that scared me. I had never had much use for the Russians, anyway. Now I was becoming more fearful of their intentions every day. Their excuse was always the same: Nothing could be done for us until the war ended. Then we would be sent to American control.

16

I spent a restless night mulling over my next move. I felt I had to try to get closer to the Elbe River in order to have any chance at all of regaining my Freedom. My fate was at a standstill here. Rumors that we'd heard before were again rampant about the Russians sending all prisoners to Siberia. More and more trucks loaded with civilians were passing through Hoyerswerda, heading eastward. I decided to leave town the next morning.

Only Roy, who always seemed willing to tag along and often looked to me for guidance, decided to go with me. The two of us slipped out of town before dawn. I had noticed that all roads in and out of town now had guard posts set up with armed guards patrolling the outskirts of town. We managed to slip by the outpost without arousing the posted guard. I must have crawled on my belly for at least 75 yards. Then I saw that it wasn't necessary because the guard was snoring loudly. We stood up and walked the final 50 yards until we were out of sight.

The two of us stayed on the road for three days. At the end of the third day, we were becoming so weak with hunger that I was beginning to hallucinate. Moreover, I was staggering like a drunken idiot, babbling incoherently at times to my partner. We had to have some food soon or we would be unable to continue. It had been three full days now without a bite to eat.

For the past two nights, we had been sleeping in abandoned barns. But at a farmhouse sitting several yards back off of the road, hunger drove us to throw caution to the winds. Darkness was falling rapidly but not fast enough for us. We couldn't wait and boldly walked up to the front door and knocked. No answer. So we immediately opened the door and stepped inside. The inside of the house was in shambles, a sure sign the Russians had preceded us.

No food was to be had in the house, so we headed out back to look for a garden. All farmhouses had gardens, and the Germans would cover potatoes and rutabagas with straw and mound the dirt over to use as winter storage for these crops. We fell to our knees and began frantically pawing through some small earthen mounds, hoping for a potato or two. But the Russian soldiers were good scavengers. The mounds had been cleared of all potatoes. We then headed for the barn. There we hit the jackpot: A nest with two eggs of doubtful freshness and several small potatoes were scattered about in one corner of the barn. We had no matches and dared not build a fire for security reasons, anyway. Too many stray Ruskies around.

I never thought I could eat an egg raw, but that night I didn't hesitate to gulp it down with a little water from the pump as a chaser. We had netted about 10 small potatoes, which we ate raw, wrinkled peelings and all. Snuggling into a small stack of hay then, we slept through the night without incident. No flashlight in my face, no gun in my gut.

We hit the road again early next morning, still following a main road I assumed was the right direction to get us to the Elbe River. About noon, though, we entered a rather large town, called Spremberg, north and east of Hoyerswerda. Walking into town, as always, we started looking for food. We were on a main street near some large bombed-out factory buildings when a column of Studebaker trucks came roaring down the street and stopped in front of the only building still standing. People began pouring out of the front door, and the Russian soldiers forced them into the trucks. As we approached the thong of people pouring out of the building, I tried to slip into the middle to keep away from two nasty Russian soldiers. But they would have none of it.

Standing out away from the buildings, we had little chance of seeking cover before the convoy came speeding by us. We tried to move away, but it was too late. Two soldiers started our way, guns at the ready and shouting commands. We stood our ground as they approached, but there was no misunderstanding their intentions. One soldier took Roy and the other one shoved his rifle into my gut and forced me to the edge of the crowd and pinned me against the side of the truck. He held his rifle against my chest, holding me against the truck until all the trucks were loaded. Then he slapped me across the back with his rifle and roughly shoved me toward the last truck. I managed to get an end seat in hopes I'd have a chance to escape. But my efforts were thwarted by a big fat Russian who squeezed me away from the tailgate. I bounced around in that truck the rest of the afternoon and far into the night.

My decision to sit at the rear of the truck proved to be a big mistake. Later in the evening, a spring downpour drenched those of us at the back. Although the truck was covered with a canvas canopy, the rain blew and poured into the rear of the truck bed. To add to my misery, that big fat Russian moved toward the front and forced me to the very edge of the seat. I had no possible means to ward off the rain. The cold wind and the splashing from the mudholes completely engulfed me. I was soon covered from head to toe with a layer of mud. Of all the miserable nights I'd spent during my Army career, this, by far, was the most miserable.

I had been separated from Roy during the loading process, so all I could do was sit huddled alone in my misery. The trucks stopped sometime during the night, but we were forced to stay in the truck until morning. The rain continued. By now, it made little difference. I would have continued to be cold and wet, regardless.

At first light, we were ordered out of the trucks, given instructions to go several blocks, turn right and proceed to a barbed-wire enclosure several blocks down the street. The big sign said, "Zagan," the place the truck driver had told us about and the other men had started toward on bicycles. I was apparently at *Stalag* VIII C, a large German POW camp in Poland. I got out of the truck and joined a good-sized group of people who walked to the compound before milling around in front of the prison gate. My buddy finally showed up, and we were ordered into a long single file line that stretched out for several yards down the street.

We stood in that line all day long with little movement forward. I'd had no food for two days now. Our last meal was at the abandoned farmhouse and barn. Why the line? I wondered. I didn't have the faintest idea. But I talked to a couple of British Tommies and learned that the camp was a collection station.

Trucks continued to arrive throughout the day. They were crammed full of men, women and children of every nationality imaginable. This was the slave labor the Germans had brought into the Fatherland from all the countries invaded by Hitler. The people were a sorry-looking lot, much like my buddy and me. My own physical appearance must have been worse. I seemed to attract many stares from the new arrivals. Some carried a small satchel containing their belongings. They didn't have much. Many, like us, carried only the clothes on their backs.

The gate was slammed shut before dark, and the line began to disintegrate in all directions with everyone looking for a place to sleep. We were told that the gate would reopen at 0900 hours the next morning. I found a bare spot on the floor of a big house a block from the gate and squeezed in between a couple of men whose ancestry I had no idea but were just as filthy and stinking as I was. With a few grunts, they moved just enough for me to find the floor. Apparently they were too tired to argue with me. Roy was sacked out somewhere in the crowded room.

The house was packed with men, women and squalling kids. I felt for the little kids because I knew they had to be hungry. Some of them already showed signs of malnutrition. Those sad, pleading eyes were enough to tear my heart out. I realized the Russians were overwhelmed by all these refugees, but there still seemed to be a total lack of sensitivity to the basic needs of these people.

After another restless, uneasy night on a hard floor, I was up at dawn and heading for that big gate. I arrived there at the crack of dawn, only to find the line was already more than a block long. Some must have stood in line all night. By noon, I had moved about 50 feet and decided this was no place for me. Leaving Roy still standing in line, I left and headed back to the center of town, hoping to be able to get into the mess hall. But I wasn't allowed in because I had no official pass. I was trying to figure out if I was better off in town or out in the countryside. I had no idea where Roy was now. I guess I completely forgot about him in my confused state of mind. Hunger was again numbing my thinking and causing hallucinations. So I headed off, west.

I had to find some kind of food before long or I knew I could not survive. I believe my strong will to live reached its lowest point about this time. Trying to assess my position, I knew also that I could ill-afford to make any mistakes if I were to have any chance at all. But I started walking, or staggering, as fast as I could.

Just about noon, I happened upon a small garden patch out near a small roadside shed. I really hit it big. Two large rutabagas lay in the bottom of a basket. They had probably been dug up by a previous occupant who had to leave in a hurry and left them behind. I rubbed the dirt off as best as I could and started gnawing away—I had no way to cut them up. I ate them both, eating the tops right along with the bulbs. Almost overdoing it this time, I soon had terrible cramps and had to stretch out to keep from vomiting.

I must have been dozing off for about an hour when I suddenly woke up to the roar of tank motors. The little shack I was in was just a few feet away from the roadway, and I thought the tanks were going to ram it down. The Russian tankers liked to play games, running over and knocking down everything in their path just for the hell of it. I stuck my head out of the window just as the last of the four tanks roared by. The last tanker stopped his tank so abruptly he nearly stood his tank on its nose.

The turret opened and a rather gigantic figure popped up, grinning like an ear of corn. He motioned for me to come out and hop on board. Fearful of being shot for noncompliance, I quickly obeyed and jumped on top to come face to face with the grinner. I was staring into the face of a woman. She barked a command, dropped down into the hull and roared off to catch up to the other three tanks.

What a wild ride! We careened down the road, hitting potholes at full throttle ahead. I grabbed a couple of iron rings and hung on for the most thrilling ride of my life. Those thrill-park roller coasters paled in comparison to the ride I was getting.

After catching up to the group, we just sort of meandered along aimlessly down the narrow road. I was trying to catch my breath and shift my body around to ease the pain from the pounding I'd been taking from bouncing around on that steel hull when I heard the eerie ear-shattering screech of a shell headed my way. I'd heard of these multi-barreled mortars dubbed the "Screaming Mimi," but I had never been under their fire before. It didn't take me long to figure out where they got their name. The round just seemed to float forever before it hit. I knew it was coming awfully close but had no idea just how close until it hit the tank on the other side of the turret.

That thud was the last thing I remembered until I woke up in the weeds along side of the road. The mortar shell was the anti-personnel type and apparently did little damage to the tank itself. I doubt that the tank even slowed down and was long-gone when I regained consciousness. The tankers probably weren't aware of any Germans in the whole area and didn't bother with them. They couldn't be more than a small pocket of diehards, holed up in the woods along the road.

I had a pounding headache and was bleeding profusely from a big gash in my forehead, but I dared not move for fear of the Germans in the woods just down the road. I tied a rag that substituted for a handkerchief around my head to stanch the blood flow. Damn, I thought, this is all I need at this point. I've staved off starvation for a few more days; now I'm going to bleed to death.

If the Germans were well dug-in and deeper in the forest, I knew they probably didn't see the hit on the tank, let alone see me flying through the air. At least that thought tended to soothe my nerves for a minute. Then I heard voices. And again a miracle. Instead of German voices, I thrilled at the sound of a British accent. Two Limeys were walking along in the opposite direction that I had been traveling. I shouted as best I could, and they came running to my aid.

If I had called them both Limeys to their faces, they might have slit my throat. One of them turned out to be from the famous 51st Scottish Highlanders. Jock McCloud had been a POW for nearly five years. He had been wounded and captured in Dunkerque in 1940. His buddy Joe Plenderleath was a British paratrooper from the 15/17th Royal Hussars who had jumped at Bone in North Africa. He had been in a prison camp since 1942.

The Highlander, also a medic, had a partial German first-aid kit and a small bit of tape he had taken from a fallen German trooper. The two men soon patched me up. They were anxious to be on their way, and I agreed to tag along. My physical condition scared me, and I was tired of traveling alone. They were seasoned veterans. That gave me a feeling of confidence and security. Nothing like having my own personal medic, either, I thought. What luck!

While we were still sitting in the ditch, I was filled in with news about the war. They felt it was winding down fast and could be over soon. Why then were they headed east instead of west? I wondered. They had been told, just as I had, that the quickest way to safety and Freedom was to get to Odessa on the Black Sea, catch an Allied freighter, ship out through the Dardenelles and be dropped off at an Allied port on the way. After learning how far it was to the Black Sea, I had ruled out that option.

These two had tried making it to the British sector in northern Germany but were turned back because of the severe fighting still in progress along the upper reaches of the Elbe River. Like me, they had had to sweat-out several encounters with both Russian and German forces and were wanting to get clear away from the fighting zone. A lot of hard-core German SS troops were still fighting and would prolong the war, maybe for weeks or even months.

My own instinct was to get as close as possible to American lines in anticipation of the end of hostilities. This war simply cannot go on much longer, I thought. But I had had those same thoughts 20 days before and still.

As soon as I felt strong enough, we three headed back down the road I had just traveled. I had difficulty keeping up with my new companions, and we were obliged to stop frequently. I knew this was annoying to both of them, but they kept their cool and continued to stay with me. By nightfall, we were in Spremberg—back where I had started from that morning. I warned the men about the growing hostility of the Russian soldiers, so we decided to spend the night in a deserted farmhouse beyond the outskirts of town.

While Jock, Joe and I were roaming about in another abandoned farmhouse later, we found an ornate metal strongbox under a bunch of clutter. The Russians, who had undoubtedly been there before us, had overlooked our find. It looked mighty inviting.

"Looks like it might have the Crown Jewels themselves in it," Joe said as we admired the box.

"Even if it does," I said, knowing that I didn't have the strength to help carry the strongbox, "it's too heavy to pack with us. So we either leave it or bust it open somehow."

"Let's forage around in those outbuildings," Jock said. "Surely there'll be a tool to do the job around here some place."

We scurried around back of the house and began searching through the buildings. Shortly, Jock let our a squeal and came running out of a shed with a long-handled steel mallet held high above his head. He flailed away at the locked box with eager abandon.

"What a bloody tough son of an ass," Jock said, blurting out the word the British seemed to use several times in every sentence they uttered. "Must be a bloody fortune in this bloody box."

With the last blow, he smashed through the lid, and we saw a piece of soft red velvet cloth. We lifted the cloth from the box, set it down on the floor and circled ourselves around it. Jock slowly unfolded the cloth to reveal several pieces of shiny jewelry. In this war-torn place, it was enough to take your breath away.

"Look at those bloody diamonds sparkle," Jock said, his breath exhaling sharply as we looked at our booty in disbelief.

"We've got ourselves a gold mine here, mates," Joe said.

"We'll have to figure how to get the diamonds out," I said nervously. "The rings and bracelets are most likely gold and silver, but the diamonds will be easiest to conceal."

We chipped away at the diamonds, prying them loose from their settings, using small pliers we'd found in one of the buildings and some small thin metal pieces to lift the prongs holding the diamonds. Each of us took an equal number. Added to the four I had taken out of rings that came reluctantly from the fingers of four German women I had met, I now had 11 diamonds.

This looting wasn't something I was particularly proud of, but I was determined to take something of value from the German people for making my life so damn miserable this past stinking winter. Foxhole mentality? Perhaps. But I had long since reached the depths of dishonesty in my struggle to survive. What was one more rung down the ladder? To hide the diamonds, I managed to make very small holes down the front edge of my blue coat, then stuffed each diamond in a separate hole.

The next several days were virtually a blank. We mostly walked in silence, I guess to help conserve our strength. During those frequent stops to let me rest, we engaged in small talk. Mostly we discussed home and family. Since none of us was married, the talk frequently turned to girlfriends of our past. On one occasion, extreme anger and bitterness crept into our conversation. Jock was usually reserved, but this time the pent-up anger broke through.

"We should steal some automatic weapons and kill every German woman in sight," he said. "How many times are we going to have to fight these bloody German bastards? My father fought them in World War I, and here I am spending five years of my life fighting them again."

I was somewhat surprised at this outburst but quickly agreed with Jock's suggestion. So did Joe. My dad also served in the Army during World War I, and here I was doing the same thing in World War II. We didn't attempt to follow through on Jock's suggestion, but just the thought of it relieved some of the frustration from his mind. It's funny how twisted a man's mind gets in such circumstances of war.

Throughout these days, we continued to have confrontations with Russian stragglers who berated us and even fired on us during some of these incidents. Somehow we always escaped with our lives. The British men had mastered the German language, but it was of little use in Poland. I still wore my red armband, which I'm sure saved our skin more than once. And my mastery of the two most important words in the Russian language helped, too.

But those days were a blurring, surreal experience. We went deep into Poland, skirting all but the smallest villages and continuously searching for food. I just had to blot out the horrible scenes of death, rape, starvation and destruction that I witnessed during our many days behind the lines, scenes too horrible and terrifying to describe. One of those gruesome scenes occurred as we passed near one of the concentration camps. I didn't remember, exactly, the name of it, just that it was located somewhere in Poland. I cared less about names and places; I had to keep walking and keep living.

The vivid picture that kept playing back in my mind was one of human skeletons, still alive, peering through the barbed wire. Every person, including the few women in the group, was completely bald. What first caught my eye was the clothing they wore. All of the people had on blue-and-white-striped trousers and long overcoats. The stripes ran vertically up and down their bodies. I cringed at the sight, remembering the pile of striped coats and trousers back at Limburg when our uniforms were confiscated. Back then, I had shied away from even touching those items, choosing instead a plain blue overcoat. The clothing with the stripes was the uniform worn in the concentration camps, I saw now. Behind the mass of humanity stood a long row of peaked-roof buildings. I assumed these were their living quarters.

It wasn't until months later that I learned that these buildings contained the ovens in which the prisoners were cremated. In retrospect, I'm pretty sure the camp we passed must have been Treblinka. At that time, no one in the outside world knew of these terrible concentration camps. I was about as close to starvation as many in the camp. I felt, however, that eventually I would survive my ordeal. I had faith in that. But for those people in the concentration camp I saw, there was no hope.

Two days later as we were walking through a small town, we happened upon a small group of British and Canadian soldiers who were resting near a deserted house. They had a small bit of food which they shared with the three of us. I was puzzled at their exuberant mood. Most of them had been in various prison camps for several years.

"Haven't you heard the news?" they fairly shouted at us when they saw the lack of exuberance in us. "The war's over! We're going home!"

With that, we all embraced, jumped up and down and had a big celebration on the spot. We sat around in a circle, discussing the future. No one even talked of prison life. The conversations were all about home, family and all the wonderful things we would do when we got home. Three or four of the British Tommies were married and had children they hadn't seen, some for four years or more. The rest of us, including me, were single. We talked fast and long for quite a while, then decided we'd better get started. We were all several hundred miles from actual Freedom with our own forces. And it was many miles more to home.

Reinforced with the wonderful news and a bit of food, I turned around, and with a sprightly step, headed west for Freedom and home. About nine of us all together started out. I was the only Yank. We managed to hitch a couple of short rides on some Russian trucks loaded with supplies for the front. But most of the time, we plodded along, resting frequently and sleeping in abandoned houses or barns.

Some of the time, we had been traveling along railroad tracks in hopes of hopping a freight train headed our way. Staying along the tracks also kept us from running into many Russians who stayed on the main highways and in the larger towns. If the rails ran through the town, we would stop at the edge, go around the town, then pick up the rail on the other side. The railroad was a more direct route west, too.

Grabbing a fast train as it whizzed by didn't pan out. But somebody came up with the idea of waiting until dark, then hanging around the edge of a freight yard to see if we could catch a ride on a train before it pulled out of the yard. That strategy worked. On the first night we spent in a freight yard, we separated and each man picked his own special car. I ended up on an open flat car that was loaded with an artillery cannon and an assortment of machinery. I crawled into a round tube that was part of one of the pieces. Although I was rather cramped in this big thing, I managed to sleep quite soundly despite the rumble and jostle of the train. The steel was cold and hard, but I had no other choice at this point. I fell asleep dreaming of my nice warm, soft bed back in Illinois.

Nothing had changed much for me, even though the war had ended, I found out before the night ended. I was suddenly awakened to shouting and felt myself being jerked out of my hiding place and staring at five or six guns, all pointed in my direction. One soldier was jabbing me in the gut with his rifle. His buddy held a bayonet within inches of my throat.

My mind was reeling. God, I thought, am I going to get this close to Freedom and then have my throat slit by another stupid Russian? Again, I was face to face with certain death. I kept taking in long, deep breaths, hoping they wouldn't be my last. After what seemed like an eternity, the one with the bayonet at my throat pointed to my tattered red armband. He fired some more questions at me and, finally, slowly, pulled the bayonet away from my neck. I was barely able to utter, "*Amerikanski,*" which seemed to sink in. The rifles were slightly lowered, and I was ordered to my feet.

Without any further ceremony or intimidation, I was hustled out of the freight yard toward an imposing-looking building, which was draped in red and had the usual pictures of Stalin and some other character I failed to recognize. There I was led into a small, empty room and told to sit on the floor. I was hoping to see some of my

British comrades, but I appeared to be the only one in the building.

After about an hour, I was ushered into another room to appear before a Russian officer, seated behind a desk so huge that he had to almost shout for me to hear. Well, it was almost that huge. He spoke fluent English—only the second time I'd heard English from any of the hundreds of Russian soldiers I had been around. The interrogation was mild, compared to the many previous encounters. I almost relaxed.

I did have to endure some 20 minutes or so of listening to him tell about the glorious fighting capabilities of the soldiers of the great Union of Soviet Socialist Republics, the USSR. He told me how this great army had annihilated the forces of the Third Reich and captured this city, the greatest prize of all: Berlin.

"You did not know you were in the great city of Berlin?" he asked, apparently noticing my look of amazement at the mention of Berlin.

"I was asleep when I arrived by train," I said.

"How was your ride? Comfortable?"

"Yes, very comfortable. First class all the way." I cringed, wondering who would allow a "thing" like me into a first-class coach.

He seemed satisfied and asked no embarrassing questions. But I'm sure he was skeptical of my answer after seeing the wretched condition of my clothing and my dirty, matted hair and long beard. I had tried to control my hair by pulling my stocking cap down over my ears, to no avail. My hair hung to my shoulders.

He signed a paper, handed it to his orderly, reached his hand across that big desk and wished me a good journey to America. I could finally begin to see a faint light at the end of the tunnel. Unknown to me at this juncture, however, I still had to face another 10 days of frantic uncertainty before seeing a friendly face again. I was led back to that same bare room to await further orders. Only when the orders came did I learn that I was being sent to another prison camp.

Until the orders came, I sat slumped in a corner, dozing. When the door flew open, I was rudely yanked to my feet and roughly shoved toward the door. Hey, I thought, but didn't say anything. More rough treatment from our Russian Allies. I was ushered out the front door and into a waiting truck already crammed full of people. But there still were no signs of the British. This truck was full of civilians, mostly women, who seemed to move as far away from me as possible. I apparently had lost my sex appeal. This crushed my ego. Oh, well, I thought, a good haircut, a shave, a shower and a new uniform and I would undoubtedly regain my lost powers.

Stupid dreams, I knew, but anything to boost my morale helped.

17

Berlin—a typical destroyed city, a sight I had witnessed every day. Rubble filled the streets; fires still burned and smoldered all around. The streets had been partially cleared in spots; otherwise, the truck just rumbled up and over the debris, tossing us around in the back like ping-pong balls. Fortunately, we were packed so tightly that our movement was minimal, and we just sort of clung to each other. The stench in the air was overpowering at times. Many bodies were still lying in the streets and yards of houses. I guessed that the Russians were still mopping up numerous pockets of die-hard resisters around the city. I witnessed a great number of tanks buzzing around, anyway. I also heard small-arms fire several times during my trip out of Berlin. Sporadic fighting had continued in Berlin for days after the official end of the war.

The truck headed out of Berlin in a southerly direction instead of west. Rumors flew that we were being sent to a collection point. Collection point for what? I wondered. Home or Siberia? Siberia seemed to be on everybody's mind. With the taking of Berlin, the Russian attitude was no longer conciliatory. I had noticed the sudden change days ago, but only after reaching Berlin did I realize the reason: A new war with the west had started long before the actual end of the fighting in Germany. People from several different countries, gathered up as the Russians advanced toward Berlin in the waning days of the war, were on the truck. And now we had no idea of where we were going or what to expect.

About mid-afternoon we found out. The truck approached yet another large, sprawling barbed-wire enclosure. The sign over the gate read, "*STALAG* III A LUCKENWALDE, GERMANY." Just inside the gate, the truck stopped, and we were ordered to unload. Was I any closer to the Elbe? I wondered. No one could tell me that, and no one seemed to be in charge. So I wondered around until I found some Americans. They did have their own fenced-off compound area. But since the barracks was full, I found that I would have to bed down on straw in a big tent.

Since I found no one I knew, I kept strictly to myself. I talked to no one but kept my eyes and ears open for any information concerning when we would all be repatriated. Rumors abounded. Who knew if there was any truth to them? Anyway, I was so exhausted and weak from hunger, I really didn't have the energy to talk. Mostly I lay around and slept or checked out the compound area in case we all made an attempt to break out and try for American battle lines.

This camp was, as rumored, a collection point for sure. The place was full to overflowing with people of all shapes, sizes and nationalities. Some estimates I later heard were as high as 35-40,000 displaced persons or DPs. At least 2,500 Americans, most of whom had been brought in by truck, were among them. The camp had originally held 6,000 Yanks I learned, but most had fled when the Russians had liberated the camp.

By the time I arrived, the Russians had secured the camp with the guard towers being manned 24 hours a day. The perimeter was patrolled constantly. Those prisoners who didn't leave Luckenwalde as soon as the Russian troops arrived were prevented from doing so. And now I was again back behind that dreaded barbed wire after about 20-some days of Freedom—not complete Freedom, but not behind barbed wire, either.

I didn't know the exact date we left Runddorf or the dates of my stays at any one place. I saw a calendar for the first time in Luckenwalde and noted the date: 20 May 1945. The war had ended on 7 May 1945, I had been told. But for many of us, it was still going on. I had had no food for the past three days and eagerly looked forward to the first evening's meal. It was thin, watery soup and a chunk of black bread. No potatoes. No complaints, though. The soup was hot for a change.

Truck after truck filled with refugees continued to come through the gate all day long and into the night. Life at Luckenwalde took on an air of tense apprehension. The only Russians visible were those manning the machine guns in the guard towers and those on patrol.

Early on the morning of the second day, a loudspeaker blared forth a message from General Dwight D. Eisenhower. The brief message said: "All Allied prisoners of war stay put; we are coming to get you." This message was repeated every morning of my stay in Luckenwalde. Just the sound of General Eisenhower's voice was a great boost to my morale. After hearing this same message repeated for several days, however, I began to wonder if this was just a ruse to keep all Americans placated long enough to ship us all to Siberia.

And every day a few more Americans would wander into our area, straining our rations and sleeping quarters. Every night men from our area and Allied soldiers from other areas attempted to break out. Some may have made it; some were shot on sight. Many more were rounded up by the Russian patrols that seemed to be everywhere and were brought back to camp. Most of those returned would take off again the next night, driven by the thirst for Freedom. Because the place was in such a chaotic condition, I had no way of knowing what was really taking place.

On the third day, several American trucks bearing the 83rd Division logo approached the gate but were refused entry. They were forced to retreat after managing to relay the message that they would be waiting a few miles away. That night a large number of Allied soldiers slipped through the wire to rendezvous with the trucks—security was practically non-existent about midnight because the guards would either be drunk on vodka or had come into the camp to rape the women.

The next morning, the men were back in camp. They had found the trucks, all right, but Russian patrols had stopped them after a few miles, somewhere near the Elbe River. The patrol forced the prisoners out of the trucks and marched them back to camp. The Americans didn't resist, and the trucks returned across the Elbe to American lines, empty.

This same procedure was repeated several times, and each time the American truck drivers put up no resistance. I often wondered why the truck drivers couldn't come up with something to outfox the Russians and try harder to get a load or two of the Americans across the Elbe. I wondered later if the truck drivers were under orders *not* to risk confrontation with the Russian army. And if so, why? I thought we were allies in this damn war. It wasn't my fault that I ended up in Russian-controlled territory at the end of the hostilities. So much for General Eisenhower's message.

General George Patton had wanted to keep on going into Berlin, but our political leaders had nixed the plan. Hence, there I was, just a pawn in the political infighting. I was never able to talk to any of the 83rd Division truck drivers to find out what their orders really were. But I was told that some of those men made the trips at night, disregarding orders, in hopes of rescuing a few POWs. They knew something rotten was going on. I did talk to some Yanks who made two attempts by truck and got turned back. According to all the rumors, the Russians on this side of the Elbe were returning Allied POWs to American hands on a one-for-one exchange: one Russian returnee, one Allied POW, for trade. No Russian returnee, no Allied POW.

And I didn't see any reduction in the number of Americans in my area. In fact, we were gaining a few new arrivals each day. The Russians were scouring the countryside, forcing all DPs and even German Nationals aboard trucks and bringing them to Luckenwalde. At first, I roamed the whole camp looking for anyone I knew from my work camp in Runddorf. Not once did I see a familiar face. I was alone in a sea of humanity without much hope of leaving.

Even though trucks loaded with people continued to arrive, the camp numbers seemed to stabilize. Somehow people were being shipped out to another destination, and I intended to find out how. I had heard an occasional train whistle during the nighttime hours. So somewhere close, there was a rail line. I set out one morning to find out what was going on and headed for the eastern side of the camp.

At the last fenced-in area on the far side of the camp, I was halted by a host of Russian guards patrolling that station. I tried to make conversation with them long enough to try to figure out why the sudden line of guards. I used every German and Russian word I could think of while pointing to what remained of my tattered red armband.

In a matter of seconds, the guards became extremely hostile. One of them shoved his rifle into my stomach so hard that I was sent flying, landing on my butt. He then cocked his rifle, pointed it at my head and shouted something in German that, translated, probably meant for me to get the hell out of there—and fast. With another loaded rifle staring me in the face, I immediately rolled over and crawled away so fast I probably spewed dirt 10 feet behind me.

I learned what I wanted to know, however. The sealed-off place was crammed with German soldiers. Still in uniform, they were a sorry-looking lot, bearded and dirty. A couple of hundred yards beyond the outside fence, I was sure I had spotted two boxcars with the doors open and several figures either already inside or entering the boxcar.

This confirmed to me all the scary rumors floating about. These Germans were undoubtedly being shipped east, toward Russia. Most civilians also were going that direction instead of back to their home countries. Still, the early-morning loudspeaker blared Eisenhower's call to all Allied prisoners to "stay put."

My days in Luckenwalde were spent trying to figure out what to do next and to keep a low profile doing it. The nights were utter chaos, filled with the sound of gunfire, women screaming and a general state of confusion from the sheer numbers of people thrown together in a swirling mass of humanity. The barracks were filled to overflowing, and the Russians had erected huge tents similar to the one I was in to help accommodate the steady influx of people.

The night of the sixth day in camp, I walked the inside perimeter of the camp, looking for the darkest corner closest to the woods from which I could escape. The land was cleared for about 200 yards all around the campsite and was saturated with anti-personnel mines and flares hooked up to trip wires. Although the guard towers were manned, there were instances during the change of guards when the tower would be empty. Other men had gotten out of the camp. I knew I could, too. The trick was staying out.

I was growing increasingly restless. The food was worse than in most of the other camps—certainly not the life-sustaining type of nourishment I needed. I was getting even weaker and was having some difficulty getting to a standing position, let alone walking. But I didn't let that stop me from making plans to leave or investigating things in the camp. Rumors abounded that the Russians were having nightly dances in the main headquarters building for all of the Allied soldiers. Looking for anything to relieve the monotony and anxiety, I decided to see for myself and checked out the rumor with a Texas paratrooper. He had talked to a couple of Dutch women who had just been brought in two days before. We invited them to go dancing with us.

I still wore my ragged clothing and was still unshaven and had long hair. I had managed only to wash my hands, but the dirt and lice were still with me. I had made a feeble attempt to wash my head under a pump once. But water was scarce, and I needed all I could find for drinking. Getting clean was secondary to keeping alive at this point, anyway, and had nothing to do with dancing.

After spending the night with the Russian soldiers outside of Rosenthal, I should have known what to expect in the way of Russian music. As we entered the building, it seemed to be shaking on its foundation from the ear-splitting volume of the music. The room was jammed with Russians, some in uniform, but many in the ragged clothing of prisoners, like myself. Taking one glance at what was taking place, I decided to retreat out the door.

I was too late. A large, buxom Russian woman dressed in a tanker uniform, grabbed me and off we went, whirling into a horde of dancers already on the floor. Now I'd had the pleasure of a short ride on that Polish tank with another big woman a few days earlier. But this episode turned out to be rougher than that or any other physical combat I had ever experienced.

This woman—and I use the term loosely—outweighed me by at least 100 pounds and towered over me by a foot, it seemed. Moreover, she had the strength of a gorilla. I don't know if I could have coped if I'd have been at full strength myself. Her continuous jabbering, in Russian, of course, added to the roar of the band made me think I was in Echo Canyon. And she used me as a battering ram. Literally. We surely bumped every dancer on the entire dance floor. Some of the collisions were so severe and her bear hugs so unrelenting that I began to get light-headed and was hardly able to draw a breath. My knees were wobbly, and I would have fallen to the floor had it not been for those gorilla arms that continued to hold me up while squeezing the life out of me.

Finally the noise stopped. I struggled to slip out of her grasp and immediately headed for the exit. She attempted to follow, but I was so desperate to escape, I managed to ditch her, flew through the doorway and disappeared into the darkness. I never looked back.

I was completely exhausted and didn't even think about my comrades back at the dance. But I knew now that I wasn't going to hang around this camp too long and take the chance of being "waltzed around" again by this or any other buxom lass. I wondered about the fate of those two Dutch girls. The Russian guards were known to take liberties with any females in the camp, following the adage, "To the victors belong the spoils."

This episode definitely motivated me to hatch an escape plan from Luckenwalde to be initiated at the earliest possible opportunity. So much confusion and ineptitude was evident most of the time that I felt I had a good chance of sneaking through. I had been looking for a pair of wire cutters for the past three days. I'd been following a couple of Russian men who seemed to be trying to get the guard-tower searchlight to work. They were less than enthusiastic about their job and left tools, wiring and junk laying around in the bed of the truck they were using. It was really a simple matter to snitch a small pair of pliers and a screwdriver from them. And I did. The pliers I needed to cut through the wire fence; the screwdriver I needed for a weapon.

While it was still daylight, I picked my spot by laying a small stick under the edge of the wire—something I could find in the dark. The Russians were beginning to clamp down with tighter security by locking the gates to the individual compounds at nightfall. Even with this tactic, though, there were still men roaming around after dark. During the day, I had let slip my plan while talking to the paratrooper from Texas. He wanted to go with me, and I agreed.

At about 2200 hours, I slipped under the wire next to my tent, headed for the perimeter and found my stick undisturbed. The paratrooper got there just as I was cutting through the first of two wire fences. The pliers were rather crude. This made the cutting difficult. The main problem, however, was sweating out two possible obstacles at the wire.

First was the electrified wire that was usually run along the ground. I was gambling that the Russians had not restored all the electric power, since only about half the lights around the camp were ever turned on. I wrapped a piece of cloth around the plier grips, hoping that would insulate me in case any wire was hot.

Secondly, the Germans had always hung empty tin cans with a few rocks in the bottom that would rattle when anyone bumped the wire. Sometimes they strung a fine wire along the ground, which when cut would sound an alarm in the guard tower. So I gently cut just under the bottom two wires. That was enough to allow us both to squeeze under.

We had managed the first hurdle. Then came the 200 yards of the mine field. By crawling slowly in single file and gingerly picking our way through the grass, we somehow missed the mines. It was tricky and slow going. I noticed a few holes where some of the mines had been activated, possibly during other aborted escape attempts. By stretching our bodies out full length, we would bring less weight to bear on the mine. It usually took the full weight of a man stepping directly on the detonator to bring about the explosion we wanted to avoid. After what seemed like an eternity, we finally reached the edge of the woods.

The weather was still chilly, and I was soaking wet from the grass. But I was sweating profusely, too. Fear, I guess. I never knew about my buddy. I knew him only as Ed. No last name. But names made little difference to either of us. We just wanted away from that place. Somehow we got separated going into the thick woods, and I never saw him again. A cold rain started falling, and I was tempted to try and find shelter. But I felt I had to keep moving, just in case someone had spotted me and sounded the alarm. If I made a wrong move and the Russian guards found me outside now, in the dark of night, one shot and I'd be one less American they'd have to look after.

My first instinct was to listen for dogs—the German police dogs the guards usually used on patrols. I didn't hear any and kept moving. Most wooded areas in Germany that I'd been in were kept clear of undergrowth, but this one had been missed. The forest was dense, the night cloudy, so I had trouble traveling in a straight line. At times, I was beginning to panic. The fear of being caught, however, spurred me on with a reserve that I didn't know I possessed. C'mon, Charlie, I thought, get a grip on yourself. Calm down. Keep your mind clear. Let's go. There, that's better. My mind kept telling me these things.

I avoided all roads, skirted the farmhouses and all open fields, trying to get as much distance between me and Luckenwalde as possible. I made my first big mistake at early-morning light. Desperate for food, I took the risk of entering a barn to look for something edible. Now near exhaustion from my flight and a little lax, I didn't notice the cow lying in one corner near a grain bin. I was filling my pockets with grain when I was startled by the movement in the corner and a loud, "Moo." I beat a hasty retreat through the back door of the barn and made a safe getaway just as the farmer came out of the house.

My second big mistake was continuing on through the fields to find a place to hide for the day. I did find a small thicket and had buried myself in the underbrush, all the while munching on the barley. I thought a little milk and some sugar would certainly have enhanced my breakfast. But that was the least of my problems. Either the farmer had spotted me leaving the barn and had seen me entering my hiding place and notified the Russians or it was just a routine patrol that came tromping through the thicket and found me. Either way, with no identification, I was just another DP. I was apprehended, roughly thrown into a truck and was back behind barbed wire in Luckenwalde an hour later. There I was routinely searched. Since I carried nothing but a pocket of grain and that small pair of pliers and screwdriver, I was released without a hassle.

I just lost myself in the tent full of Yanks and rested. But when I made the chow line later that day, I found myself a quiet corner and emptied my pockets into that bowl. The soup was hot enough to soften the barley a little, so I had a full bowl *and* a full stomach for a change.

Later, I checked the fence and found nothing disturbed from the night before, so I made plans to go out again that night. I was hoping to find an extra shirt or short jacket for added warmth, but I had nothing of value to trade and could only hope for warmer weather. I was getting so jumpy that I couldn't sit still. With nothing else to do, I spent the rest of the daylight hours walking around, waiting for darkness. I had to play smarter this time and travel only at night and hide during the day. I had seen only one small map of the whole of Germany and had calculated it to be a good three-day journey to the Elbe by traveling directly west. To hide my escape from the camp, I needed dark, overcast skies. Later on, I would need the stars for guidance.

My luck held out. It started to rain before dusk, so I moved through the fence early. A couple of hours later, the skies cleared. I found the North Star through the trees and fairly flew through the forest, thanks in no small measure to that last big bowl of soup, fortified with the grain. For the first time in a month, I felt my chances for survival were fair.

I had decided that I would travel fast, rest sparingly and make no attempts to forage for food, hoping that I still had enough endurance to last three or four days. During the nights, I heard several trucks and felt relatively safe. The Russians were employing foot patrols only during the day. By this time, their army was gathering in the cities and celebrating their victory, anyway. I planned on them being a bit lax for a while.

I had experienced much brutality during combat and while I was a "guest" of the Germans. In addition, I had heard about, and witnessed, the total disregard the Germans had for the lives of all Russians. Armed with this background, I was sickened, but not surprised, at some of the harsh retaliation carried out by the Russian army at or near the cessation of hostilities in Germany. I had survived the past two weeks or more under this Russian mentality and had seen first hand some of the cold-bloodied killings, but one episode painted an especially gruesome picture.

As I wandered about, trying to reach the Elbe River, I tried to always avoid even the smallest of villages. But at one point I had entered the very edge of a small hamlet, driven by a desperate need of food. I was foolishly scrounging for whatever I could find in a basement when I was confronted by three Russian soldiers, pointing three loaded rifles at me. I quickly went through the usual ritual of trying to identify myself as an American.

"*Amerikanski*," I said while pointing to the ragged red armband. I hoped they understood me before they lost their patience and got trigger happy. I apparently made believers of them, because they herded me out of the basement and into the center of the village at gunpoint.

The narrow road through the village was lined with the civilians, probably the local inhabitants. More than 100 Russian soldiers were lined up at the far end of the road. To my right there now appeared about 20 German soldiers marching in two columns, guarded by Russians. The two columns halted near the center of town. The Germans were then forced to lie down on the road, each about two feet from the other, in a single line. Their heads all faced to the left. The Russians then gathered around the prone Germans, broke into a loud, raucous song and began dancing wildly around and through the Germans. I was standing with the civilians, about 30 feet from where the Germans were prostrate on the road, my Russian guards still hovering near me.

After a few minutes of these barbaric antics, three Stalin tanks roared into town and proceeded to pulverize the soldiers strung out in the roadway. The crowd of Russians shouted and cheered. Thank God I was just out of range of the shower of blood, guts and brains that came shooting out from under the tank treads.

The poor townspeople shrieked with horror, many fainting in their tracks. I attempted to look away but was prodded by three gun barrels and forced to watch the carnage. I gagged several times but didn't vomit on the spot, although that was my inclination and undoubtedly would have had their been any food in my gut to vomit. Civilians ran pell-mell in all directions, screaming and wailing. As they did so, it gave me the chance to slip away from the three Russians. I left town still hungry and found no food along the way.

For three nights I walked west with no other big surprises except falling over a dead cow and walking into a couple of grazing live ones. But on two occasions, while scrounging for food in what I thought was an abandoned house, I discovered the house was occupied by women who were hiding in the attic or basement. They feared the Russian soldiers who thought nothing of raping any female they came upon. Age was no factor.

Upon discovering I was an American, filthy as I was, the women begged me to stay the night and sleep with them as protection from the soldiers. I didn't know what protection I would be, but it meant a warm night's sleep. With my thin, ragged clothing, there had been few nights I slept warmly. So I accepted the invitations and slept in a warm bed under a big fluffy comforter, next to a warm body. And sleep I did, for in my emaciated condition, sex was just not possible, even though it was available for the taking. The women begged me to stay come morning or to take them with me. At the time, I didn't need any excess baggage to be responsible for on my way to Freedom. I always awoke early, grabbed a chunk of bread and slipped out the door and away like a thief in the night. I had to keep moving west.

On the third night of travel, I had decided to follow one of the larger streams. I stayed just a few yards back away from the path along the river bank. Combat had taught me never to walk in a path through a forest. The retreating enemy always mined all easy access routes for the lazy soldier to get trapped. The stream I had followed was in a heavily wooded area and afforded cover from prying enemy eyes. The terrain became more rugged as I moved along, giving me renewed hope that I was approaching a river valley. It had to be the Elbe River.

And just as the sky was getting gray, signaling daybreak, on the third day out, I reached the crest of a hill. Resting for a moment there just before dawn, I looked out and saw that I had stumbled onto a big, wide, fast-flowing river running south. The Elbe! I hoped. Could this be the river I had been searching for since the end of the war? I had waded through several small streams that all seemed to flow in the same general westerly direction. Using all my natural instincts, I knew that as these streams became larger and larger they would eventually lead me to their mother, a larger river. While I wasn't sure that the Elbe was the only river running south in this area of Germany, I had to have faith that I was going in the right direction. This has to be the Elbe, I thought.

At the riverbank, I searched for any kind of a boat or raft, to no avail. I was a poor swimmer, and that river was wide and swift. No way was I going across that way. I hadn't come all this way to drown. A faint glow of light to the south meant a town, so I started walking down the river. When I came up over the top of a hill, I looked down into the valley below and saw that it was teeming with people. I had to speculate that the mass of humanity had gathered at this point, one of the main crossings from Russian-held territory on the east of the Elbe to allied territory on the west bank. Why else would they congregate in such numbers?

From my vantage point, I could see an American-built Bailey bridge stretching across the river with only three of four figures on the far side. Approaching the milling crowd, I was able to identify what looked like four or five GIs standing near a large American military truck. As quickly as I could, I descended into the throng and pushed my way into a line near the big pontoon bridge. The whole area was full of people of all descriptions. The shock came when I discovered that Russian soldiers patrolled the edges of the crowd.

I was so desperate that I practically fought my way through until I came to the small group of what turned out to be four Americans, Army Air Corps officers. They had all made their way to the Elbe individually as I had done. Although no one knew at the time that the area had been set up as the demarcation line between the Allies and the Russians, many allied POWs had been roaming east of the Elbe and trying to get across the river just as I was. I had difficulty proving my identity to them.

Even my dog tags weren't enough to persuade them that I was an American GI. Who knows, I could have taken them off a dead GI, for all they knew. At this time, I didn't know I looked like an apparition, so I guess I couldn't blame them. But finally, after some talk about things we all knew about the States, I was accepted as one of them.

Thank God, I thought.

Someone in the group gave me three crackers when I told them I hadn't had food for the past three days. Physically, mentally and emotionally, I was about at the end of my rope. But I had reached my long-sought goal: The Elbe River. The final hurdle, now, was crossing to the other side—and FREEDOM.

18

We stood near the pontoon bridge that had been built by American engineers, but we were barred from crossing by the Russian soldiers. The American officers explained the situation. This was one of the sites for the exchange of prisoners—on Russian terms.

An American truck would pull up on the far side of the river and discharge its cargo of Russian prisoners repatriated by the Allies. As one Russian would start walking across the bridge, one Allied soldier would be allowed to start from this side, the two passing in the center. It was a slow, agonizing process that had been going on every day since the declared end of hostilities and was just like the rumors I'd heard in Luckenwalde.

The officers I was with had been at the crossing for more than two days already. I was fortunate that I was able to push my way to the front of that huge group waiting to cross that bridge. The majority of those congregated here were civilians. I really think many of the people were shocked at my appearance and that fact allowed me to edge my way to the group of Allied soldiers nearer the bridge. I was eternally grateful to the Americans for allowing me to squeeze in among them and ahead of others who had waited hours and days for their turn.

Because the Russians had made no provision for food or water for the waiting throng, many were beginning to get ugly. The guards were having a problem keeping some people from charging across the bridge. It was this confusion, I think, that enabled me to work my way up near the front. I could see Freedom just a few yards away, and I was determined to make it there one way or another.

But as I stood gazing across that wide expanse of water, I was still worried about whether I would ever get to climb aboard that big old GI truck. I stood and looked while all sorts of memories consumed my mind. I wondered if my mother had survived her bout with cancer. Was she still alive? Was Dad still around? I'd received no word from home since I had left Holland in late October 1944, a long seven months ago.

Everything came rushing to my mind at once, and I was overwhelmed. What would be in store for me if and when I actually reached home? I wondered how I would be accepted by my family once I got back to the States. I knew I was skinny and drawn looking. Would I be able to function back home as a normal human? Would my mind be twisted as a result of witnessing so much death, destruction and bestiality? What could I expect from the severe concussion and head wound I had suffered?

Slumping to the ground, I began to cry uncontrollably. It was getting close to dark when I heard that the Russians closed down the operation at nightfall. I knew I had to regain my composure and had to start thinking positively. I spent that night lying on the ground, huddled close to men in American uniforms. That helped, and I felt safe that night. I was closer to the magic edge of that bridge to Freedom.

At the first sign of dawn, I was stirring, stiff from laying on the cold, wet ground and weak from hunger. I had to be helped to my feet, only able to stand with the help of my fellow soldiers. My mind was wandering again, and I was apparently babbling incoherently when someone pointed to two sets of headlights coming to the river on the other side. Then I heard the sound of 6x6s roaring up the road. Somebody told me that each day fewer and fewer trucks were arriving with Russian prisoners to exchange. When the Allies run out of Russians to exchange, then what? I wondered. Nobody seemed to know.

Some people in the crowd were more impatient than others. There appeared to be a faction that would just as soon storm the bridge and take their chances of being shot by the Russian guards. But being on the other side, dead, wasn't what any of them wanted. So they waited with the rest of us.

Two men who had befriended me seemed to always be at my side, and they helped me to edge closer to the crossing point. The two truck loads of Russians on the other side brought me to the place where one more batch of Russians should be able to allow me to be exchanged. Within an hour, another truck arrived and with the help of my two new friends, I was about the 10th man to be allowed to navigate that bridge. Still, I had waited more than a day and a half before they gave me a shove to be the next man across. And it seemed that the American truck had contained only 12 Russians. Again, my luck was holding. I was exchanged for the next-to-last man in the truck, and there was no way of predicting when the next truck load would arrive.

The Bailey bridge was constructed primarily for the crossing of tanks and trucks. It consisted of two narrow steel treads about 18 inches wide, attached to floating rubber pontoons for buoyancy in the swift river. The bridge swayed a bit with the rush of the current. With no railings or supports of any kind, the bridge presented quite a challenge to the one navigating it on foot. This was especially true for this old infantryman. I was so excited and yet so physically exhausted that I fell to my knees several times and had to crawl a few feet before I was able to regain my feet.

I would have crawled on my hands and knees if I'd have had to, but somehow I found that last bit of strength to proudly walk to Freedom. I'm sure I must have had a helping hand from the Lord above. He gave me the strength to stand up and take those final steps across the river. Tears of joy streamed freely down my face as I made those last unsteady steps across the Elbe from captivity and death to Freedom and life. Stepping off on the other side, I stumbled and collapsed into the arms of two American soldiers. As they were supporting me, my eyes locked in on the most beautiful sight imaginable: A big, silver Timberwolf insignia emblazoned on the door of the truck. I was home, back among my own. I had crossed the Elbe River and was Free.

Whenever I think about the Elbe, the bridge and the exchange of prisoners, I am once again in awe of finally crossing that Bailey bridge to Freedom. I had no feeling before or have had none since that came close to what I felt that day.

I barely remember the long ride into Halle, headquarters for the 104th Division. When we arrived, I was carried off the truck to a tent and immediately attended to by a medic. An American officer who was questioning me informed me that my old L Company was just a block down the street. He told me that after the medic checked me out and I got a little food, someone would take me to my company command post.

The medic checked my vital signs and insisted that I get on the scales as part of the information he needed. When he read the scales, he wouldn't tell me what they showed. After a few more questions, I was beginning to get incoherent. He had already asked me more questions than I was able to answer: name, rank, serial number, date of capture and my normal weight. At that point, he took one good look at my eyes. The last thing I remember was him calling for a litter.

So I never made it down the block to L Company. Instead, I was loaded into an ambulance. My next recollection was the roar of an airplane. It was dark. A bright light flashed through the small window. It was then that I realized I was airborne. Our plane had been picked up on a ground search-light beam. I was hoping that the ground crew recognized us as American and didn't blast us out of the sky; I didn't want to be blown to hell on my way home.

An Army nurse appeared, pushed up my sleeve and gave me a shot of some sort. The last words I heard were her saying, "You'll sleep better now, soldier."

The hum of the plane's engines were like a lullaby, and I was soon in dreamland. I hadn't been informed of my destination, so when I awakened sometime the next morning, I wasn't sure I was still alive. When I first opened my eyes, everything in my field of vision was pure white. I could hear low voices speaking a strange language. My vision was foggy, but I began to see the outline of two faces bending over me. The light over the bed was exceptionally bright, and I couldn't focus my eyes very well. For a few seconds, my mind again played tricks on me. I imagined myself in Heaven, being tended to by two beautiful angels.

As the fog slowly cleared, I blinked a couple of times to see two nurses, all in white, leaning over my bed. They had to be two of the most beautiful women in the world. I recognized their language as French, but I still had no idea of my situation.

Had I been flown back to the States? I wondered. Was I back in a prison hospital or had I actually been freed and this was America? I had yet to reconcile myself with the facts. When the nurses realized that I was awake, they quieted down their rapid-fire French. I learned that I was flat on my back in Rheims, France.

Through the use of French, a smattering of English and much gesturing of sign language, I got the message that they wanted to give me a bath. I had been deloused upon arrival and my clothes immediately burned. There had been no time to outfit me with an Army uniform when I had arrived at Halle. Because of my extremely weakened conditioned, it had been urgent to get me to the hospital in Rheims as soon as possible. The uniform had had to wait. I had been hustled aboard a waiting C-47 for France just as I was, with a nurse waiting in attendance.

I had gone to sleep on the plane. It was only when I woke up the hospital in Rheims that I realized that my prison clothing had been burned. Because they were full of lice, fleas and bedbugs, this had been the only way to dispose of them. For the first time in seven months, I was going to be free from that incessant itching associated with lice, fleas and other insects that made their home in my hair and beard. One of my first thoughts, though, upon learning of the fate of my prison clothing was, "There went the diamonds." Oh, well, I thought, I didn't have too much invested in them, anyway. Or maybe I had a great deal invested in them. It's according to how you look at it, I guess. But losing the diamonds didn't matter.

Being quite unsteady on my feet, the nurses half carried me into the next room where there was a large, ornate bathtub. Before they gently lifted me into the tub, they stood me in front of a full-length mirror. I was stark naked and a bit embarrassed in the presence of two females, forgetting for a moment that they were nurses. I took one fleeting look in the mirror and quickly looked away. When I took a second look at the image in the mirror, I was shocked at what I looked like. My shoulder-length hair and long beard were matted with filth; my ribs showed through my chest; and my knees were bony. I hardly recognized my own face. I just didn't realize, until that moment, the terrible toll starvation can take on a man, even though I'd seen what it had done to others throughout the last several months.

One of the nurses confirmed my weight at 109 pounds. When I was captured in November, I had weighed in at 175 pounds. After I was weighed, buckets of warm water were brought in and poured into the tub, which sat in the middle of the room so that a nurse was on either side of me with a big brush and soap. When had I last seen soap? I wondered. Hohenstein, maybe? The nurses scrubbed and scrubbed, especially my hands which were nearly black with ground-in dirt.

Following the bath, I was placed in a big straight chair to have my hair cut. They started on my head, cutting to the bare scalp. Next they chopped the beard off and clipped every hair on my body. One of them shaved me with a straight razor, no less, nicking me only once. I was a bit tense. Then they smeared a white ointment on me to heal the lice-infested areas. By this time, I was completely exhausted and was helped back into bed where I was served breakfast. My first *real* meal since... hell, since I couldn't remember when.

I was so nervous and excited that I was barely able to hold a spoon in my hand without slopping milk all over me. The nurse showed a great deal of concern, but she gave me encouragement and let me struggle with the bowl of cereal. I tried my best to watch my manners and eat it slowly. It would have been easy to resort to the animal instinct I had developed as a prisoner.

After nearly nine months of combat and prison life, now I was getting breakfast in bed. I could hardly believe it. But the memory of it was one that I knew I would always cherish and remember: A bowl of cereal with real milk, toast with marmalade and butter, a biscuit with honey and real coffee. What a treat! I had a nurse at my bedside almost constantly for the five days I spent in Rheims. Because of my extreme malnutrition, the food was sparse but wholesome. Surprisingly, I was quick to regain some of my strength. And when I was outfitted with a new uniform, I almost felt human again.

Of course, I fell madly in love with both my nurses. But alas, after the fifth day in the hospital, orders came through transferring me to Camp Lucky Strike at Etrétat, near Le Havre, France. A jeep arrived early in the morning, and I didn't even get a chance to say goodbye and thank the nurses for all their tender-loving care. I was on my way home at last, although at the time I didn't realize all the detours that lay ahead on the long journey to home.

We made the run to the coast non-stop, whizzing through small villages at a fast clip. I enjoyed the scenery and dozed off occasionally. At this speed, I thought, I'll be home in a few days. My train ride—*really* in first class this time—was uneventful except for the celebrations that got a bit wild. All passengers were American military troops who were being rotated to the States after long tours of duty on the Continent. And they were ready to celebrate. By the time we reached Le Havre, the men were really wild. Most everybody carried souvenirs of some kind, including Lugars and P38 pistols.

As we sped along beside the farm fields of France toward the coast, several men took potshots at the civilians working in the fields. The workers were primarily women and children. I saw several fall to the ground, either from being hit or from a learned sense of survival from gunfire. At this time in our lives everyone was still the enemy. The firing continued until the men ran out of ammo. Killing had been such a part of our lives these past months—years in some cases. What was one more corpse?

Arriving at Camp Lucky Strike, I was assigned a cot in the pyramidal tent city. The weather had warmed up, I had a wool uniform and overcoat and I slept up off the ground. It was pure heaven. I was assigned to go through four separate procedures in four separate sections of the camp. They were lettered A through D. Section A consisted of a complete physical, Army style. Sections B and C consisted of orientation classes which, after three years of Army life, were boring and a waste of time—mine and theirs. Then came D Section.

I was seated at a desk across from a captain and a sergeant from the Army Office of Strategic Intelligence or OSI. The interrogation started off friendly enough. The questions were routine. Then the captain asked me to describe conditions in the various camps I'd spent time in. I told him just exactly the conditions I'd endured in the work camp. They do want the truth, don't they? I thought. The sergeant was rapidly taking notes as I was describing the conditions.

"Listen, soldier," the captain said, abruptly halting me in mid-sentence after several minutes of listening to my story, "this *couldn't* have happened to you. We have monitored the POW camps and know all about the conditions in these camps. You received Red Cross parcels, were allowed to write letters home, received mail and were given adequate food."

My shock at his statements quickly turned to anger. I rose to my feet and asked him if he knew all about my treatment at the hands of the Germans and the Russians, why ask me and waste my time.

"You, sir, have called me a liar," I said in an even voice. "I have been interrogated by Germans and Russians enough to last a lifetime. I don't need another like those from my own Army. I request permission to leave."

He stood up, but before he uttered another word, I saluted him, made an about face, pushed my way through the tent flap and headed to my own bunk. I fully expected the MPs to be at my bedside at any minute. But they didn't show up. Instead, I lay around camp for another three days, waiting for a ship to the States. I checked in at headquarters every morning to see if my name was on the list for the next sailing. The officer in charge could sense that I was becoming more irritated each morning.

On the fourth day, he booked passage for me on a coastal schooner and issued me a seven-day delay-en-route pass to England. He knew my division had landed directly in France and thought a few days in merry old England would be a nice diversion for me. It sounded like a good deal.

I was one of the last POWs to pass through Camp Lucky Strike, and I think my belligerent attitude was striking a few nerves. Headquarters officers' main objective was to ship as many soldiers as quickly as possible back to the United States and on to fight the Japanese. So I held a low priority. And since they were closing the section of the camp reserved for returned POWs, they wanted to get rid of me. Hence, the idea of sending me to England. I hadn't been issued any pay yet. As I picked up my boarding pass, I was given a few English pounds along with the location of the American Army Headquarters where I could apply for some back pay.

The ship landed at Bournemouth on the southern coast of England, and I immediately hopped a train for London. My first stop in London was Rainbow Corners, the main Red Cross Club there. I had read many stories that Rainbow Corners was the place to obtain food and free passes to all of London. The club was considered the best in the city. Also, I had been thoroughly briefed concerning my physical condition while undergoing my first physical in Section A at Camp Lucky Strike and had been warned that it would take many more days for my stomach to adapt to real food again. I soon learned that eggnog seemed to be the best nourishment and wouldn't upset my stomach.

My days in London were a complete joy. I got a map of the London underground rail system, plus free passes to various historic sites in and around the city. I intended to make the most of my stay in the city. My money held out for most of the week. I lived off the Salvation Army kitchen where they never charged a cent, therefore spending as little as possible on food. This was in direct contrast to the Red Cross which charged for coffee and donuts and for a bed at night.

Occasionally, I got in line at a British Army mess hall. But I could never eat very much at any of these places because of the condition of my stomach. The food always tasted good. I just had to be careful and not overeat. A night's lodging in one of the several American and British Red Cross Clubs cost a whopping 40 cents, American. Most nights I spent at either Covent Gardens or Hammersmith, two large theaters that had been converted to dance halls for the Americans. The price was reasonable with live music until midnight.

Before I had come to London, I had frequently complained of severe headaches. I thought they were the result of the episode on the Polish tank. The head wound had healed quite nicely without ever having any stitches. That Scottish medic knew his business. But the headaches persisted and continued while I was enjoying my delay-en-route pass. An added side effect to the headaches was occasional periods of blurred vision and even total blindness for short periods of time. I had carried a large knot on the back of my head as a result of being slammed against the turret of the tank. The usual diagnosis and treatment was, "That bump will eventually recede; take a couple of aspirins."

The bump was still there, and the aspirin didn't do much for the headache. The whirlwind week in London may not have helped things. My last night of furlough was spent dancing at Covent Gardens. Sometime close to midnight, I became extremely light-headed and finally passed out on the dance floor. I came to about 1000 hours the next morning, lying flat on my back in a British hospital.

A little while after I woke up, a nurse making her rounds came to the foot of my bed to check my chart. I bombarded her with questions. What day is it? What time is it? Where am I? She politely answered my questions. I knew I'd made a big mistake. I was scheduled to appear at an airfield north of London at 0700 hours for my flight to the States. It was now 1100 hours, and I was AWOL, absent without leave. The penalty for missing movement in wartime was a court-martial. I just knew the hospital staff had checked my leave papers and were already aware of my predicament.

After being served a relatively good breakfast, I was informed that a doctor would be in shortly to examine me. The nurse seemed to have no idea why I was brought to the hospital, except that I was unconscious on arrival. As I lay there contemplating my options, I decided I hadn't seen enough of England. The penalty for desertion was a court-martial, too, and probably even more serious in war time than missing movement. My uniform was neatly hanging on a rack near my bed. I got up, dressed and climbed through the nearest window, which put me in a garden-like recreation area at the rear of the hospital. Several patients were milling around, taking their morning walk. I merely joined them and nonchalantly walked through the main lobby, acting as a visitor, then walked out the main door. No one questioned me.

I spent my days bumming around London, taking in as many sights as possible—the Tower of London, Madame Tussaud's Wax Works and a variety of other things I knew I'd probably never see again. I even took a pleasant, leisurely tour, partly by boat, to Stratford-upon-Avon. And I usually found a dance to go to every night. My leave papers were now worthless for drawing any back pay, so I found myself penniless and had to get by as best as I could. I continued to have my dizzy spells, accompanied by shorts stints of blindness. Any excessive physical activity seemed to bring on this condition. Thinking back to that night at Covent Gardens, I decided I must have engaged in some strenuous jitterbugging and so toned down my dancing to more slow numbers.

Bumming around in London also gave me plenty of time to reflect on the time I'd spent as a POW and things that I'd forgotten or buried for one reason or another. I had done a few things I didn't particularly like to think about. I knew I had sunk pretty low during my days behind the Russian lines. I was a scavenger of the lowest form. I would take anything valuable I could find, although the Russians had usually been there ahead of me. For a while, I had a P-38 pistol for protection that I'd picked up somewhere. It was finally taken away from me by a drunken renegade. Like me, he was merely living much like everyone else caught up in the war.

When I was captured back in Aachen, or actually Eschweiler, and as I've said earlier, I had a wrist watch of my own, plus another given to me by my buddy to take back to his mother in New York City. He had died in my arms as soon as he gave me the watch and before I could get him a medic. I also had a small picture of my mother, one of my father and a silver dollar minted in 1892, my father's year of birth. Although they did take the two watches, explaining that I wouldn't be needing one watch, let alone two, where I was going, not once during my numerous interrogations by the Germans did they attempt to keep the pictures or the coin. I would explain the significance of the coin and they understood. Souvenir is the same in German and English. I carried my wallet with the pictures and the coin all through prison camp. But the Russians later took the coin, leaving my wallet and the two pictures.

I carry those pictures to this day as a token of good luck, although my parents have been deceased several years.

Of course, I never made it to England with any of my loot I had split with the two Britishers after we had found the diamonds in a strongbox in the abandoned house near Zagan and the others I had taken that had been lost with my prison clothes when they were burned at Halle. But I always managed somehow.

In my wanderings about London I sometimes bumped into some Canadian soldiers from the 4th Division and was able to spend some time at their billets. I had fought beside them when the 104th as attached to the Canadian Army and was always welcome to join their chow line. Because of my severely malnourished state I wasn't able to eat very much at one time, but I slowly began to regain some strength through these repasts. And before I ran out of money, I managed to secure an Italian Beretta .25 caliber pistol and a black, leather-covered German SS blackjack. My Canadian friends made these available to me for a very nominal price—a few steins of stout at one of the local pubs.

"You're going to need some protection, bloke," the Canadian who gave the weapons to me said.

Although London was safe enough to roam during the daytime, after nightfall the streets became a dangerous place in certain areas of the city because so many men were without any means of income. In that environment, I felt I needed some protection. I finally ran out of money after a few days and didn't have the 40 cents a night to sleep at the Red Cross clubs. Because of that and the MP bed checks at the clubs nearly every night, I had to find another place to sleep. Being AWOL, I was forced to keep a low profile.

Before running out of money, I had frequented the Columbia and the Mostlyn Red Cross clubs and had become good friends with the night clerks in both clubs. When I ran out of money, these friendships paid off. On certain nights of each week, these two women would see to it that I had a bed for the night. I would stop by each club early in the evening to see which one had managed to save me a bed. If one was available, there was a small note posted on the bulletin board which spelled out the floor, room number and bed number. It never varied; it was always spelled out in these terms: Timberwolf—2-R206-B16. They accomplished this little trickery by having one of the cleaning ladies declare a certain bed as "broken and out of service for the night."

Between these two women, I managed about three nights a week in a soft, clean bed. The ruse worked during my entire stay in London. Evidently the Red Cross management really had no way of checking on the women. What was one bed in a 10- or 12-story hotel, anyway? I wondered. If no notice was posted, I slept wherever I could find a secluded spot. I slept in the rubble of bombed-out buildings or in the bushes at St. James Park; I slept in bus stations and occasionally at a British army barracks.

Sometimes I slept in a church, preferably in a church that had padding on its pews. In one church in particular, I gathered up four or five pads and made a nice soft mattress. Of course, I had to get up early before the rector arrived for morning mass. And I was always gone by the time he arrived, but I'm sure his kind, benevolent heart wouldn't have let him be too rough on me.

England was full of soldiers from many nations. Men from all around the world had made their way to England to fight on the side of the Allies. They were conscripted into the British ranks and all wore British uniforms with the only identification being a small black arc with blue letters spelling the name of their country of origin. It was worn at the top of the left sleeve, just below the shoulder. Some fought in small regiments as a people under British commanders; others were integrated into regular British units. There were many released POWs who would never return to their homeland for one reason or another. As repatriated prisoners, we were all known as Recovered Allied Military Personnel or RAMPs.

In that kind of atmosphere, I walked the streets at night in certain districts with the Beretta in my left hand and the SS blackjack in my right hand. I walked the curb, away from the darkened doorways and would challenge anyone who approached me closer than I thought they should. At times, I felt I was back in a combat situation. But I just couldn't get enough of being Free. I had the Freedom to roam and daily ignored the rainy, foggy London weather. It wasn't going to dampen my spirits at this stage of the game.

One day I decided to go to a village northeast of Glasgow near Loch Lomond where my Scottish friend Jock MacLeod had told me was his home village. I hitchhiked rides on trains and trucks to reach the place. Once there, however, I was unable to locate him, although the village was full of the MacLeod clan. Disappointed, I headed back to London to survive as best I could.

At Covent Gardens one night, I asked a pretty young woman to dance. We struck up a conversation, and I learned that she was on holiday, the British term for vacation. She was visiting friends in Chelsea, a section of London proper. Her home was in a small village up in the Midlands near Leicester. Her name was Clarinda, and she worked for a bottler and distributor of Scotch whiskey. A light came on in my head. Before the evening was over, I had a deal to make some money.

If I could somehow scrounge up enough American dollars, I could buy six or eight bottles of the whiskey at a wholesale price and a cut on the side for her. I could easily transport the stuff back to London in my kit bag and sell it at a fancy price on the black market. New Yanks arriving from the States always had plenty of cash. And they were eager to get drunk and would pay any price for a bottle.

I traveled unnoticed on the train. I had learned that only the conductors collected tickets. By simply avoiding the conductor, I rode many a trip without purchasing a ticket and found one more way to use my wits to the utmost to survive from day to day.

Prior to going in the whiskey business, I'd met another young woman—at a dance, naturally—who was employed by the Army and worked in the exchange office down near #10 Downing Street, the heart of the government and ministry district. She was in charge of a section of foreign exchange. Her job was to supply British pounds in exchange for American dollars, French francs, Dutch guilders and any other foreign money brought in by American soldiers.

Each currency had its own exchange rate of value for the British pound. She could also exchange the pounds for dollars. I felt I could effectively do what she was doing. The only problem was that I had to present actual leave papers in order to make the transaction. No problem, really, as Nettie, short for Annette, always managed to have a couple of extra blank forms for me to sign. I was in business.

All I had to do was manage to be around the exchange office at a slack time. We didn't want any snoopers. I was able to make one or two transactions per day if I really needed the money. What I did as I built up a bit of surplus cash was to approach fresh, new GI arrivals and make a deal to exchange the British money for dollars. My rate was a bit higher than what they'd get at the army exchange. But they were always in a hurry to see the sights and start partying. None of them ever had the knowledge to question my rate of exchange. Anyway, there was usually a long line at exchange HQ, and a GI didn't like to wait in line.

I also stole from the American PX whenever I had the chance—

but not too often. I stocked up on small cans of orange juice, candy bars, gum and nylon stockings. These items and a few dollars extra I gave to my two employees, Clarinda and Nettie. It gave me a great deal of joy and satisfaction as I observed them relishing a candy bar or drinking the juice. But probably the supreme happiness for them was a pair of nylons.

All these things I gave them were rationed during the war and still were. I couldn't even buy anything for my mom and dad because everything required ration tokens. I did buy these things at the PX when I had the money—I wasn't always a thief. My helpers were so grateful for these little favors I could give them.

Once, briefly, I had to slow my exchange business for a couple of weeks because of an Army Intelligence investigation. I'd used several aliases on the leave papers and got a bit jumpy. The reason for the investigation, however, was that someone else was trying the same scheme I was using. But he didn't have the inside help I had with the clerk and got caught.

Even during the investigation, I continued to make exchanges at a slower rate—only about twice a week. The whiskey, though, continued to flow. I'd be back in London by early afternoon, sell my wares within the hour and head for the dance hall. I still didn't make enough to survive really well and still had to spend some nights without a warm bed. Rain was always a nagging problem then.

On three different occasions, I was picked up by American MPs. In the first instance, I was sentenced to three days of Army orientation—eight hours of lectures with a 10-minute break each hour. The second day, I was able to sneak away during one of the breaks. Security was lax. At the time, there were a number of repatriated POWs roaming around in England. Actually the lecturers didn't want to lecture any more than I wanted to listen to them. But had I stayed the full 3 days, someone would have checked my status and probably kept me. That's the reason I had to take off through the window.

The second time, I asked to see a chaplain. I gave him a great story about how I was going to marry this British woman who had waited for me throughout the war. I even had her picture and address at Knightsbridge in East London. The chaplain bought my story, gave me a three-day pass and happily agreed to perform the ceremony free of charge. I thanked him and promptly forgot the date I was to be back for the ceremony. My starvation diet was still affecting my thinking. Or something was—I just wandered around, never even giving a thought to writing home. I didn't even know if my parents knew if I was still alive; I never even thought about that.

Sometime in late July, I was in the chow line at a Salvation Army canteen when I was approached by a gentleman with a microphone. The interview was brief. He asked only my name and hometown. I thought nothing of it. I figured it was just a local radio station and forgot about the interview. But my name was picked up from a BBC broadcast interview by some Ham operators. A message was then relayed to my father, by letter, from a couple of complete strangers in the States. Now my parents knew I was alive, but I wasn't aware of this until later.

The one really memorable experience that came from my stay in London happened one afternoon while I was strolling down a street, going nowhere in particular. Turning a corner, I spied a cluster of people queued up outside a tea shop. I had stopped in the shop a couple of times and had noticed it was quite an elaborately decorated restaurant.

I walked up to the crowd and discovered that the people were awaiting the arrival of the queen, who made occasional stops at this, her favorite tea shop. I squeezed myself in one side of the line and hoped to get a glimpse of the queen of England. After about 10 minutes, an ornately decorated horse-drawn carriage appeared, the handsome horses trotting our way. The carriage pulled up to the cheering thong. But as soon as the queen stepped out, all grew quiet out of respect to her. She was a most gracious lady as she acknowledged her subjects while making her way to the entrance of the tea room.

I was standing about halfway to the door. Being the only soldier present, I must have stood out in the crowd because as she pulled even to where I stood, she stopped and walked toward me. She offered her hand and said, "Yank, I want to personally thank you for coming over here and saving England."

I was in a state of shock. I took her hand but didn't know whether I should bow or fall to my knees. So I just stood there holding her hand and stammering. She then turned and walked through the doorway into the tea shop. As for me, I stood there wondering how I should have reacted. I knew I'd always remember the scene.

19

One drizzly afternoon after I'd been in London for a time, I was quaffing a few ales with my new-found Canadian buddies at the Golden Pheasant Pub. We were discussing our fighting days in Holland. An incident, nearly forgotten, popped into my mind, and I proceeded to let them in on another little secret of mine.

After some very severe fighting, my outfit dug in for the night on the outskirts of the town of Breda. It wasn't long before K Company moved through our forward positions, and we found ourselves in reserve for the rest of the night. We felt fairly secure in our reserve position, so a couple of men and I decided to roam through the rubble of the town. Just for kicks.

It was a typical dark, rainy night. But this one seemed darker than most. Thanks to the Canadians and Americans throwing up a continuous artillery barrage, however, the sky was pretty well lit up. We poked around a partially destroyed building.

"Hey, guys," I said, "looks like this was a bank."

"What makes you think so?" Henry Finnegan asked.

"Well, this big square thing the bombs couldn't blow up looks like a vault to me," I said with the experience of having been in the bank with my dad many times. "The bank in my hometown had a vault just about like this."

"Hey, look," George Will said as he fiddled around with the vault door. "The thing isn't even locked. Guess the explosions sprung the locks."

Without much effort on our part, the door swung open. Once inside, we were able to use our flashlight to search for souvenirs. We frantically pulled out drawers and smashed metal strongboxes, looking for anything of value. Surprisingly, we found no coins, but one strongbox was jammed with Dutch guilders of various denominations.

"Oh, great," Finnegan said. "Just look at all this loot and us with no way to cart it off."

"Let's bury it," I said.

"What for?" Will asked. "Finders keepers I always say."

"Yeah," I said, agreeing, "but we can't get out of here with all these guilders. I think the best thing to do right now is bury it and make a map that we can split three ways. Then when this mess is over we can all come back and divide it up."

"Sounds good to me," Finnegan said. "How about you, Will?"

"Okay, but we'd better get at it and get back to the unit. Reserve doesn't last forever, damn it."

Will was right. We never knew when we'd be moving forward again. So we went to work, stumbling around in the darkness outside the vault, looking for some prominent landmark to be used as a reference point. We chose a small monument honoring some hero or prominent Dutchman as our reference point. It was a hunk of marble small enough not to be too noticeable, yet one we could easily find again. Or so we thought.

I stepped off seven paces in what I perceived to be straight north of the small monument. We quickly dug a hole with our entrenching shovels, wrapped the metal box in an old GI blanket and hastily covered the hole. Then I scribbled a crude map of the area on a scrap of paper, using points I could see in the black night. My stub of a pencil was so light that I could barely make out my drawing. But this was it.

"This is a good map, Dukes," Finnegan said.

"This is the first place I'll head when the war's over," Will said.

"Okay, guys," I said as I ripped the paper into three pieces and gave each of them one. "Good luck to all of us."

With that, each of us stuffed his portion in his shirt pocket and shook hands on our deal before heading back to our positions. We arrived just as the squad was pulling out on another bayonet attack.

Sitting in the pub some nine months later, stimulated by a couple of more ales and the retelling of the incident, I was haunted by the thought of all those Dutch guilders going to waste. I had long ago lost that small scrap of paper, and the other men had both been killed in Holland a few days after we had buried the money. Will had died in my arms. So I was the only one who knew about the secret cache, and it loomed larger in my mind as I recalled the events of that night. I decided then and there I would go look for that money.

Joan, a girl I had been seeing, loaned me some of her brother's civilian clothes. He was away in India in the army. I donned the civvies, left my uniform with her and headed for the English Channel where I boarded the ferry to France. I felt I would be less conspicuous in the ill-fitting civilian clothes than in an American uniform.

France, Belgium and Holland were still in a state of utter chaos and confusion, so it was fairly simple to hitch rides in American trucks traveling in all directions. In fact, my second truck ride took me within a few miles of my destination: Breda. It was nearly dark when I finally found my way to what I perceived to be the are of the bombed-out bank.

Man, was I confused! The landscape had changed drastically from all subsequent bombings, no doubt, and there was not a sign of the small monument or the bank vault. I searched the area in vain until complete darkness enveloped me and halted my search. Then I curled up on the floor of an abandoned and partially destroyed house and slept the night away. I arose at daybreak and continued my search, futile as it was, and soon became completely disoriented. I dug several small holes before finally giving up. I threw my shovel away and headed for the main road back to England. I had a round-trip ticket on the ferry and managed to catch the last ferry of the evening back across the channel.

During those two days, I was never challenged by anyone. The people were just too engrossed in the business of survival to notice my presence as I vainly searched for the treasure. Like everyone else, I scrounged in the fields and empty houses for scraps of food.

Back in London, I retrieved my uniform, then joined the Canadians for our usual gathering at the Golden Pheasant where I recounted my escapade of the past two days.

"You're damn lucky you weren't caught out of uniform, Yank," one of them said.

"You didn't even have leave papers, did you, Dukes?" another man asked.

"Hell, no," I said. "Good thing the Man upstairs looks after fools and Yanks out on treasure hunts, isn't it? Let's have another round on me."

They laughed and admonished me, and we had another round. I realized the sheer stupidity of the whole venture. But I still couldn't help but wonder if anyone had ever or would ever come upon that strongbox of Dutch guilders. It would have been quite a find for someone.

Much later in my wanderings, I came upon the Canadians at the Golden Pheasant Pub again. We were good friends and downed a couple of steins of stout at the pub. Since it closed from 2-4 p.m., we wandered over to the Hare & Hound for a few more stouts. Conversation turned from war stories to stories of Aldershot, a giant amusement park in the east end of London. It had a carnival atmosphere. Some of the Canucks felt they had been cheated at some of the games of chance just because they were wearing a Canadian uniform. Most of the Colonial Armed Forces had little love for the British soldiers. Some that I met that day had been away from home for more than six years, fighting for the British.

Fortified with a few more steins of stout, we all decided to go to Aldershot and either win back some of their money or else to wreck the place. So we headed for the park and played a few games. We lost every time. That's when the party started. Of course, we were soon outnumbered. It wasn't long before a multitude of London Bobbies were on the scene, and we were all hustled off to the lockup. I'd now left a little of my blood on the soil in yet another foreign land. Now I could count the third time I was picked up since going AWOL.

I spent a couple of days in solitary confinement. In fact, my first news of the Japanese surrender in August 1945 came from the shouts of a newsboy hawking the London *Times* headlines on the street outside my cell window. The next morning, the American MPs came after me. This time I was scheduled for a general court-martial. I was called before a five-member board of officers. In short, I was sentenced to six months at hard labor and two-thirds forfeiture of all pay and allowances. And I was immediately hustled off to serve my time in the stockade at the Third Replacement Depot in Litchfield.

There I was searched, stripped of my uniform and issued dungarees. I worked three days in the kitchen washing pots and pans for 10-12 hours per day. Then I got an infection in my right hand from the strong lye soap used in the kitchen—I still had two sore spots on my right hand from white phosphorus shells that burned me in Holland—and was switched to the garbage detail.

The guards at the stockade were really a mean bunch. I was subjected to every bit as much physical harassment in the American Army stockade as I suffered at the hands of the Germans. In fact, conditions were so bad that several articles were written about the horrendous conditions at Litchfield. Several of the guards were court-marshaled as a result of the investigation of brutality. It was double time every step of the way in moving from one place to the next.

At 0400 hours in the morning of my eighth day in the stockade, I was rousted out of my bunk and ordered to appear before another board of officers. This session consisted of a three-man tribunal from the 29th Division. The charges against me were 43 days absent without leave, or desertion, since it was more than 30 days. But after a thorough review of my case, the tribunal concluded that, considering my good combat record and my experiences as a prisoner of the enemy, my sentence would be rescinded. I would be shipped to the United States immediately and under guard. As one officer explained, the decision was based on my condition of apparent battle fatigue; therefore, I was not fully responsible for being AWOL. The court-martial would not appear on my record, either.

I saluted and, amazing to me, the three officers stood and shook my hand, all wishing me a quick, safe trip home. I was issued a new uniform, my arms were bound in chains and I had an MP escort to Barry, South Wales. The MP was given strict orders to have me at dockside by 1800 hours or else he would have to serve the balance of my sentence. I didn't realize that I was that dangerous, but it surely scared the hell out of that guard.

On our way south, I wanted to stop in London to pick up a little money I had stashed in the safe at the Columbia Red Cross Club near the Marble Arch underground station. But he would have none of it, even when I offered to share. It was really a small amount of money anyway, so it was just as well that the guard refused.

At dockside, I boarded the James R. Turner, a 7,000-ton liberty ship which had been converted into a troop ship. She was already full to capacity as far as sleeping accommodations. But I, along with 12 other RAMPs, some of whom had been AWOL like me, were put aboard anyway. To add insult to injury, the entire contingent consisted of Air Corps ground-crew personnel.

As members of the Air Corps, they all carried rank from corporal on up. Not a private in the bunch. One whole section was for officers only—off-limits to privates. The 13 men in my group were all combat infantrymen and all were former POWs. Some had married English women and had taken their leave time with their British wives. A couple of the men had gone AWOL. We all became close friends on that long 11-day voyage home.

When the ship reached the 3-mile limit after leaving port, my chains were removed. One more step to being really Free.

Being excess baggage, the 13 of us had no sleeping quarters and were compelled to sleep on the open deck. Three or four days out to sea, some of the merchant seamen became aware of our predicament and offered us their quarters when they went on night watch. We had to be careful, however, since this was against regulations. But we managed. Anything but that open steel deck.

The first night at sea I was discovered sleeping in a life raft. The seaman explained to me that maybe the raft would not be a good place to be. "We nearly always hit one storm in the North Sea," he said, "and the raft might be torn loose, and you'd wake up floating in the ocean."

I was convinced. I spent the rest of the night snuggled up against a gun turret.

The 13 of us felt like outcasts on that ship. We were always last in the chow line but first for KP duty. We banded together and refused to obey any and all orders given to us during the entire trip, even with the threat of court-martials upon docking in the United States. We decided we had had enough from the Army, regardless of the consequences. Just let us relax and look forward to home. Why should the Air Corps men take precedence over us, anyway? we wondered.

Those giving the orders eventually tired of badgering us. From that point on we spent the remainder of the voyage sitting around playing Hearts. We made friends with several of the crew, and they allowed us to share their table. Again, this was against regulations, but discipline was starting to slack off a bit in the European Theater.

I was up early on the 11th day at sea, eagerly scanning the horizon for the sight of land. I was hoping to see the Grand Old Lady, the Statue of Liberty, rise up out of that vast ocean. I wanted to tell her, "Hello! It's good to be home." I remembered when I said goodbye to her many months before. When I saw her, I'd know I was close to home again.

About noon, I saw a tiny speck of America in the distance and excitement began to build in my veins. But to my disappointment, we were going to arrive at Boston Harbor, not New York. As we approached the harbor, all men were ordered below decks to secure baggage for disembarking. That left the "outlaw 13" the only ones still on deck. So we were handed brooms and mops and ordered to sweep down fore and aft to prepare the ship for inspection by port authorities before being allowed to dock. This we refused to do, amid threats of punishment upon landing. The major in charge was livid with rage, but he was forced to recruit from below decks for the sweeping-and-cleaning crew. And when the ship docked, we were the first men ashore.

I boarded a train and was served coffee and donuts by the Red Cross. It was a short ride from the dock to Fort Miles Standish where I was immediately checked into the base hospital for a medical evaluation. As the medical technician was securing my history, I was informed that I was to have a free three-minute phone call to my mother in Illinois, courtesy of the Red Cross.

I was ushered into a phone booth while the operator was making all the necessary connections to cross nearly half the United States. After about five minutes, I heard the phone ringing in Georgetown. Finally, I heard a weak, faraway voice say, "Hello."

I had to swallow hard to get the breath to answer, "Hello, Mom. It's me, your son. I'm back on American soil."

For the next three minutes, Mother cried and was unable to carry on any conversation with me. I tried to talk to her but received no answer, except for her weeping. We were both choked with emotion at this moment, the moment she'd been praying for since June when she and Dad learned that I was in England. Nothing I said seemed to comfort her. This surprised me some because, as a rule, Mom was stoic and unemotional. I knew what I'd been through, but I hadn't given much thought to what they'd been through.

At the end of the allotted three minutes, the phone went dead and ended my chance to tell her I was okay. The call had been placed from an Army hospital, so there was nothing I could do. But as I started to walk away from the phone booth, the phone rang. I picked it up and a cheerful voice said, "Charlie, I have your mother on the other end of the line again. You may talk now."

It was most thoughtful of the operator to reconnect me. Evidently she had heard the previous conversation, realized the situation and took it upon herself to give me another three minutes. I was so stunned that I didn't even think to thank her. This time Mom was more composed. I was able to explain my situation, but I couldn't tell her exactly when I'd be home. My closest guess was within a week. But I told her I would call again when I reached Chicago, before boarding a train to Danville, where they could meet me.

Looking back, I realized that I hadn't taken into account that Mom and Dad had been waiting since June, when I'd gone AWOL in London, for some word about my whereabouts, my safety and my mental and physical condition. They'd been waiting and praying for three months. They didn't know what shape to expect their son to be in when they saw him. I thought I was okay, but they were at the mercy of time, and it had been a long time for their worries about me to increase. In another week or so we would be united. And if I wasn't okay yet, I would be then.

After a five-day sojourn at the base hospital, orders came through for Fort Sheridan, Illinois. Another day's delay there, and I boarded the train for Danville and arrived at the Wabash Station around noon. My mom, dad, sister and a crowd of family, friends and neighbors from Georgetown made my homecoming complete. It was 2 September 1945. I was back home after all those months overseas.

I returned to Georgetown with a full-barracks bag, including a steel helmet, minus a Garand M-1 rifle. I received 30 days hospital leave, 60 days POW leave and orders to report to L Company, 413th Infantry, 104th Division stationed at San Luis Obispo, California, by 2 December 1945. The division was training for duty in the South Pacific Theater. Within 30 days of arriving home, however, I received a change of orders. I was now to report to Fort Sam Houston in San Antonio, Texas, at the end of my furlough.

My dad was a rather prominent figure for many years in our small town. During the time I was missing in action with the uncertainty of my survival, loyal family, friends and supporters among the townspeople rallied around Mom and him. After I returned home, that support was so strong that Dad had to rent three spaces at the local food locker to accommodate all the extra meat and foodstuffs that people brought in to fatten me up. Everyone was so thoughtful; they just couldn't do enough.

While I was forever grateful to all of them, we just didn't have the heart to tell them that I couldn't eat it all because of my ongoing stomach problems stemming from the severe malnutrition I'd suffered. If I just could've eaten all those goodies ... , but I still weighed only 130 pounds. It would take a full year to bring my weight up to 155 pounds, still 20 pounds short of my combat weight.

I was an oddity of sorts to the people in town. They had never seen a prisoner of war before. I was the only one from town. And I know I wasn't the easiest person to get along with. I thought that when I got home, I could relax, fit right in and live normally. That was not to be, though. My nerves were so frayed, I had trouble keeping any food on my stomach. It was back to eggnog.

The Army had tried to fatten me up too quickly by giving me rich food and by giving me vitamin pills that made me sicker. I was also issued, or prescribed, several bottles of nerve medicine which didn't help, either. I spent many sleepless nights reliving the nightmares of the preceding months. Finally, when nothing else helped, I turned to alcohol. I always felt better when the alcohol took effect. But, of course, it did nothing to help my stomach—or my nerves.

I was full of pent-up anger about everything, about nothing. I would explode at the least little incident and was causing my mother great anxiety. While I was overseas, Mom had developed cancer again. I wasn't aware of this. Nobody ever talked about cancer at the time. All I was told was that the problem was in the female organs. And all of my antics in England and my delay in coming home had only added to her health problem. She didn't know how to relate to me, and I wasn't as normal as I thought I was. It wasn't a pleasant situation.

I wasn't the kid who had left for the Army in 1942. She didn't know this man who'd returned four months after the war was over—the one she had to throw a shoe at to wake him up in the morning, because if she touched him, he'd come up swinging.

Finally, my dad informed me of her illness. He said she was going into the hospital for treatment and maybe it'd be best if I went back to the Army. So on 17 November 1945, I boarded a train for Texas. Once there, I reported to Fort Sam Houston.

My orders stated that I was to be discharged at the convenience of the government. But since I was technically still on furlough, the process couldn't start until 2 December. So the Army assigned me a bunk on the base. I hung my hat there but spent every day in San Antonio.

The system used to qualify a soldier for discharge was based on the number of points he had amassed during his years of service. There was one point for each month of service, two points per month for overseas service, five points for each medal awarded and five points for each Bronze Battle Star, denoting a major campaign. I could come up with only 87 points, despite having more than three years total service, and didn't qualify for discharge.

I was awarded three more medals and one more Bronze Battle Star several years later when I asked for a review of my service records. I was awarded the Purple Heart "posthumously" for some reason. My mother received it on my behalf in February 1946, nearly two months after my discharge from the Army. Naturally, these awards were too late to boost my point total when I really needed the points.

Shortly after arriving in Fort Sam, I was subjected to a physical exam as part of the preparation for discharge. The results showed that I was still suffering from a nervous stomach disorder, a prostate infection and a slight concussion that affected my oculary nerve system. I was given a place in Brooke General Hospital and was immediately given a series of penicillin shots. I was restricted to a VD ward for the next two weeks until the prostate infection was cured. By this time, my furlough was up, and I was put in line for discharge.

The first day in line, I quickly realized that I was once again up against the Army Air Corps. Each morning, a point total was put up on the bulletin board, and all men with a point total higher than the one on the board could line up to be processed. The point total was lowered each day, but more new men kept arriving at the process center every day. Most of them were Air Corps with higher point totals than my measly 87 points.

After about 10 days of this frustration, I approached one of the officers in charge with an ultimatum: "I haven't been home for Christmas for three years. I am either going to be granted a furlough or a discharge, or I'm going AWOL in time to be home for Christmas."

The officer took note of my request, and two days later I was in the final line for discharge. I was issued an Honorable Discharge, a Ruptured Duck (a pin signifying that I'd been discharged) and $75 in travel pay. Somebody at Brooke General must've felt sorry for this beat-up old infantryman, because my point total was still not high enough, according to the posted list that morning of my discharge.

That magic day was 14 December 1945. With $75 in cash, I hustled down to the train station and bought a ticket to Danville, Illinois, just 10 miles from my home in Georgetown. Now, for sure, I'll be home for Christmas, I thought, as I jumped on the train and headed for Illinois.

The train chugged along all that afternoon and into the night. Early the next morning I changed trains in St. Louis and boarded the C&EI for the final lap to Danville, arriving there in mid-afternoon. Then I hired a taxi to take me the last 10 miles home. The taxi pulled up in front of The First National Bank just at the 3 p.m. closing time. Dad, unaware that I had been discharged, was overjoyed to see me walk through the door. It was great to shake his hand and embrace him.

After a warm welcome home from all the employees, Dad tossed me the car keys and we left immediately for home to see Mom. It was three whole blocks to 225 Walnut Street. It felt great to be driving, even that short distance. It was the first time I'd been behind the wheel of a vehicle as a civilian for some 38 months.

I just knew Mom would be in the kitchen. But she'd caught a glimpse of the car through the dining room window as we pulled into the driveway. She started for the front door, but our reunion took place in the living room. She was wiping her hands on her apron as we neared each other. Dad was grinning from ear to ear with his surprise. After hugs all around and a few joyous tears—unlike the tears Mom shed when I had called from Boston a few months earlier—I slowly began taking in all the familiar surroundings: the dark-stained grand piano that dominated the living room and always needed tuning; Dad's chair with his ashtray stand close by; Mom's ladder-back chair against the wall at the entrance to the dining room; the long table where aunts, uncles and cousins would join us for Christmas dinner a few days from now.

Lots of memories came flooding back. I was home. All was right with the world. "There's nothing 'twixt life and death save to enjoy the interval," I thought, remembering a quote from George Santayana (1863-1952). I planned to do just that.

Afterword

Regaining my strength was a slow, tedious process. I tried to relax but continued to be troubled by nervous stomach disorder and uncertainty about my future. My last payday (before combat and before being a POW) had been August 1944. When I finally got back on Uncle Sam's payroll in November 1945, I had about 15 months back pay due me. With this windfall, I lost no time ordering a new Chevy convertible, squandering most of the bonanza on the down payment. Almost three years later, in the fall of 1948, I got my new car—a 1947 beige Chevy convertible. I named her "Esmeraldy." She was a real gem to me when I finally got her.

After a wonderful Christmas season with family and friends, I decided to go back to Indiana University in the spring and pursue a degree in business administration. I got a rather rude awakening on the morning I approached the enrollment desk at the IU fieldhouse. I had pre-enrolled for a normal 17 hours of class but was informed by the head registrar that the Army had strongly suggested that I enroll for a maximum of nine hours for the first two semesters back on campus. So my schedule consisted of only three three-hour business courses. The only explanation I received, in Army terminology of course, was that I was "psychologically unfit to handle a full course of study at this time." I'll have to say that the Army was correct in this evaluation because I had a very difficult time concentrating on my assignments for any length of time. Even sitting through an hour lecture became quite difficult. I didn't have the concentration to stay on task.

Readjusting to civilian life became more of a challenge than I ever imagined it would be. However, I was able to make a C average in order to stay in school. Fortunately, while on leave in September, I had made arrangements for a room in my old fraternity house with the hope that I would be mustered out in time for the spring semester of 1946.

It was a struggle for me those first two semesters, even with the small class load. Frequent nightmares played havoc with my attempts to get a good night's sleep. I was restless and took many long walks out into the wooded hills surrounding Indiana's beautiful campus. Usually darkness had fallen long before I returned from these solitary walks.

During that first summer home from college, I went into the woods near home, built a small campfire, and with my back against a bluff and a rifle or a pistol at my side, I would just sit and stare into the fire for most of the night. I was trying to readjust to the friendly sounds of nature and reassuring myself that there were no enemy soldiers out there, staking my position.

Returning to Indiana University for the fall semester, I found myself becoming immersed in the activities of various campus organizations. During the next two years, I served two terms as president of Sigma Pi Social Fraternity; was president of the Junior Class Honorary and vice president of the Senior Class Honorary and was president of the Interfraternity Council. In addition, I served on various committees throughout the university system. All this participation, I think, was the reason I was able to get back in the mainstream of civilian life. My mind was occupied with something other than the horrors of war and prison life. Thus, those ugly memories of war were being supplanted with the pleasant activities at hand.

The fall semester of 1948 came and went. Spring semester of 1949 was to be my last on campus. After Spring Break in late April, I met a beautiful 18-year-old freshman girl from Connecticut. Her name was Gracie Schwab and from day one, she was the girl of my dreams. Within 20 days of meeting and being together at every opportunity, we decided we wanted to spend the rest of our lives together. This sudden commitment on my part was a real surprise to me because, knowing so many GIs whose girls jilted them, I had studiously avoided any commitment with anyone I dated. No way was I going to lose someone I cared about. I had cried so much over the deaths of so many of my combat buddies that I really wouldn't let myself get close to anyone. I did have many friends on campus but also had the reputation of being a loner by my fraternity brothers.

Gracie graciously accepted my fraternity pin as a sign of engagement. We hastened to Georgetown to share the good news with my parents and younger sister.

It took some planning to arrange our trip to Connecticut so I could meet her folks. Back in those days, it was unheard of for a single, teen-age girl to travel across the country with a man unchaperoned. Our trip required a night to be spent in a motel. Gracie's folks approved the plan of her married roommate, Phyllis Teeple, who was going to Schenectady, New York, to join her husband, being our chaperone. So we picked her up in Fort Wayne, Indiana, and were on our way. After dropping Phyllis off in New York, it was a short hop to Plainville, Connecticut.

During the five days I spent there, plans for our marriage were solidified. The only thing missing as the engagement ring, which I was able to afford later and sent by mail in July when I'd scraped up enough money.

September 17, 1949, was our wedding day, and it was beautiful. Now, after 48 years of a wonderful, happy married life, we have two daughters, two sons and eight grandchildren, all living within a 100-mile radius of Georgetown. Life has been, and continues to be, very good to me. But to this day, the nightmares from those days in World War II and German prison camps have never ended.

For the past 10 years or so, I have arranged to speak to history classes in junior and senior high schools. I have found the students to be most receptive to my story. I speak to these classes because our young people need to know just how their precious Freedom was secured and how important it is for them to be ever vigilant. History books don't contain facts such as those I share with them.

And I intend to remain a "living link to history," as one reporter called me, as long as I have breath to do so.

— *Charlie Dukes*